ALSO BY LORI D. GINZBERG

Untidy Origins:
A Story of Woman's Rights in Antebellum New York

Women and the Work of Benevolence:
Morality, Politics, and Class in the Nineteenth-Century United States

Women in Antebellum Reform

ELIZABETH CADY STANTON

ELIZABETH CADY STANTON

AN AMERICAN LIFE

LORI D. GINZBERG

HILL AND WANG

A DIVISION OF FARRAR, STRAUS AND GIROUX

NEW YORK

Hill and Wang
A division of Farrar, Straus and Giroux
18 West 18th Street, New York 10011

Library of Congress Cataloging-in-Publication Data
Ginzberg, Lori D.
    Elizabeth Cady Stanton : an American life / Lori D. Ginzberg.
        p.   cm.
    Includes bibliographical references and index.
    ISBN-13: 978-0-8090-9493-6 (hardcover : alk. paper)
    ISBN-10: 0-8090-9493-2 (hardcover : alk. paper)
    1. Stanton, Elizabeth Cady, 1815–1902.   2. Feminists—United States—
Biography.   3. Women's rights—United States—History—19th century.   I. Title.

HQ1413.S67G43 2009
305.42092—dc22
[B]

                                                            2008054395

Designed by Jonathan D. Lippincott

www.fsgbooks.com

1   3   5   7   9   10   8   6   4   2

For Kate and Eli

CONTENTS

ELIZABETH CADY STANTON

INTRODUCTION

Brilliant, self-righteous, charismatic, self-indulgent, mischievous, intimidating, and charming, Elizabeth Cady Stanton was the founding philosopher of the American movement for woman's rights. She comes across as larger than life, a woman driven by her commitment to rouse herself, and everyone else, to rethink and remake women's status in politics, law, religion, and marriage. There was not one thing that Stanton considered so large, or so trivial, or so sacred, that it could not be illuminated by her close scrutiny; no occasion escaped either her wit or the serious lesson she meant it to cushion. When her friend Susan B. Anthony traveled on the ship the *Prince* to meet her in Europe in 1883, Stanton quipped that her friend should have taken the *Queen*.[1] If a host called on her to say grace before a meal, Stanton offered a prayer of her own composition: "Heavenly Father, Mother," she would intone, "make us thankful for all the blessings of this life & make us ever mindful of the patient hands that often in weariness spread our tables & prepare our daily food: for humanity's sake, Amen."[2] Surely the bowed heads hid a range of expressions, but having a place at her table, literally or metaphorically, meant being in the presence of a probing, flashing, breathtaking mind.

Stanton was, to many, a dangerous radical, whose words threatened the stability of marriage, the sanctity of religion, and men's exclusive control over politics. Others, taken with her cheer, her confidence, and her curls, imagined her as a safe and comforting figure.

To be sure, she was charming even when she was cutting. Once, in Nebraska, a man in the audience declared that his wife had borne him eight children, and wasn't that "a better life-work than that of exercising the right of suffrage?" Stanton "slowly viewed him from head to foot" and replied, "I have met few men, in my life, worth repeating eight times."[3] But every time she expressed a new idea, something—a tradition, a strategy, a friendship, or simply an old way of seeing things—seemed to blow up. That nearly all of her most radical ideas would one day be widely accepted is all the more reason to try to understand why they seemed so outrageous at the time.

As a historian who has written about more ordinary women, I have found wrestling with Elizabeth Cady Stanton's life and legacy a compelling, and infuriating, process. Stanton and I go way back, for I have been arguing with the woman about one thing or another for my entire adult life. I do not identify with her or revere her or hate her. I do not want to celebrate her every utterance or, alternatively, rat her out. But while I have admired various nineteenth-century women in the course of my career, it is Stanton I fight with, for she butts in even when she is not part of the story. We have argued about the meaning and usefulness of voting; whether and how deeply she was racist, anti-Semitic, intolerant, or self-absorbed; how she could talk as if all women were wives and mothers when her best friend was neither; and whether to support Abraham Lincoln for reelection in 1864. Such arguments forced Stanton in her own time to articulate her grandest ideals, and their echoes are ongoing today: What principles should we compromise in order to gain an immediate goal? How broad a platform can a movement sustain before it loses too much of its following? How should we balance national politics with local? Arguing with a dead woman is an odd experience, of course. When we argue, Stanton always thinks she's right; she never has to deal with my critiques. On the other hand, I get the last word.

Elizabeth Cady Stanton looms large both personally and historically, and perhaps historians of American women will expect to learn little from my taking up her story again, especially since I have compressed it into several hundred pages. I hope that I have written a book that addresses her place in the discussions in which scholars still engage, and that I have opened up, rather than foreclosed, debate on issues—slavery, racism, feminism, individualism, class, and reli gion, to name a few—that absorbed Stanton and that vex us still. But educated Americans who have asked "Who was she?" offer historians an even broader challenge. Their question underscores how removed our historical icons and scholarly discussions have become, especially when those icons are women. But it also highlights that the radical ideas that Elizabeth Cady Stanton promoted so passionately in her own time are utterly commonplace in ours. When Stanton embarked on a life demanding woman's rights, including the right to vote, the opposition she faced was fierce, and personal: "I passed through a ter- rible scourging when last at my father's," she admitted to Susan B. Anthony in 1855. "I cannot tell you how deep the iron entered my soul. I never felt more keenly the degradation of my sex."[4] These days, hardly any adult woman's father opposes his daughter's public speak- ing, as Daniel Cady did that day, or young women's access to higher education, physical activity, or comfortable clothing; married women's control of property, credit, or children; the right to a divorce; or women's presence in voting booths, jury boxes, and courts of law. For virtually every American alive today, woman's rights are ordinary com- mon sense; that this is so is, in large part, because of Stanton's life work.

Even in her own time, many of Elizabeth Cady Stanton's ideas fit neatly into one framework of thought while they challenged other deeply held beliefs. Like the men we call the nation's founders, Stan- ton took what she viewed as simple truths ("All men and women are created equal," she famously declared in 1848) and wove them into a philosophy of rights that, once expressed, seemed almost too obvious to debate, though they might still, and for a frustratingly long time, be denied. Like other thinkers and movement builders in American history—Thomas Jefferson, for instance, or the abolitionist William Lloyd Garrison—Stanton did not invent the notion that women had rights, but she grabbed the ideas that floated around her, shook them hard, shaped them into words that were strong and accessible, mixed the whole with a good dose of charm and charisma, and flung them back into the world forcefully enough to launch countless others into action.

American political and intellectual history had always contained competing frameworks of thought, and was as much defined by "inegalitarian racial, patriarchal, and religious" categories as by liberal demands for equality.[5] By Elizabeth Cady Stanton's day, the conviction that it was women's nature and duty to remain in a "private sphere" of piety, domesticity, and motherhood was widely held. Such views fit securely into the body of thought that assigned status on the basis of race or gender, that justified some people's dependence and inequality as natural or divine, and that viewed marriage itself as the crucial source of women's standing. In challenging women's separate and subordinate status as wives, mothers, and citizens, Elizabeth Cady Stanton posed a serious threat to some of Americans' most cherished beliefs.

Like Jefferson and Garrison, Stanton lived a long life (she died just before her eighty-seventh birthday), and she never stopped thinking or talking or writing. No one book can cover every aspect of her career, every idea she articulated or rejected, every speech she gave, or every challenge she faced. Nor can it drop the name of every person who passed through her well-populated life: I have studiously avoided mentioning every politician Stanton met and charmed and cajoled, or every dinner party she attended. It is enough to note that Stanton herself relished such events, and was always certain that she had been the life of the party.

Elizabeth Cady Stanton considered herself a model for all womankind, and as such was determined to guard against any sign of frailty that would, she knew, be cause for public judgment. She spent a significant part of nearly every day scribbling petitions, letters, articles, speeches, and, late in life, a diary and several books, but she left few traces of her most intimate thoughts. Stanton's "insistence on the privacy of emotions," as her daughter's biographer puts it, "was reinforced by her condemnation of weakness and dependence, vulnerability and need, especially in women."[6] Pregnancies were difficult, husbands became boring, friendships became strained, children went astray or even died; in public and in her extant writings, Stanton barely flinched. If there were letters describing the pain of such losses, they no longer exist, perhaps because her children, having learned their mother's lessons well, destroyed them. Thus we catch only the barest whisper that Stanton's youngest son, Bob, had an accident in his youth that "crippled him for life." We hear almost nothing about her oldest child, Neil, as he descended into corruption, divorce, and death. Marital regret and frustration make only oblique appearances. And if there was a cry of agony at the death of her daughter's small child, it comes not from the adoring grandmother, but in the letters of Susan B. Anthony.[7]

Elizabeth Cady Stanton, for all her openness and cheer, worked very hard to present to the world the image she thought befitted a leader of women. Since "I usually preserve the exterior of a saint," she wrote a friend, only partly tongue in cheek, "there is no use of everybody knowing how like a fallen angel I often feel."[8] As a matter of both duty and inclination, she transformed each painful, infuriating, or demoralizing experience into a new understanding of women's wrongs and, therefore, their rights.

But Stanton's personality does come through, as alternately appealing and maddening as the woman herself. Drawn as she was to the pleasures of intellectual combat and rational analysis, she was a woman with strong physical tastes and unexamined prejudices. Raised in wealth and comfort, she was unabashed in the gratification she got from material possessions: a comfortable chair, fine clothing. Short and plump, she relished food and sleep as much as she did a brilliant turn of phrase. Theodore Tilton once described her (in print) as a woman whose "figure . . . suggest[s] a preference for short walks rather than for long," and Stanton made little effort to resist "muffins, and oatmeal, and cream . . . [and] powdered sugar." Decades after her introduction to abolitionists Angelina Grimké and Theodore Weld, she recalled the "cheerless atmosphere" of their home for those like her "who were not yet weaned from the flesh-pots of Egypt" and who were forced to rely on "memories of tea and coffee for stimulus." Stanton also adored napping, and regarded her preference for "the horizontal position" as the source of her physical and psychological health.[9] Unlike her friend Susan B. Anthony, who believed in the virtues of self-denial, Stanton saw no reason to apologize for her indulgences.

Given Stanton's utter confidence that anything she loved must be for the best, a comparison with another daunting personality is instructive. In *The Most Famous Man in America: The Biography of*

Henry Ward Beecher, the son of Lyman Beecher, brother of Harriet Beecher Stowe and Catharine Beecher, and minister of the prominent Plymouth Church in Brooklyn comes across as self-confident to the point of arrogance, full of enthusiasms and charm and excesses and perhaps a not-quite-Christian pridefulness. Except for Beecher's propensity to have affairs with married women, he and Elizabeth Cady Stanton seemed remarkably alike. I was gratified but not surprised, then, to come upon the middle-aged Stanton's own description of herself: "Mine is an impressible magnetic soul," she wrote, "that feels joy and grief, that weeps and laughs at the same moment. Those who know us both say I am in temperment like Henry Ward Beecher, who makes his congregations laugh and cry alternately all through his sermons."[10] Ironically but characteristically, Stanton was far less well disposed toward the famed Beecher self-regard when it appeared in Henry's sisters, Catharine and Isabella. (Catharine might not have become "the narrow, bigoted, arrogant woman she is to day," Stanton once suggested rather crudely, if she had "ever loved, with sufficient devotion, passion, abandon, any of Adam's sons, to have forgotten herself, her God, *her family*, *her propriety*, & endured for a brief space the world's coldness, ridicule, or scorn."[11]) Although she believed that society had drastically limited women's education and self-esteem, she never doubted that her own self-regard was fully earned, and she could be cutting about actual women whom she considered less brilliant, less radical, or less self-confident than she. Thus while she argued passionately for the rights of all women, Stanton expressed little affection for women as a group; indeed, condescension rather than warmth characterizes much of her attitude toward most women. Generally she preferred the company and the competition of men. Asked once if she played chess, Stanton bragged about her skill at the game and then complained that women "all say it is too hard work, as if thinking were not one of the pleasures of life."[12] People who reached conclusions more slowly than she—which is to say, pretty much everyone—often struggled to keep up, and she undoubtedly let her impatience show.

Elizabeth Cady Stanton was an extraordinary American who, in many respects, lived a very ordinary life. A proponent of extending the nation's promise of radical individualism to women, she herself remained embedded in a fairly conventional family life and suburban home. And while audiences applauded her "maternal" presence on the stage, and Stanton referred at times to the power of motherhood, she struggled mightily with the responsibilities posed by her seven children and a home. She embodied other contradictions. In calling for a woman's rights convention in Seneca Falls in 1848, and adding the demand for suffrage to its resolutions, she helped launch the movement for woman's rights, but she squirmed in organizations, and avoided conventions when she could. "I would rather be burnt at the stake (under the influence of an anaesthetic!) than go through another," she griped to her long-suffering friend Susan B. Anthony. (In contrast, Anthony, who relished organizational life, "says she wants to drop suddenly on the platform, like John Quincy Adams on the floor of Congress.") Part of a generation of joiners, Stanton was not communal by inclination, though she loved the acclaim, the money, and the publicity that being a public figure could bring. She authored no single tome, left no monument in our national consciousness, and yet she helped articulate a philosophy of woman's rights that has shaped our world.[13]

Elizabeth Cady Stanton was an absolutist; she viewed everything through her unconditional "oppos[ition] to the domination of one sex over the other." Like absolutists of all kinds, she granted little moral complexity to those whose views swerved from her own. Other reformers found her both thrilling and exasperating, for she could be an excellent ally and a bothersome menace, sometimes both at once. She was sweeping in her intolerance, applying it as emphatically to people's grammar as to their politics; she especially disliked the common usage of *woman* as an adjective (as in "woman doctor") and, citing Webster, declared a *suffragist* to be *"one who votes."* (I have felt entirely free to criticize Elizabeth Cady Stanton in this book, but I have avoided the term she found doubly exasperating, *woman suffragist*.) She was certain that "the next generation will not argue the question of woman's rights with the infinite patience we have for half a century," but her own patience was limited; she tended to grow bored at precisely the moment when her ideas began to seem respectable.[14] Her own "settled maxim," she declared, was simply "that the existing public sentiment on any subject is wrong." Elizabeth

Cady Stanton was, she admitted, happiest when "hurling my thunder" at opponents.[15]

But Stanton was no armchair radical who remained entirely above the fray, nor a high-toned philosopher with no public appeal. She was a visible presence in American public life, a force to be reckoned with, a household name. Women crowded legislative halls to hear her speak, gathered in San Francisco's Golden Gate Hall to honor her on her eightieth birthday, and sought her advice about marriage, babies, and the laws of divorce.[16] She was unsurpassed, in Anthony's admiring view, at giving her audiences "the rankest radical sentiments, but all so cushioned they didn't hurt." Even fictional characters adored her. Marietta Holley, the author of the wildly popular Samantha and Betsey Bobbet series, had one of her characters "meet" Elizabeth Cady Stanton, and find in her "jest about as noble a lookin' face as I ever see, with short white curls a fallin' all round it." Stanton was, the character gushed, "an earnest noble woman, who had asked God what He wanted her to do, and then hadn't shirked out of doin' it . . . She was givin' her life for others, and nobody ever did this since the days of Jesus."[17] The irony of being identified with Jesus must have tickled the secular Elizabeth Cady Stanton to no end.

Although Stanton considered herself "a leader of thought rather than numbers," she faced crises that were strategic as well as theoretical, and that went well beyond the demand for woman suffrage.[18] These included debates about dress reform, marriage, and divorce in the 1850s; the conflict and schism over the Reconstruction amendments and black male suffrage following the Civil War; and her attack on organized religion, epitomized by her publication of *The Woman's Bible*. In each of these moments, as in her overarching insistence on women's right to be fully realized and rights-bearing human beings, Stanton shaped nineteenth-century feminism even as she addressed the founding principles of American political life and the meanings of citizenship, rights, independence, and equality. Both in her appeal to universalism and in her elitism, she exemplified the complexity of American thought, which in turn defined the kind of citizen and self Stanton aspired to become.

The outlines of Elizabeth Cady Stanton's life are familiar, even conventional; it was what she made of that story that set her apart. From a girl embittered by her father's narrow expectations, a wife frustrated by small-town life, a mother facing the demands posed by seven children, and an intellectual emerging as the leader of a new movement, she has served as a template for understanding nineteenth-century women's discontents and the demand for their rights. Her own experience was, Stanton implied, as universal as it was inspirational; it was every woman's log cabin myth, her bootstrap-pulling climb from insult to rebellion to independence. How she sculpted that iconic story has ever since shaped the scope and the limitations of the demand for woman's rights.

Elizabeth Cady Stanton had shown (she probably thought) characteristically good sense to be born in the early nineteenth century. It was a time when talk of universal justice and emancipation pervaded public discussion, when female reformers on both sides of the Atlantic were engaged in every aspect of struggle. That Stanton was arguably the most important female activist-intellectual of that era, and one of her generation's most charismatic leaders, is therefore no small claim. Her own circle included such reform luminaries as Angelina and Sarah Grimké, Lucretia Coffin Mott, Abby Kelley Foster, and Lucy Stone, not to mention the thousands of women who adopted and promoted woman's rights. Long before Stanton became prominent on the reform scene, the Grimkés had asserted women's equality as moral agents; Lucretia Mott had declared that the very notion of a female sphere limited women's potential as human beings; Abby Kelley had boldly confronted virulent, even violent, opposition to women acting alongside men; and Lucy Stone had embarked on a speaking career that gave distinction to the cause of woman's rights. But in a time and place that was bursting with reformers, when new radicalisms seemed to enter the current of intellectual life almost daily, Stanton was the first person to devote her considerable intellect solely to developing the philosophy and promoting the cause of woman's rights. She essentially invented and embodied what we might term stand-alone feminism, devoting her life to challenging the ways that ideas about gender shaped women's place in society, politics, law, and marriage. Undistracted and undeterred, she spent more than half a century elaborating the nature of women's subordination and providing the verbal ammunition to anyone who wanted to join her to change it.

Like those other national icons, the founding fathers, Elizabeth

Cady Stanton failed, or refused, to look too closely or too critically at her own complex place in the society she wished to change. She understood women's wrongs, and therefore their rights, in terms that reflected her particular experience; her notion of "universal" woman-hood, defined largely by wifehood and motherhood within the Protestant middle class, was both broad and shallow; and while she insisted with great passion that the liberal ideal must include women, her understanding of the world was flawed by assumptions about the superiority of her own class, race, religious culture, and nation. While historians, following Stanton's lead, have tended to stress her intellectual courage and independence—no one, she was sure, was ever quite as radical as she—Stanton herself epitomized both the strengths and the limitations of the Protestant middle-class worldview from which she emerged: claiming universal standing from the vantage point of her own experience and having enormous faith in the ability of the law to make fundamental social change. Above all, Stanton, like other leading American thinkers, believed devoutly in the power of the individual to make, remake, and save herself. "Nothing adds such dignity to character as the recognition of one's self-sovereignty," she declared; "the right to an equal place, everywhere conceded—a place earned by personal merit, not an artificial attainment by inheritance, wealth, family and position."[19]

Elizabeth Cady Stanton's confidence in her positions underscored an acute sense of her own historical significance. Tuesday, November 2, 1880, was not a particularly notable presidential Election Day; the victor, Republican James Garfield, would be remembered mostly for his assassination and replacement by the hardly more distinctive Chester Arthur. Still, the day was memorable for Stanton. Her husband, Henry, and their sons were away from home, and so, when the "republican wagon and horses all decked with flags and evergreens, came for the male part of the household," she was dressed and ready: "I told the driver that my legal representatives were all absent, but I would go down and vote," she wrote her son. Susan B. Anthony, who had been tried and convicted for voting two presidential elections earlier, "went with me and we had great fun frightening and muddling these old Dutch inspectors" and "arguing with the judges of elections." Stanton, then age sixty-five, insisted she had done a great, radical thing—"The whole town is agape with my act," she boasted—but by 1880 many women had already voted, and even the local men had "taken sides about equally." More telling than Stanton's actually casting a ballot was what happened later that evening: "the post-man said he would give five dollars for that ticket that I proffered [to vote]; he would have it framed and hung up in his house." More than a century later, Elizabeth Cady Stanton's 1880 election card sits among the boxes of suffrage memorabilia in the Library of Congress. With it is a witness's transcript of the event that concludes: "Believing that this will become historical I have written this out for the benefit of posterity and having submitted the same to Mrs. STANTON and MISS ANTHONY I now subscribe my name, EDWARD P. FURLONG."[20] Stanton would not have been surprised.

Stanton's faith in her intellect and her persuasive powers was matched only by the sheer volume of her words. Late in life she estimated that she had written more than one hundred speeches "on all questions of government, reforms, religion and social life," but that does not begin to account for the paper trail she left behind. Even with culling by her and her children, the written documentation is daunting. Theodore Stanton and Harriot Stanton Blatch, who shared their mother's eagerness to control and shape her historical legacy, divided Stanton's letters between them, transcribing some and circumspectly destroying others. ("One never criticizes one's family in public," Harriot Stanton Blatch later told her own granddaughter, reflecting her mother's teaching and her own practice.) Their plan, which they took up erratically, was to publish a definitive collection of their mother's private and public work, a common tribute by the children of nineteenth-century reformers. The result was the two-volume *Elizabeth Cady Stanton, as Revealed in Her Letters, Diary, and Reminiscences*, published in 1922.[21]

Thus chopped up, dispersed, and edited, the papers of Elizabeth Cady Stanton ended up in numerous locations. Harriot's share, as well as her own correspondence, landed at Vassar College and the Library of Congress. Theodore tried to leave his share to his alma mater, Cornell University, with the caveat that he serve as its unpaid curator; when that negotiation fell through, he turned to Rutgers University, seeking lodgings in exchange for his share of the library. Eventually he donated "the Elizabeth Cady Stanton Memorial Collection" to the New Jersey College for Women, later Douglass College. "Mr. Stanton is personally most objectionable," reported the Rutgers librarian, adding an epitaph that would, mostly, have made his mother proud: "He is a radical and an atheist and he is not nice."[22]

Stanton's words were more widely scattered throughout various attics, libraries, and archival collections than her children could imagine. A heroic effort by Patricia G. Holland and Ann D. Gordon to gather some fourteen thousand documents resulted, in 1991, in forty-five reels of microfilm, but the project of making Stanton's correspondence and speeches accessible is ongoing.[23] Ann Gordon's *The Selected Papers of Elizabeth Cady Stanton and Susan B. Anthony*, a model of professional editing and annotation, beautifully identifies hundreds of people and events, untangles misinformation, and sorts through various versions of letters and speeches to reflect their primary purpose. Still, as Gordon notes, only a small portion of Stanton's and Anthony's papers could be included in the projected six volumes, and questions of selection necessarily stress some stories, debates, and individuals over others. The effort to narrate Stanton's story and to assess her historical significance invites an ongoing conversation, of which this book is only a part.

Still, counting and publishing Stanton's speeches and letters cannot begin to measure the effect of her words. No one was as certain as Stanton herself that her public speeches, private writings, and even the most casual interactions were having an enormous impact on changing public opinion about women's status, abilities, and rights. "Her gift of gifts," Theodore Tilton declared, "is conversation." She never much cared to measure that impact in electoral victories, nor would she quiet down on those occasions when progress was frustrated by political reality. She would have spoken out anyway, for the sheer joy of it: "We cannot estimate the good that a fearless utterance of our best thoughts may do," she wrote a friend.[24] It is a fitting epitaph for a woman who never failed to utter her thoughts, even when her closest friends sometimes wished she would keep them to herself.

1

THE TWO WORLDS
OF ELIZABETH CADY

(1815–1840)

To hear Elizabeth Cady Stanton tell it, Johnstown, New York, where she was born in 1815, was a place of comfort and convention, privilege and patriarchy. Her parents, Daniel and Margaret Livingston Cady, were devoted to family, tradition, and the Federalist Party. They were strict and stodgy, and their children were raised according to old-fashioned norms of childhood, religion, class—and, especially, gender. Church, school, and family taught only "that everlasting no! no! no!" and conspired to enforce "the constant cribbing and crippling of a child's life." It struck the young Elizabeth Cady that "everything we like to do is a sin, and . . . everything we dislike is commanded by God or someone on earth." Only with her sister Margaret's complicity was she able to get over her "infantile fear of punishment" in order to have fun.[1] It was a perfect setting against which to rebel, and, as Elizabeth Cady Stanton recalled fondly, she rebelled with gusto.

Provincial it was, but the world of Elizabeth Cady Stanton's birth, while it seemed only to reinforce the traditional, pastoral life her father enjoyed, was far from static. The inhabitants of the town, an 1824 gazetteer reported, "seem to be very industrious and intent on keeping pace, in every improvement, with the progress of things around them" and, indeed, Johnstown was a local center for the industrial changes that had skirted other small towns. The nation's first glove and mitten factory had been founded there, in about 1808, and manufacturing was at the heart of Johnstown's economy; the very

air of Stanton's childhood must have smelled of progress.[2] Nor was
the local elite of long standing. The family and Episcopal church congregation of Johnstown's founder, Sir William Johnson, all Loyalists,
had left for Canada after the Revolution, leaving an open door for the
likes of Daniel Cady.

For all their sense of established respectability and community
leadership, the Cadys were, like most white residents of Upstate New
York, new blood. Daniel Cady had been born in Columbia County in
1773, studied law in Albany, and moved the forty miles to Johnstown
in 1798. Margaret Livingston, a dozen years his junior, had been born
in the Hudson Valley to Revolutionary War hero James Livingston and
his wife, Elizabeth Simpson Livingston. Although their own Elizabeth
believed that the laws, norms, and values that structured men's and
women's lives in her childhood were unchanging and unchallenged,
Daniel and Margeret Cady had already seen changes of various kinds.
Not all of these were progressive in nature. Churches that had shown
some openness to women's speech in the mid-eighteenth century
were, by the early nineteenth, reasserting traditional forms of male
authority. Near Margaret Cady's birthplace, Dutch traditions that had
given married women greater property rights had been largely superseded by more stringent English common law that declared the whole
of a woman's inherited property her husband's. Even in politics, the
barriers of sex had been less rigid, less seemingly absolute, in 1800
than they would be during Elizabeth Cady's youth. In New Jersey,
women who owned property could vote until 1807, when the legislature restricted suffrage to white men, reflecting a growing consensus
that women had no role in political life. Indeed, the Revolution itself,
while underscoring the political equality of greater numbers of white
men, saw a narrowing of elite women's conventional access to public
authority. Daniel Cady, stubbornly conservative, wished to hold on to
what authority he had gained (cultural, familial, political, and economic) as long as possible.[3]

Historians tend to mark 1815, the end of the War of 1812, and the
year of Elizabeth Cady's birth, as the start of a new era in American
history. It was a time that would, before too long, seethe with changes
in law, religion, trade, politics, transportation, class structures, and, of
course, ideas about women. Vast changes would take place that the

Cadys could not possibly imagine or predict. Indeed, among Elizabeth Cady Stanton's generation of Americans would be the first women to attend college, once Oberlin formally admitted them in 1837; the first female doctors, once sisters Emily and Elizabeth Blackwell earned their medical degrees; and an astonishing array of female speakers, antislavery reformers, writers, editors, labor activists, educators, and, of course, advocates of woman suffrage.

But before imagining the change that would occur, consider the world, and the rules, into which these women, citizens of the United States, were born. In 1830, when Elizabeth Cady was fifteen, the common-law notion of coverture—that is, the idea that wives were "covered" by their husbands' protection—virtually defined the laws of marriage. Once they married, women could not own or inherit property, sign a contract, or pursue their business interests in court. Although women tended to bear somewhat fewer children than they had a century earlier, childbearing was still frequent and deadly. Legal divorce, as opposed to less formal desertion, was rare, and custody of minor children went to the husband, who essentially "owned" their labor. The opportunities for middle- and upper-class women to live independently of men—whether husbands, fathers, or brothers— were few indeed, and it would not be until the very late nineteenth century that significant numbers of them could do so. Unmarried women paid taxes just as men did, but they could not vote for the representatives who set their tax rates or give advice about how those taxes were spent. Women could not serve on a jury, though they were tried often enough for crimes; nor could they speak out about such crimes in most religious assemblies. They were barred both from men's colleges and from a wide array of occupations—and not surprisingly, those they dominated, such as domestic service and prostitution, were among the lowest paid. In cities, new commercial markets presented both opportunities and pitfalls for women; they ran shops and small manufactories, operated millinery businesses, opened schools, and did the grueling work that the growing upper classes expected of seamstresses, servants, and nursemaids. But if these enterprising women married, their wages were no longer their own, but their husbands'. Over the next century, much of this—first and mostly among the upper and middle classes—would change. In the meantime, for all the rhetoric about the common man, Elizabeth Cady's world was in many respects characterized by greater restriction, reinforced hierarchies, and frequent declarations that what America needed was more stability and tradition, not less.

The Cadys, who married in 1801, when Margaret was sixteen, flourished in Johnstown and in this larger world, living in a large house on a corner of Main Street. Aided by his ties to Margaret's brother-in-law, the fabulously wealthy Peter Smith, Daniel Cady established himself as a lawyer, landowner, state legislator, and judge. In the year of Elizabeth's birth, his neighbors elected him to Congress, where he served one term. The couple had eleven children, of whom only six would survive childhood; the only son among those, Eleazar, would die at twenty.

The Cady family's economic privilege and social authority are nearly invisible threads running through Stanton's recollections, unquestioned and, to Stanton, unproblematic. It was, rather, her father's intransigence about gender that formed the core of the story Elizabeth Cady Stanton told about her childhood. Her most vivid, and oft-repeated, story was that of a brilliant, boisterous, rebellious little girl, eleven years old, whose only living brother, Eleazar, had just died. How dark the household must have seemed. Distraught, she crawled into her father's lap, seeking to give and receive comfort. But her grieving, distracted father put his arm around her and sighed, "Oh, my daughter, I wish you were a boy!" The sting of the father's remark, whether spiteful or unfeeling or simply careless, lingers. Every girl who has yearned to impress an accomplished or demanding father, every woman who has felt the slight of being thought less promising than her brothers, can relate to the insult. Elizabeth Cady, as it turned out, had more than enough reserves of self-esteem to survive the slap, though she never forgot it; not only was she as brilliant as the boys and men around her, but she knew it. She was, as one historian puts it, "singularly unafflicted with psychological insecurity," and she quickly put her extraordinary self-confidence to work.[4] The child, as the woman later recalled, vowed to make her father happy by being all a son could have been, thus providing a rationale for her grand ambitions. But the political moral that she took from this childhood affront was the germ of something even larger: her recognition that society's preference for and pride in boys dwarfed girls' lives, limited their opportunities, and were used to justify the denial of woman's rights. She took this insult very personally indeed.

Is it possible to sympathize, however grudgingly, with Judge Cady? There is every evidence that he loved his daughters, and even in sighing over the limitations of Elizabeth's sex, he surely knew that this one was especially bright. But the man had just lost his only living son, at an age when the young man's promise was evident but his path not clearly marked, and at a time when a man such as the judge could reasonably rest his ambitions for succession only on boys. Surely he envisioned Eleazar, who had just graduated from Union College, following in his footsteps, perhaps joining him in the law office or at court. It is possible to read Daniel Cady's comment to his daughter not simply as a putdown, though it surely was that, but also as an acknowledgment that her intellect and her wit would in fact have found more expansive arenas if she had been a boy. Elizabeth's father was neither so wrong nor uniquely old-fashioned in feeling a twinge of regret that this gifted child was a girl, for in the judge's world, and pretty much everyplace else, the barriers that limited her sex were real indeed.

To hear Stanton tell it, she spent her girlhood days trying to impress her learned father, live up to the standards set by her brother, and learn from the law students who wandered through the house. That the household was not composed exclusively of men seems largely to have escaped her notice. There is little of Margaret Livingston Cady in her daughter's account, and her appearances are generally fairly passive. To her daughter, Mrs. Cady was simply "a tall, queenly looking woman," a female enforcer of the "Puritan ideas," and the reason that "fear, rather than love, of God and parents alike, predominated" in the household. It was she, presumably, who often placed the young Elizabeth "under punishment for what, in those days, were called 'tantrums'" but that Stanton insisted were "justifiable acts of rebellion against the tyranny of those in authority."[5] But Margaret Cady demonstrated both a strong will and the capacity to change; years later, in 1867, she signed a woman suffrage petition and was, according to her granddaughter Harriot, "a dyed-in-the-wool Abolitionist," even a "Garrisonian extremist."[6] However distant and disciplined she may have been, it was not Elizabeth Cady Stanton's "queenly" mother alone who upheld the family's conservative attitudes. Unfortunately, neither Stanton's account nor other historical documents offer clues about what ambivalence Margaret Cady might have felt about her rebellious daughter.

If, in Stanton's recollections, Judge Cady embodied the hard-line patriarchal attitudes that shaped his daughter's rebellion, Mrs. Cady was the regal exemplar of discipline, and Elizabeth Cady's younger sister Margaret was her "fearless and self-reliant" companion, the other women in the Cady household appear largely as the enforcers of conventional attitudes about women's place. Sister Harriet Cady, later Eaton, maintained a tight grip over Elizabeth Stanton's decisions even late in life, and often made the Stanton children miserable with restraint. Tryphena, the eldest, was conservative to her very bones. Not only would she oppose her younger sister's radical proclamations and actions, but, as Harriot Stanton Blatch recalled, " 'Aunty By' had a leaning to the southern side in Civil War days." Even Margaret Cady was, as her granddaughter recalled, "much freer and finer . . . without the aunts weaving nets of convention about her."[7]

Gender conventions were not the only vestiges of tradition in the Cady household. Among Stanton's most quoted reminiscences are stories about the "three colored men, Abraham, Peter, and Jacob, who acted as menservants in our youth." Peter in particular evoked the "most pleasant recollections," for Stanton recalled that the little girls followed him to "the negro pew" at their otherwise all-white church, to celebrations of the Fourth of July, and on various river-rafting expeditions. But Peter Teabout was not simply a "manservant"; he was a slave—and he likely remained one until 1827, when the last slaves were finally, grudgingly, emancipated in the state of New York.[8]

Daniel Cady was hardly unique in holding slaves in Montgomery County, New York. Johnstown's founder, Sir William Johnson, had brought slaves to central New York in the mid-eighteenth century, and by the time the Cadys arrived, revolutionary declarations of liberty notwithstanding, the practice of holding people in bondage had expanded. Five hundred and eighty-eight enslaved African Americans lived in the county in 1790, and 712 in 1810; by 1820, when Elizabeth Cady was five, 40 percent of the 152 African Americans in

Johnstown still lived as slaves. Only in 1799 had the state legislature passed a law for gradual, and compensated, emancipation; a very few years before Elizabeth's birth, an African American man or woman in her county remained almost twice as likely to be a slave as to be free. Finally, on July 4, 1827, slavery was ended in New York. African Americans, refusing to have their day of emancipation eclipsed by their white neighbors' own independence, pointedly waited until the following day, the fifth of July, to hold celebrations around the state.[9]

Stanton never mentioned that day of emancipation, neither to reflect on its implications for her father nor to consider its meaning for the supposedly greatly cherished Peter. Is it unfair to have expected an eleven-year-old to notice? By her own account she was an unusually alert child, exceptionally sensitive to injustice and matters of law. Even as a young girl, she claimed, she found in the restrictions on married women's property ownership deeply personal insults, and had plotted to cut them out of her father's legal tomes. Certainly she seethed when one of the judge's law students, Henry Bayard, upon being shown Elizabeth's new Christmas gifts, teased, "if in due time you should be my wife, those ornaments would be mine."[10] Surely a young woman who could be so vexed about some coral trinkets would be affected by the knowledge that a beloved companion and chaperone of her youth was himself her father's property.

Furthermore, it is hard to imagine that the momentous emancipation day passed her by entirely. The young Elizabeth Cady was enthralled with public events, and loved "attending court" with Peter, learning about the law, and participating in the "numerous and protracted" gatherings surrounding each Fourth of July.[11] One wonders how she could have remained untouched by the celebrations and fêtes that took place in honor of emancipation. She felt no qualms, then or later, about criticizing her father's adherence to convention where the status of women was concerned. But her sensitivity to injustice and her outrage at the laws of property seem not to have extended to Peter Teabout and the other enslaved men in the Cady household.

Like many ambitious young girls, Elizabeth Cady chose men as her role models. Feeling slighted by her father, whom she revered, and apparently unimpressed with what her mother could teach her, she turned to her neighbor, Presbyterian pastor Simon Hosack, for guidance. Apparently he enjoyed the little girl's company, and tolerated her frequent visits and unceasing questions. When Eleazar died, and Elizabeth decided "that the chief thing to be done in order to equal boys was to be learned and courageous," Rev. Hosack agreed to tutor her in Greek and Latin. Horseback riding, the child's measure of heroism itself, she would have to learn on her own. In Stanton's recollection, Hosack thought nothing of dropping his other duties to teach a grieving little girl Greek, and she soon outstripped the local boys, winning prizes for her accomplishments. Her father, "evidently pleased," nevertheless repeated, "Ah, you should have been a boy!" and the child ran to Hosack for solace. Only he, she recalled, offered the "unbounded praises and visions of [her] future success" that she so desperately wanted.[12]

As hard as Elizabeth was working to persuade her father that she was "as good as a boy," her student years at the Johnstown Academy actually allowed her to be one of them. Until she graduated at sixteen, she was "the only girl in the higher classes of mathematics and the languages," and relished as well the "running races, sliding downhill, and snowballing" in which there was "no distinction of sex." When upon graduation the boys left for Union College, the young Elizabeth Cady's "vexation and mortification knew no bounds."[13] Later she believed that her thwarted ambition made her more determined to fight the suppression of women; at the time, she was simply furious at being left behind.

If the young Elizabeth had not later turned that exclusion into a philosophy of woman's rights, we might simply shrug at her teenage self-absorption. After all, the child was indulged in her rebellions, had found an otherwise busy adult to teach her Greek and sing her praises, and enjoyed the attention of young men who were willing to argue with her on all subjects. And although she was barred from Union College, she was hardly deprived of a formal education. In 1830 she entered Emma Willard's school, the Troy Female Seminary, and there received the best education available to girls—not merely a "fashionable" one, as she later sneered.[14]

For all the constraints on women in Elizabeth Cady's youthful world, there had been dramatic change in the area of girls' education.

Throughout the nation, a lively conversation about female education—about women's abilities to reason and to learn, which subjects were most appropriate for their "sphere," and what women should actually "do" with their learning—infused discussion in newspapers, parlors, and pulpits. Philosophers of female education—Catharine Beecher and Mary Lyon, most famously—insisted that schools could simultaneously expand girls' intellect and train teachers and missionaries for the larger good, while sustaining women's traditional place in a gendered world. Their students gathered in schools and literary societies to test the proposition that women's intellects were, in fact, equal to men's. Even as she griped about her father's limited expectations, Elizabeth Cady lived at a time when female academies were offering girls of her class much of what was being provided to their brothers.[15]

The Troy Female Seminary had had a rocky start at its founding in 1814, but by 1821, when the city of Troy granted it $4,000 in funding, it was solidly launched as a premier educator of elite and middle-class girls. The school's founder, Emma Willard, one of the pioneering educators of her generation, introduced these young women to a rigorous academic education, balancing intellectual achievement with a conventional approach to women's domestic roles. The school served as a model, and indeed a training ground, for the next generation's founders and professors of women's colleges. Elizabeth Cady's own classmates were, like her, the daughters of the elite and professional classes; her younger sisters, Margaret and Catherine, would follow her there in 1834 and 1835, respectively. The school's catalogue of its early graduates reads like a "Who's Who" of the daughters and, later, wives of lawyers, politicians, and merchants. Frances Miller, who later married politician William Henry Seward, had attended the school a decade earlier, as had her sister Lazette, later lawyer Alvah Worden's wife. Their father, like Elizabeth Cady's, was an Upstate New York judge, and they, too, would move into antislavery and political circles; both Miller sisters, by all accounts, were the intellectual equals of their prominent husbands.[16]

But Elizabeth Cady liked boys, and she thought the prospect of an all-girls school "dreary and profitless." She admired boys' energy, envied their freedoms, and aspired to their achievements; she badly wanted their approval and admiration as well. But she was not, or not only, a flirt; mostly, she wanted to be one of them, to compete with them on their terms. She would always relish any chance to best "the young masculinity," whom she found so often "mistaking bluster for logic." Elizabeth Cady spent her time in Troy only vaguely attentive to academic pursuits; she claimed she had "already studied everything that was taught there except French, music, and dancing." She was far more interested in debating with the local boys and gaining the adoration of girls: "I loved flattery," she admitted. Both she and the more conventionally feminine girls were happy to cast her as a heroic male figure. In one foolish escapade, she swapped her essay for the less excellent composition of one of her young admirers; discovered and disgraced, she found, decades later, that the memory could still evoke that horrible adolescent mixture of mortification and pride: the girl "put her arms around me affectionately and kissed me again and again," said, " 'Oh! . . . you are a hero. You went through that ordeal like a soldier,' " and announced, " 'You are so good and noble I know you will not betray me.' "[17] And Stanton never did.

Argumentative, heroic, and self-confident, Elizabeth Cady was not particularly bold in imagining her own life. At seventeen she was home again, her formal education complete. She had no particular plans for her future—but then, girls of her class were not expected to—and for all her later calls to rebellion, she showed little inclination to forge a new path. There were, after all, only a few appropriate choices for someone like her, at least before marriage: teaching, charitable activity, domestic work, and religious enthusiasm. None appealed.

Elizabeth Cady had already rejected religion as a possible outlet for her energies. The Second Great Awakening was in full swing, and thousands of young people were inspired by its religious preachings to commit themselves to a spiritual, and social, mission. Yet Elizabeth Cady's own flirtation with religious conversion did not go well. As she recalled, the great revival leader Charles Finney himself came to Troy for a six-week revival when she was at school, and she fell "victim" to his declarations about "the total depravity of human nature and the sinner's awful danger of everlasting punishment." Terrified by the sight of Finney's "great eyes rolling around the congregation and his arms flying about in the air," she underwent a conversion full of "mental anguish," followed by a near breakdown. A six-week trip to Niagara with sister Tryphena, brother-in-law Edward Bayard, and Judge Cady was prescribed, where a rigorous reading of rational philosophers replaced any discussion of religion. Stanton's mind, she reported happily, was "restored to its normal condition," cleansed once and for all of any "religious superstitions."[18]

There are problems with this story, not least that Charles Finney did not preach in Troy for any length of time while Elizabeth Cady was there. But in telling it, Stanton had made the point she intended: just as she described her life as a series of steps toward her awareness of women's oppression, so she explained her lifelong distaste for orthodox religion by stressing the harm that befell women (herself the prime example) who fell under its spell. In her memoir, Stanton took special delight that her family's "old church was turned into a mitten factory, and the pleasant hum of machinery and the glad faces of men and women have chased the evil spirits to their hiding places."[19] (That the "glad" men and women who worked there might not have felt the same way apparently did not enter Stanton's mind.) In any case, religion would offer Stanton neither comfort nor a calling. At a time when religious faith propelled many women of her generation into work for charity, antislavery, temperance, and woman's rights, Elizabeth Cady had serious qualms about its teachings. For the time being, no higher purpose presented itself.

There were, of course, other ways Elizabeth Cady could have kept busy. But unlike most of her future coworkers in the reform community, she was never encouraged, and certainly not required, to do much work. Her father was more than willing to support her and her sisters, and was, all in all, remarkably indulgent; he probably enjoyed Elizabeth's chatty and inquisitive presence in his study. Nor did Margaret Cady seem to expect much labor from her daughter; the girls were required only "to keep our rooms in order, mend and make our clothes, and do our own ironing." Although Elizabeth Cady Stanton recalled that their home was filled with "barrels of apples, vegetables, salt meats, cider, butter, pounding barrels, washtubs, etc.," that there were "tallow candles," and that a "laundress or the nurse" sewed the girls' outfits of "bright red flannel, black alpaca aprons, and, around the neck, a starched ruffle," she gave little thought to the labor involved. While her contemporaries had to support themselves in work of various kinds—Susan B. Anthony was a teacher, Harriet Hanson Robinson a mill worker, and Lucy Stone an antislavery lecturer— and countless others did prodigious amounts of housework, cared for smaller children, helped out on their parents' farms, and sewed for charitable societies, Elizabeth Cady partied, rode horses, and enjoyed "the most pleasant years of my girlhood."[20] Like many a pampered girl, she seems to have waited for her future to land in her lap. Which, of course, it did.

During these years after she finished school, Elizabeth Cady made frequent visits to her cousin Gerrit Smith's home in Peterboro, a place that indulged both her love of fun and flattery and her passion for debate. It was there that her partying proved to be more fruitful and fateful. Smith was an extremely wealthy landowner: his father was Peter Smith, who had amassed a great fortune in New York real estate after the Revolution, and his mother was Margaret Cady's sister. Gerrit Smith himself enjoyed a long business relationship with his uncle, Elizabeth's father. But in striking contrast to Judge Cady, Smith was also a radical reformer. By 1835, Gerrit Smith had become convinced by the impassioned teachings of William Lloyd Garrison and his newspaper, the *Liberator*, to embrace the cause of immediate abolitionism. Peterboro became the local center for antislavery radicalism, as Smith and his wife, Ann Fitzhugh Smith, devoted their household and much of their wealth (one estimate is $8 million) to entertaining, organizing, and expanding a community of reformers. Their visitors at a given time could include prominent antislavery reformers (James and Lucretia Mott visited in 1835), members of Upstate New York's Dutch elite, free African Americans, and fugitive slaves on their way farther north. With characteristic warmth, they opened their home to the lively young Elizabeth Cady, and welcomed her friendship with their own accomplished Elizabeth, known as Libby. (For the rest of their lives the two cousins would correspond under assumed male nicknames: Libby Smith Miller was Julius, named for the "witty" character in a Christy Minstrels play they had seen, and Elizabeth Cady Stanton was, appropriately, Johnson, the philosopher.)[21]

The Smiths enjoyed congenial company, but they had a more serious purpose as well: they undertook to convert their many guests to the cause of emancipation, instructing one fugitive slave, Harriet Powell, to "make good abolitionists of them by telling them the history of your life." Although one biographer insists that Elizabeth Cady "instinctively . . . rebelled against slavery," Stanton herself "recorded no memories of meetings there with black villagers or visiting activists," and seems to have been simply enraptured by the scene: "Mr. Bayard and cousin Gerrit argued all the time upon the subject of *abolition*," she wrote her uncle Peter Smith. "I enjoyed it very much as they both argue well and without the least impatience either in word or manner. Every member of their household is an abolitionist even to the coachman."[22] If the Smiths' antislavery preaching changed Elizabeth Cady's life, it was only indirectly, and she did not experience the dramatic conversion to abolitionism that transformed the lives of so many of her contemporaries.

Visits to the Smiths were simply among the many pleasures of those years, for Elizabeth Cady continued to enjoy parties, outings, and the company of a never-ending stream of law students who were delighted to tease the feisty girl about woman's rights. Recalling these debates, as well as her victories in chess and the lively flirtations in her father's law office, Stanton later admitted that she "did not study so much for a love of the truth or my own development, . . . as to make those young men recognize my equality." Not surprisingly, Elizabeth Cady's ease with young men, and her eagerness to be accepted as their intellectual equal, soon blurred with her desire for romance—these years were, she recalled, "the period . . . when the emotions rule us, and when we idealize everything in life." It was then, when she had begun to attract a different kind of attention, that she fell in love. While some might remember their earliest romance as a crushing disappointment, Elizabeth Cady's only added to her self-regard: "What dignity it adds to a young girl's estimate of herself when some strong man makes her feel that in her hands rest his future peace and happiness!" she recalled happily.[23]

Although Elizabeth Cady Stanton never identified the person who evoked her "long[ing] for one more such rapturous dream of bliss," a future biographer described an uneasy romantic crisis, a "beautiful, tempestuous, impossible thing." Edward Bayard, ten years Elizabeth's senior and a classmate of her brother, Eleazar, had long acted as a surrogate brother; he loved nothing more "than to get a bevy of bright young girls about him and teach them how to think clearly and reason logically." He was just the kind of man to arouse Elizabeth Cady's ardor. By the time she returned home from Troy, Edward had married her sister Tryphena, but he continued to play an important role in her life until finally, when she was visiting the Bayards, who had moved some 150 miles away to Seneca Falls, Edward "impetuously revealed his secret, told her that he loved her, and she knew that she had always loved him." Apparently the two continued to declare their love "on moonlight nights" and discussed running away together, until Elizabeth finally, in a sober moment, broke it off and returned home. Years later she would live briefly with Edward and Tryphena in their apartment in New York, though family lore insisted that Bayard "never allowed himself to be left in a room with her alone."[24]

Leaving aside Edward Bayard's behavior—what *was* he thinking, and would he really have given up his wife, career, and reputation for this girl?—it is hard to know what to make of this story. Aside from Stanton's own oblique reference to that "season of supreme human love and passion," there are few sources for it. In 1873 Stanton complained bitterly to her coworker Isabella Beecher Hooker that she had betrayed a "moonlight talk" that had been "as sacred as if it had been with God himself," which may have involved Stanton's confession of her secret love. Certainly Stanton herself recalled her brother-in-law with more than a twinge. After his funeral in 1889, she was moved to reflect, "Oh! how much of my happiness in those years I owe to to [*sic*] the dear one whose eyes have just closed forever."[25]

A second source is more explicit. Stanton's early biographer, Alma Lutz, printed the story at the insistence of Stanton's daughter, Harriot Stanton Blatch, who had two motives for telling it. For one, Harriot could not stand Tryphena. It was she, "tall, handsome, severe 'Aunty By,'" who tried to squelch Elizabeth's daughters' own boisterous spirits. ("What a trial that aunt was in all our lives," Harriot recalled years later, without a hint of forgiveness.) It is certainly plausible that by repeating or even embellishing the story, Harriot had "devised a unique form of retribution." Second, a youthful affair with Edward Bayard portrayed Stanton in a way her daughter, a "new woman" herself, wished: as a real live sexual person, a "juicy radical," in Harriot's words, rather than as a staid and prudish Victorian in whom the post-suffrage generation showed little interest.[26] There is no way to know how deeply involved Elizabeth and Edward got, or who knew of it, but it seems likely that their relationship moved beyond a shared passion for philosophical texts.

Regardless, or perhaps because, of Elizabeth Cady's indiscretion, in the fall of 1839 a new man of interest appeared at Gerrit and Ann Smith's, where Elizabeth had sought refuge. Henry Brewster Stanton was an effective and thrilling antislavery lecturer who used Peterboro as a base while he toured Upstate New York. Because he had shown up with another young woman, Elizabeth Cady and her friends viewed him "as not in the matrimonial market" and so "we were all much more free and easy in our manners with him than we would otherwise have been." Henry Stanton was thirty-four years old, ten years Elizabeth Cady's senior, "with the advantage," she recalled, "that that number of years necessarily gives." Elizabeth was smitten: "spell-bound" at his talks, happy in his company, and distracted from Edward Bayard. Riding horseback with Henry aroused in her "new ideas of individual rights and the basic principles of government," as well as "charming revelations of human feeling." He also wrote passionate missives to his "sun-flower," thus incidentally bestowing on her the pen name with which she would sign numerous articles in defense of woman's rights. With "so much happiness crowded into one short month," the two became engaged.[27]

Like Elizabeth Cady, Henry Brewster Stanton came from old Puritan stock, as the phrase went; his mother, Susan Brewster, was a direct descendent of William Brewster of *Mayflower* fame. Henry was born in 1805 in Pachaug, Connecticut, the second of six children and oldest son of a merchant, Joseph Stanton, who had increased his wealth through manufacturing cotton and wool and establishing country stores, and who owned a slave.[28] Of Susan Brewster Stanton we hear only that she was a vigorous woman who "thanked God she was born before nerves were invented." That she lived in nearby Rochester, New York, until she died in 1853 does not figure much in Henry's and Elizabeth's stories of their lives.[29]

Henry Stanton's early career resembles the plot of an antebellum novel about a young man on the make. It offers a stock combination of bootstrap pulling, manly independence, and timely meetings with famous and charismatic men. Like thousands of other young men from New England, in 1826 Henry was lured to the expanding city of Rochester by the promises of the Erie Canal. There he became a clerk in the canal office. He seems always to have been where the action was: on Friday, November 13, 1829, he was among the thousands of people who witnessed daredevil Sam Patch's jump to his death from the Genessee Falls, after a speech Stanton considered "ridiculous."[30] Soon he made the acquaintance of newspaper editor (and soon founder of the Whig Party) Thurlow Weed, for whom he wrote a number of articles. In the course of working for John Quincy Adams's reelection campaign in 1828, Stanton crossed paths with another aspiring young politician, the red-haired William Henry Seward. Delighted to be in the bustling new world of Upstate New York, and confident that his talents would serve him well there, he was open to anything.

Politics was Stanton's first love, and he would have remained faithful to it if he had not been distracted by the Second Great Awakening. Charles Finney came to Rochester in 1830, and if he did not inspire the young Elizabeth Cady with a lifelong religious zeal, his call to personal salvation moved Henry Stanton so much that he would later devote a long passage in his *Random Recollections* to that day. "His sway over an audience was wonderful," recalled Stanton, no slouch at oratory himself. He felt deeply Finney's call to confront the moral challenges of the day and so decided to train at the Rochester Manual Labor Institute. It was there that he became close to another Finney acolyte, Theodore Dwight Weld, from whom Stanton "learned more . . . than from all other men and books." Gradually the two men, both of whom claimed to have opposed slavery since childhood, decided that their spiritual futures lay with the emerging cause of antislavery. Thus in 1832 Henry Stanton entered the newly endowed Lane Seminary in Cincinnati, headed by the Reverend Lyman Beecher and funded by wealthy abolitionists Arthur and Lewis Tappan.[31]

Stanton's academic intentions never quite panned out. Soon after he arrived in Ohio he joined the Lane rebels, whose devotion to the cry of immediate abolition tore the school apart and transformed the cause. These young men would abandon the seminary for what Lyman Beecher called that "muddy stream of vinegar that went trickling down to Oberlin," and Stanton intended to join them.[32] First, however, he agreed to speak at the American Anti-Slavery Society's first-anniversary meeting in New York City in 1834. It was there that he received, and accepted, a more intriguing offer than that of aging student activist: for about eight dollars a week, room and board with strangers, and relentless travel throughout the North, he became one of the society's first full-time agents.

Henry Stanton was, by all accounts, an extraordinary speaker and organizer, although even his closest friends thought he could stand to "correct his air of *recklessness* and *'harem-Scarem.'* " His words were "like living coals" and his style was "tremendous." Years later, Lydia Maria Child would recall "his spontaneous eloquence." True, abolitionist Debora Weston thought his speeches "rather too violent at times," and Charles Finney considered his fiery words in "the spirit and the language of a slave driver."[33] But Frederick Douglass, whose initiation into the antislavery organization included hearing Stanton speak, considered him "unquestionably the best orator" the movement had. A rising star, he would soon be called on to train seventy agents, including the Grimké sisters, who became "the driving force of abolitionism." William Lloyd Garrison himself would call Henry the "Napoleon of our cause."[34]

Such harmony and universal acclaim had already passed by the time Henry Stanton met Elizabeth Cady, for Henry was a central player in a bitter rift in the American Anti-Slavery Society over the strategy of using electoral means to end slavery, clerical influence in the movement, and woman's rights. As a leader of the so-called new organizationists, who opposed William Lloyd Garrison's leadership and platform, he was swamped with work, organizing a new antislavery association, grappling with financial difficulties, and helping to fund and edit the *Massachusetts Abolitionist*. He threw himself wholeheartedly into the work, but he had lost the trust of many former admirers, including the movement's leading women, and this must have hurt.[35] It was in the midst of all this that he stopped in Peterboro, and was met with greater female enthusiasm than he had recently enjoyed. Only much later would this meeting—between someone on the anti–woman's rights side of the schism and the future leader of the woman's rights movement—come to seem so ironic.

In the highly charged autumn of 1839, Henry Stanton offered much that appealed to the young Elizabeth Cady. Aside from being tall and "fine-looking," he was a veteran of exciting antislavery battles, an experienced activist who had faced down some two hundred mobs, and a lovely talker. For the twenty-four-year-old Elizabeth, a young woman with "a passion for oratory," his "remarkable conversational talent" and intensity of conviction were extraordinarily persuasive.[36] Indeed, what comes across from their courtship and the early years of their marriage is how his conversation stirred her. "I never knew any one who could on the spur of the moment rise and express himself more appropriately on all subjects and on all occasions," she told their son Theodore after Henry's death.[37] People embrace a cause or a lover for many reasons; for Elizabeth Cady, Henry Stanton's gift of gab was sexiness itself.

Gerrit Smith had wanted young Elizabeth to adopt his antislavery views, but he was understandably nervous about being thought responsible for her new romantic attachment. He warned Elizabeth "in deep, solemn tones, while strongly eulogizing my lover, that my father would never consent to my marriage with an abolitionist."[38] But Judge Cady, wisely waiting until Elizabeth had returned home, where she would be without either lover or cousin to sway her, objected mostly on practical grounds. "I understand Mr Stanton now has some employment in an Abolition society which yields him a living—," he wrote Gerrit Smith. ". . . If the object of the Abolitionists be soon accomplished he must be thrown out of business—and if success does not soon crown their efforts—the rank and file will not much longer consent to pay salaries." Daniel Cady was an indulgent father, but Henry Stanton seemed a poor choice for his tempestuous and spoiled daughter.[39]

Henry objected strongly to being thought an irresponsible or impecunious radical: "Since I was 13 years old I have been thrown entirely upon my own resources, especially as to money," he assured Elizabeth. "I have never received a dollar's gratuitous aid from anyone, though it has been frequently pressed upon me." Elizabeth herself was confused by friends who suddenly warned of the "dangers and disappointments" of marriage. To Henry's distress, these friends included Edward Bayard, who weighed in against the marriage. Although she resented her father's intervention—it was, she declared, more evidence of his efforts to impose his "downright tyranny" over her—she was susceptible to arguments about her material well-being. Apparently Elizabeth Cady had failed to consider the sacrifice that marriage to Stanton might entail, and by March, convinced that "I was too hasty," she broke off the engagement. "We are still friends," she assured Ann Smith, "& correspond as before & perhaps when the storm blows over we may be dearer friends than now." Still, she was in love, and after "a season of doubt and conflict," perhaps complicated by Bayard's own declarations, when Henry announced that he was sailing to London for the World's Anti-Slavery Convention, she chose not to wait.[40] As would always be the case, her father relented at once, supporting the marriage while shrewdly making sure to keep some property legally separate in Elizabeth's name.

It was not only an anxious father and a jealous brother-in-law who considered Elizabeth and Henry less than ideally matched, even "an odd couple." One British abolitionist found Henry somewhat aloof, but raved about his wife: "one in ten thousand . . . such eloquence, such simplicity of manner—such naivete, a clearsightedness, candor, openness, such love for all that is great and good." Angelina Grimké, who was "very much pleased" with the young woman, nevertheless "could not help wishing that Henry was better calculated to mould such a mind."[41] Henry for one had no idea what he was in for.

For all the agonizing, opposition, and indecision, the wedding happened quickly and without much fanfare. On Friday, May 1, 1840, they married, though the record is silent on what they expected from each other besides ardor and talk. Henry found his wife adorable, lively, and full of enthusiasm for his oratory, and he admired her "superior . . . mind and enlarged heart." She, in turn, had found someone who enjoyed intellectual exchange as much as she did. Both of them, she admitted, were "endowed with a good degree of self-esteem."[42] When she refused to say the word *obey* at their marriage ceremony, Henry likely found it cute, and congratulated himself on his open-mindedness. He was accustomed to brilliance, was in his element among famous men—Weed, Seward, Finney, and Weld were

only a few of the names he could drop—and the antislavery movement's leading women. He could not possibly have imagined, in the
self-assurance of his ambition, his celebrity, and, of course, his sex,
that his wife would match or surpass them all in intellect, following,
and fame.

The World's Anti-Slavery Convention in London is legendary
in the history of woman's rights, in large part because of Stanton's
description of the impact it had on her. In other respects, the convention was unusual only for its size (some five hundred delegates
attended) and for the multitude of countries from which delegates
came. Men made speeches, long-winded and long forgotten, on West
Indian emancipation; on ending the slave trade; and on emancipating
the slaves in America, which all present agreed was the most intransi-
gent of slave societies. After all the travel and the talk, however, the
convention became far better known for excluding the female delegates who had come from the United States and for bringing together
Elizabeth Cady Stanton and the famed Quaker abolitionist Lucretia
Mott.

But first there was the three-week voyage on the *Montreal*. Travel
to Europe was no small undertaking in 1840, with the upper-class
practice of making a grand European tour some decades off. Stanton's
parents, wealthy but provincial, had never gone abroad, nor had her
wealthy relatives Gerrit and Ann Smith. Europeans, if they encoun-
tered Americans at all, met mostly missionaries and merchants, not
tourists. Accounts of foreign travel were popular in the United States,
but it was a vicarious exploration. Certainly the rise of steamships in
the 1840s would make travel more common, but exposure to foreign
lands was still far from a requirement for public office or intellectual
stature. Editor Horace Greeley would first sail to London in 1851 to
attend the Crystal Palace exhibition, and Susan B. Anthony first
crossed the ocean in 1883, while Abraham Lincoln, six years Elizabeth Cady Stanton's senior, never set foot off his nation's soil. A few
wealthy reformers such as Maria Weston Chapman had been educated in England, and William Lloyd Garrison had "wafted safely
across the deep" to an antislavery meeting in 1833, but most of the
forty or so American abolitionists who attended the London convention were making the trip for the first time.[43]

The logistics were daunting. Some prominent abolitionists would be absent or delayed: Maria Weston Chapman was having another baby, and William Lloyd Garrison decided to postpone his trip until after the American Anti-Slavery Society's annual meeting, which promised to be bruising. Even once the American societies had chosen their delegates, raising the necessary funds was a challenge. Henry, who now had a wife to take along, had to scrape up more than $200. "What can be done for poor Stanton?" Theodore Weld had asked when he heard of his friend's approaching wedding, since *"Almost the whole of his salary* for the last two years" was owed him.[44] Elizabeth Cady Stanton knew or cared little about these mundane concerns. For her, the combination of marriage, reform, and world travel seemed to promise a lifetime of exploration and freedom.

Although respectably married, Elizabeth Cady Stanton was quite recognizably herself as she embarked on this adventure: a young woman who knew that "some amusement . . . was necessary to my existence" and whose final act in port was "a standing game of 'tag' " around the ship with her brother-in-law Daniel Eaton. "As I was compelled, under the circumstances, to conduct the pursuit with some degree of decorum, and he had the advantage of height, long limbs, and freedom from skirts, I really stood no chance whatever," she recalled laughingly. Once they had set sail, being the wife of an anti-slavery delegate somewhat cut into her fun, for "it was deemed important that I should thoroughly understand the status of the anti-slavery movement in my own country." Henry, in company with future Liberty Party presidential candidate James Birney—how he must have pursed his lips at the game of tag—"felt it important that I should be able to answer whatever I might be asked in England on all phases of the slavery question," and set her on a course of "reading and talking on that question." Henry found his lively wife endlessly fascinating, but Birney did not; he thought the young Elizabeth Stanton "needed considerable toning down," and made it his pet project to teach her some decorum: advising that she not call her husband by his first name in public, that she not cheat at chess, and that she "feel [his] rebukes more deeply."[45] Nor did Birney share in the fun in a lady's accepting the captain's dare "to be hoisted to the top of the mast in a chair." He apparently considered it "very undignified," and even

Henry Stanton admitted that Elizabeth had been "a little too gay." Although sometimes Henry wished his wife were more like Gerrit Smith's wife, "neither the praise nor the blame of mankind was over-powering to either" Stanton, so mostly they cheerfully ignored Birney's advice.[46]

Elizabeth Cady Stanton had probably visited her sister Harriet Eaton and her family in New York City, but she was still a provincial young woman. In any case, there was no place like nineteenth-century London, "the metropolis of the world," in the view of an awed Mary Grew, a delegate from Philadelphia. Stanton must have felt enormous excitement at entering this wider world. But although she performed "the traveler's duty" of exploring "the top and bottom of everything," she admitted to the Grimkés that she felt "more interest in [poet] Amelia Opie than in Westminster Abbey."[47] What mattered most was the talk, the controversies, and, above all, her new friends.

Abolitionist Mark Moore's lodging house in Cheapside, London, was rather grim, but the day after the Stantons got there the female delegates from the United States arrived, and things brightened considerably. Elizabeth Stanton was thrilled to meet these women, most of them already well known for speaking and acting alongside men in opposing slavery. Although, like Stanton, they were new at world travel, they were hardly political innocents abroad, and they had come to London prepared for a fight. Active participants in the battles raging within the antislavery movement, Stanton's new friends, she quickly learned, represented the pro–woman's rights side of the debate. Her shipboard tutorials had taught her something of the rifts in the movement, but she may not have realized until that moment how, and how much, it all mattered to her.

Elizabeth Cady Stanton had not been initiated into the inner workings of the antislavery cause by an impartial teacher. As a leader of the anti-Garrisonians, Henry Stanton was allied with those who proposed an electoral strategy to end slavery and who refused to endorse any "extraneous" issues that might harm their already wildly unpopular cause. All this infighting may at first have struck Elizabeth as tiresome. But the issue that had precipitated the schism was Abby Kelley's election to the American Anti-Slavery Society's business committee, and the resulting debate was over women's equal membership in the cause. The dispute had sailed across the Atlantic faster than the delegates themselves, and everyone, except perhaps for the young Mrs. Stanton, knew that a battle would occur over woman's rights. Now she found herself, in her words, "unwittingly . . . by marriage on the wrong side."[48]

On Friday, June 12, when the convention came to order in Freemasons' Hall with the women delegates seated behind a bar, Wendell Phillips, cautioned by his wife, Ann, not to "shilly-shally," claimed the "right to interpret 'friends of the slave,' to include" female as well as male delegates. Professor Adam of Massachusetts concurred, adding that his credentials had no more authority than the women's, and that he would not be "entitled to occupy such a position" if theirs were denied. Colonel Miller of Vermont boasted that his state "has never been troubled with the woman question" since it was women themselves who were its first abolitionists. The English delegates, though they insisted defensively, and repeatedly, that they had the "highest possible regard for the ladies," ignored Phillips's ringing affirmation that excluding women was identical to excluding black delegates, declared that the "custom of this country" should hold sway, and defeated the Garrisonian delegation with ease.[49]

The vote to exclude the women only further roiled the waters, both public and private. Reflecting a bitter disagreement among the Americans about both principle and strategy, the debate over the exclusion of the female delegates was vociferous and widespread, taking place inside convention halls, at tea parties, and in private conversation. Certainly it put the newly married Henry Stanton in a sticky situation. Elizabeth Cady Stanton later claimed that Henry "made a very eloquent speech in favor of admitting the women delegates," but he did no such thing—at least not during the convention's formal proceedings. William Lloyd Garrison, who had not yet arrived in London, heard that Stanton "voted right" on the question, and Elizabeth Cady Stanton later included her husband's name among the women's supporters, but both Birney and Elizabeth Neall later claimed that he had voted in the negative.[50]

Given Henry Stanton's opposition to Garrison's leadership (he held that Garrison's "no-government doctrine" was "worse than Fanny Wrightism," that is, infidelity and radicalism), his negative vote seems

more likely. Although he was understandably eager to maintain the
goodwill of his new wife, Henry Stanton's record on woman's rights
was decidedly mixed. He was not conspicuously conservative on the
woman question, but he feared alienating the antislavery movement's
clerical allies—whom he clearly, reflexively, considered of greater
importance than its female adherents.[51] He certainly did not feel, as
Garrison did, that "if women should be excluded from its deliberation,
my interest in [the convention] would be about destroyed." Indeed,
he probably felt relieved when Garrison and three other men
(Nathaniel Rogers, Charles Remond, and William Adam) joined the
women in exile behind the dividing bar. Did Henry realize that the
London convention signaled the beginning of a profound shift in his
wife's allegiances? The record offers no clue. Both may have been too
caught up in that summer's excitement to notice that Elizabeth Stanton already considered "no question so important as the emancipation
of women from the dogmas of the past."[52]

Whatever her husband's role, London provided the most wonderful talk Elizabeth Cady Stanton had ever heard, and she soaked it up.
Her own social network, even in Peterboro, had not exposed her to
women like these, "who believed in the equality of the sexes and who
did not believe in the popular orthodox religion." Most of the female
delegates were Quakers, and were themselves caught up in a denom-
inational struggle with British Friends, a skirmish to which Stanton
referred only briefly. All were Garrisonian loyalists, "ultraists," in the
usage of the day. They had not considered woman's rights only in the
abstract, but had struggled over women's status in their antislavery
organizations and Friends meetings. So long had they been woman's
rights women that they were already tired of being urged to wait to
gain those rights: "Four fifths of the abolitionists now are for *womans
rights* or so far on the road that they will get there soon," Theodore
Weld had assured an impatient Angelina Grimké several years earlier
as he pleaded with her not to "put the cart before the horse." Indeed,
while Elizabeth Cady Stanton was being lectured aboard ship about
the basics of the antislavery schism, the other women's ocean crossing
had allowed them to "exercise our *combativeness, veneration, conscien-
tiousness,* or *self-esteem,*" as they "roam[ed] at will" over topics that
included woman's rights. On one of their last days at sea, the gentle-

men toasted the "ladies of America" and then asked the women, who had been peering into the all-male festivities from a doorway, to assign a man to return the favor. "They were told that the women of America did not deputize gentlemen to do their business, but did it them-selves, which reply elicited laughter and cheers for American ladies," Mary Grew wrote firmly.[53]

How Elizabeth Cady Stanton would have loved *that* voyage. Now in London, she found such talk, spiked with the righteous anger trig-gered by the women's exclusion, even more thrilling. It touched a chord. She found it "intensely gratifying to hear all that, through years of doubt, I had dimly thought, so freely discussed by other women." Stanton's reverence for Lucretia Mott ("a broad, liberal thinker on politics, religion, and all questions of reform") was immediate and unconditional. Mott in turn thoroughly enjoyed meeting Stanton. "I love her now as one belonging to us," she told friends the following year, pleased to have introduced her new friend to a wider circle of radical reformers. In Mott, Stanton discovered her first female role model: a freethinker, an advocate of woman's rights, and a patient mentor, who encouraged the younger woman to pursue "all the enquiries of thy open, generous confiding spirit."[54]

The differences between the two were vast, however, and went beyond the gap in their ages. For one thing, as much as Mott might have enjoyed being a tourist in London and chatting about woman's rights with the "bright, open, lovely" Stanton, she had work to do. She was insulted, though not surprised, by the women's exclusion from the "World" convention, but she had a broader perspective than her outraged young friend and, characteristically, remained calm. She refused to challenge the ruling openly, recognizing at once that the women's banishment, merely by publicizing their position, had advanced their cause. "We had many opportunities with members of the 'New-Organization,' & with the com. & with individuals, to pre-sent to them their injustice to us," she assured Maria Weston Chap-man, who was trying to follow the proceedings from Boston. Stanton was delighted to be part of the general indignation, though it was hard to be stuck with Henry's associates. Years later, her fury at English abolitionist John Scoble, who repeatedly "denounced" Mott, still ran-kled. "In all my life," she reported to Mott's son-in-law after forty years of feminist agitation, "I never did desire so to ring a man's neck as I did his, & I never enjoyed anything more than his agonizing sea sickness crossing the channel."[55]

Elizabeth Cady Stanton felt no more shyness making her views known in London than she had in her father's law office, and even then struck antislavery leaders as a "fearless" woman who "goes for woman's rights with all her soul." But she was also happy to observe the fray, and mostly "sat there quietly and listened to all that was said and done." Surely Stanton's age set her apart—Mott was almost twice her age, and Sarah Pugh was fifteen years older. More important, she was not part of the networks and battle-scarred cliques that bound these women to one another. The younger women in the group had literally been born into the cause: Abby Southwick and Emily Winslow were both daughters of founding antislavery families in Boston, and Elizabeth Neall, barely twenty-one, could boast of three generations of "impeccable abolitionist credentials."[56]

Their years of friendship mattered less than maturity and commitment in separating the other women from Stanton. Philadelphia delegates Abby Kimber and Mary Grew, though barely older than Stanton, had been central to the Philadelphia Female Anti-Slavery Society since its founding, as had Ann Greene Phillips in Boston. And in the process of dedicating themselves to the cause of abolition, these women were longtime defenders of woman's rights as well. In 1837, when Elizabeth Cady was just discovering antislavery at Peterboro, seventeen-year-old Lizzie Neall traveled to New York City to attend the First Anti-Slavery Convention of American Women; Grew, Mott, and Pugh had gone, too. It was there, Lucretia Mott would later suggest to Stanton, that "the battle began." Stanton, a political lightweight by any measure, could barely fathom what these women had already experienced. They had known the thrill of the Grimkés' public speaking and the backlash against them; they had been mobbed in Boston and seen Philadelphia's Pennsylvania Hall burned to the ground by anti-abolition mobs; they had debated among themselves whether single- or mixed-sex meetings were better suited to teach people to "lose sight of distinctions of sex"; and they had engaged in rancorous debates within the antislavery movement over women's equal participation.[57] Furthermore, although the infinitely patient

Lucretia Mott developed a warm affection for the lively young Stanton, and Stanton and Elizabeth Neall would become friends, the others made little mention of their new acquaintance. Even Mott's diary, so full of meetings and negotiations and pleas from male delegates, suggests that her time with Henry Stanton's new wife was brief, erratic, and not crucial to the business at hand.

That is not the way Elizabeth Cady Stanton remembered the events in London. Years later, she claimed that she and Mott, walking "arm in arm," resolved on returning home to call a convention to advocate the rights of women. Mott recalled instead that it was in Boston in 1841 that Stanton had "asked if we could not have a Convention for Woman's Rights."[58] London may have been the turning point in Elizabeth Cady Stanton's life, but it is unlikely that the idea for the first woman's rights convention emerged there. When it did arise, however, the idea was clearly hers.

But all that was far off, and no one imagined at the time that it would be the moral of the London story. For most of the abolitionist delegates, there remained a great deal of work to do. The Stantons traveled with some of Henry's colleagues (including the infuriating Scoble) throughout Britain and to Paris, where Henry lectured widely, both to earn their expenses and to solidify the new organization's position abroad. By December they were happy to head for home. The trip on the ship *Acadia* was cold and dull, and seemed to last forever, and the Stantons were relieved to reach New York for Christmas. After almost eight months of traveling, they arrived as they had left: irrepressible, full of stories, confident in the magnitude of their experiences, and ready for adventure, but without much that resembled a plan for the future.

2

"LONG-ACCUMULATING DISCONTENT"

(1840–1851)

Returning from the "Old World," Elizabeth Cady Stanton did not immediately embrace a new one. On the contrary, within a month, she and Henry, still "quite undecided as to our future occupation & place of residence," had settled in Johnstown with her parents. Henry needed to build a career worthy of his father-in-law's respect and his wife's needs, and so he added the study of law to his antislavery duties. Elizabeth moved easily back into her childhood milieu. Living with Margaret and Daniel Cady offered her "two added years of pleasure" with friends and family; she read books on "law, history, and political economy" and enjoyed "occasional interruptions to take part in some temperance or anti-slavery excitement." For all her later declarations of independence, Stanton would recall of that time, "How rapidly one throws off all care and anxiety under the parental roof" and it was a pattern she would follow for decades to come.[1]

Elizabeth Cady Stanton's father had starred in her life as a girl, and he remained a ubiquitous character in her adult drama as well. For one thing, by sharing his home and property with his daughter, he steadily subsidized Henry's erratic earnings, an arrangement that would go on long after the judge's death. In addition, whether he kept his household in Johnstown or Albany, he provided Elizabeth with a refuge, with his attention, and with an emotional ballast. Elizabeth Cady Stanton recalled that Judge Cady objected vehemently to her views on woman's rights; he was, and remained, her staunchest critic and most faithful opposition. Indeed, his antagonism only fueled her determination to speak, to impress, and to excel. (Henry's family, in contrast, was a connection and a duty he bore on his own; he sent several hundred dollars a year to Rochester, helping to support a mother and sister whom Elizabeth Stanton never mentions.) Significantly, the Stantons would name their first son after the judge.

Living in the Cady household provided Elizabeth Stanton with much-needed entertainment. Henry's main interest lay with the anti-slavery movement, and he was frequently on the road, lecturing, attending conventions, stumping the campaign trail for Liberty Party candidates, and studying the law in between. Hostilities with the Garrisonians over the questions of electoral politics and women's activism had only worsened, and Henry relished the battle. Perhaps he welcomed the challenge of facing Garrison on his own turf, or perhaps he had simply grown tired of living with his in-laws, but in 1842 he decided that Boston offered greater opportunities. He passed the Massachusetts Bar that fall, and the Stantons, along with baby Daniel (called Neil), who had been born in March, took steps to move to a home of their own.[2]

No one has ever described Boston as a friendly place. If it is unfair to depict it as "a deviant, stagnant, caste-ridden community," the old guard did tend to wrap itself in a cloak of insularity and self-regard. Certainly the city was changing, however creakily: the old Puritans no longer held absolute sway over its cultural life, having been challenged by transcendentalists, Unitarians, and other religious liberals. But Bronson Alcott's delight, a dozen years before the Stantons' arrival, at finding a city "upon which the light of the sun of righteousness has risen" was not a comment about Boston's social warmth.[3]

Even if Boston's antislavery elite—the "Boston clique," as Lawrence J. Friedman has aptly labeled them—had been an especially welcoming community, the Stantons were not simply newcomers, but competitors. It is difficult from this distance, with Elizabeth's shadow so thoroughly obscuring her husband's, to appreciate Henry's place in the tumultuous reform world they inhabited. Henry Brewster Stanton had been a leader in the abolitionist struggle from its earliest days; as an antislavery agent he had been an accomplished speaker and fundraiser; he was well known by the reformers Elizabeth admired. Yet as Elizabeth had learned in London, Henry's quarrels with the Garrisoni-

ans had put him on the outs with some of the women she most
wanted to befriend. Lucretia Mott, who could hardly bring herself to
say anything unkind about anyone, only referred sadly to Henry's
"error" and continued to wish him the best, but others, including the
Weston sisters and Garrison himself, were less forgiving. To many
Boston abolitionists, Henry Stanton was not simply mistaken in his
allegiances; he was a traitor. "I hope the sad divisions in the anti-
slavery cause in Boston will [n]ot deprive you of the pleasure of being
acquainted with the noble women [w]ho are on the other side," Sarah
Grimké had written Stanton that year; it may have served more as a
warning than a wish.[4] Not surprisingly, more than a little coolness
tempered the community's welcome of Henry Stanton's lively, and
only lightly abolitionized, young wife.

Whatever slights she may have felt, however, Boston offered Elizabeth Stanton intellectual excitement, fascinating debate, and the
prospect of new friendships. In her first winter there, she attended
some of Margaret Fuller's fourth season of "Conversations," where
she met transcendentalist luminaries such as Elizabeth Peabody, anti-
slavery authors such as Lydia Maria Child, activists such as Maria
Weston Chapman, and Fuller herself. Discussions ranged widely, and
some were admittedly hard to follow, but Stanton must have been
ecstatic at the talk about individual "genius," religious liberalism, and
women's role in "millennial peace and universal harmony." She
attended antislavery lectures, and she sat in the Massachusetts State
House listening to debates about the law against intermarriage, reporting to Elizabeth Neall that "'The old Bay State' is doing nobly" in
repealing such a law.[5]

For these leading radical activists and thinkers, the abolitionist
movement represented hard work, tedious petitioning, and painful
schisms as much as it did intellectual excitement. By the early 1840s,
seasoned reformers might not have expected new recruits to declare
themselves (as Angelina Grimké and Abby Kelley had once done)
martyrs to the cause, but they were surely impatient with newcomers
who failed to throw themselves fully into its labors. Not surprisingly,
the already embattled Garrisonian women were less enthralled by
Elizabeth Stanton than she was by them. What is striking in retro-
spect is not what they said about her but what they did not; abolition-

ists hardly ever referred to her, except, occasionally, as "H. B. Stanton's wife."[6]

Elizabeth Stanton must have known that Henry's position in the movement caused abolitionist women to view her with some suspicion. Even before the couple moved to Boston she had tried to associate with Garrisonian women; still, she occasionally felt snubbed. Of course, she wrote her friend Elizabeth Neall huffily, she would have gone to "a womans [*sic*] business meeting, where I might have seen the faces & heard the voices of Abbey [*sic*] Kelley & Lydia M [*sic*] Child." Unfortunately "no one told me" about any. Stanton was indignant at Neall's suggestion that she might have been "disinclined to go" to such a meeting. Did her friend imagine that she would be reluctant "because Henry might not have wished me to go?" This was too much: "You do not know the extent to which I carry my rights. I do in truth think & act for myself deeming that I alone am responsible for the sayings & doings of E. C. S." Now in Boston, she "enjoy[ed] myself more than I ever did in any city," but she remained an observer, even a dilettante. "I attend all sorts & sizes of meetings & lectures," she wrote Elizabeth Neall happily and without irony. "I consider myself in a kind of moral museum & I find that this Boston affords as many curiosities in her way as does the British museum in its."[7] If London symbolized Stanton's initiation into a community of woman's rights women, her time in Boston underscored how marginal she remained to the antislavery movement of which they were part.

Historians have long noted that the movement for woman's rights drew its core constituency and its ideas from the antislavery movement; the "school of anti-slavery" provided these women with the rhetoric, the resources, and the experience to examine their own status as women. Elizabeth Cady Stanton was unusual, the story goes, only for extending those insights in new and far-reaching directions. And yet, for all the excitement of meeting, marrying, and traveling with Henry, and the buzz of London and Boston, Stanton was an abolitionist by marriage and proximity, more a fellow traveler than a convert. She moved in abolitionist circles, attended lectures, and thrived in the company of the strong-minded activist women she found in the antislavery movement. She immersed herself in their passion and their oratory, soaking up learning like a sponge; clearly her experience in the movement made plausible her own rocketing analysis and career. But the injustices and brutalities that characterized slavery and racism were not what got her mind racing and her heart thumping. She did not seriously stretch her thinking, sacrifice wealth or comfort, or evince a strong or urgent concern for those who were actually enslaved, and she remained remarkably calm in the face of their stories. In most accounts of her life, including the one she told, three decades of antislavery struggle serve mostly as the backdrop to the cause about which she felt truly passionate. What Stanton loved, at Peterboro, in London, in Boston, and throughout her life, was the talk—first Edward Bayard's, then Henry's, Mott's, and Garrison's— and the excitement of being at the center of the action. For her, the story of slavery and the emancipation of the slaves would serve primarily as a lesson in women's own status, degradations, and rights.

Elizabeth Cady Stanton, "in a hungering, thirsting condition for truth," loved Boston, but for all its intellectual bustle, her years there were tumultuous.[8] For one thing, Henry was frequently busy. While he established a law practice and sought to enter politics, Elizabeth traveled back and forth to her parents, who had set up household in Albany. In New York's capital, she observed debates and signed petitions in favor of reform of married women's property law, and thus took a step toward applying her interest in the law to her growing passion for woman's rights. Oddly, here she found herself on the same side as Judge Cady, who, like other wealthy fathers, sought to protect his property from erratic or irresponsible sons-in-law.

He may not have had his own son-in-law in mind, but he must have known that the Stantons' marriage had its strains. Even their friends feared that these two strong personalities might collide. As Elizabeth capered around Upstate New York with baby Neil in tow, Henry, for once, was "sad, solemn, & disconsolate." On his part at least, their correspondence included flirting, and longing, and sexual allusions. Once, after begging her to write him if she "or the Kiddy" were ill, he mentioned that he had dreamed of her: "I do think of you very, very often; & I long to be with you again, to enjoy your smiles & kisses." Then he pouted: "You have the sweet little Kiddy to play with & embrace, & so you forget all about 'the peppy.' But, reflect," he went on, "where would the Kiddy have been but for me?!" Usually, after some argument, they made up: "I *do* love you Lizzie!" he wrote from Boston. "Will you forgive all my coldness & unkindness?"[9] Apparently she did, since for a time, again with her father's money, she returned to Boston and set up a home of their own.

But Boston did not make room for Henry Stanton and his ambitions. The couple claimed that it was Henry's health that sent them back to the "more genial climate" of Upstate New York, but even before they moved, Henry's health had improved. Anyway, Elizabeth Stanton wrote her cousin, "he dreads the change from Boston to Seneca, & I fear he will long for the strong excitement of a city life." It may well have been the political climate that drove them away. Once again Elizabeth's father offered a solution: a large farmhouse that Edward Bayard owned, overlooking the river in Seneca Falls, would, with some work, be perfect for their needs; the property, which the judge made certain to put in Elizabeth's name, would be legally hers with the passage of a married women's property act the following year. This time when Daniel Cady handed his daughter money, he dared her to prove " 'woman's capacity to do and dare' " by restoring the house and yard, which, with no little pride, she did.[10] And so, in 1847, the Stantons took the train to Seneca Falls, where they would live for the next fifteen years, and which Elizabeth Cady Stanton would make synonymous with the movement for woman's rights.

If you visit Seneca Falls today, you might imagine that Elizabeth and Henry Stanton had moved to a sleepy village, one with quiet waters and pristine views. Small wineries now dot the map, and a Women's Rights National Historical Park invites tourists to contemplate a presumably simpler time. Stanton's own writings supported this impression when she blamed small-town life for her domestic boredom. But the Seneca Falls of the 1840s was a far more bustling place than it is now; even the view from the Stantons' home on the hill was different, overlooking considerable traffic, industry, and noise.[11] Water rushed to power machinery in the mills along the Seneca River that ground flour and produced woolen cloth, and the young female workers in those mills made the hardships faced by wage-earning women hard to ignore. Along with local industrial production, the larger world of commerce was literally at the Stantons' doorstep, since the canal near their hill connected with the Erie Canal and the railroad linked the town to both Albany and Rochester, a mere two-hour journey. There were stores selling all sorts of goods, tradespeople offering various services, and two hotels. A Woolworth store had recently opened, selling "the best qualities, and cheapest goods ever offered in Western New York." The four-page *Seneca County Courier* brought news of Congress and cures for baldness, and residents could receive the *New York Tribune* or the *Liberator* as well; the *Albany Patriot*, the Liberty League mouthpiece supported by Gerrit Smith, likely made its way to numerous households.[12] Although it was by no means an urban scene, it bustled with commerce, business, and noise, and the movement of goods, people, and ideas.

Nor was Seneca Falls as isolated intellectually as Elizabeth Cady Stanton later implied, though she did not instantly find a place for herself in the local community of reformers. Most local woman's rights supporters were Quakers or Garrisonians or both, and the political abolitionists and temperance reformers, ambivalent as they were about women's role in their respective movements, offered no clear outlet for Stanton's intellectual aspirations. Stanton did become friendly, and combative, with neighbor and Free Soil activist Ansel Bascom, Seneca Falls's most visible reform politician. Still, there was no obvious intellectual circle with which she might have been compatible. In Johnstown several years earlier she had received the *National Anti-Slavery Standard* from a neighbor, and the *Liberator* from Sarah Pugh ("the only woman's rights food I have for myself & disciples," she had written), and presumably she continued to subscribe.[13] But she had not yet found new "disciples" with whom to discuss her reading, her frustrations, or her growing interest in woman's rights.

And what Seneca Falls lacked in adult stimulation was more than made up for with domestic challenges. At first, running a household absorbed Stanton's prodigious energies. With her usual self-regard, energy, adaptability, and hubris, she embarked on an approach to childbirth and child raising that she viewed as a model for all womankind. She boasted to Henry that her own wisdom compared favorably to that of the local doctors. Elizabeth Cady Stanton was nothing if not a skeptic, and she was not about to rein in that skepticism just because the experts were men. An avid reader, she had surely seen the works of popular health reformers, from Mary Gove Nichols's *Lectures to Ladies on Anatomy and Physiology* (1842) to Sylvester Graham's *Lectures on the Science of Human Life* (1839), and these could only have deepened her doubts about what passed for received wisdom.

And if she thought the line between doctors and quacks a thin one, who could blame her? Pharmacists in Seneca Falls advertised such medical wonders as "Vaughn's Lithontriptic" to dissolve stones, and sarsaparilla to cure "scrofula, Dyspepsia, Jaundice, Liver Complaint, Humors, Canker, Costiveness, Rheumatism, Cancer, Debility of the system" and more. Townshend's sarsaparilla, another ad promised, "immediately counteracts the nervelessness of the female frame, which is the great cause of barreness [*sic*]." It could also, of course, make root beer. Stanton preferred to trust her own judgment. She nursed her children through the usual array of—often life-threatening—childhood diseases and injuries, and noted complacently that they were emerging as an uncommonly healthy pack. Thoroughly convinced of her own medical system, she undertook a lifelong practice of offering young mothers advice, a habit her children would find embarrassing when they traveled with her. Years later, having offered extensive advice to her pregnant daughter-in-law, she would muse that "I can see all my faults and short comings repeated in my children, which oftimes fills me with self-reproach"—but there was little evidence of such humility at the time. She was a whirlwind of projects and plans, an adherent of mild punishment, and quite definite about the virtues of ventilation, causing her husband to joke that "when he died all that need be put on his tomb was 'Henry B. Stanton, died of fresh air.' "[14] All this frenzied domesticity evokes a charming image of Elizabeth Stanton opening windows, loosening her children's garments, inventing games for them, and refusing to restrain them according to traditional notions of discipline.

The vote on her decidedly forward-looking child-rearing strategies was mixed. Henry's nephew Robert Brewster Stanton, who remained irritated well into old age that one of Stanton's sons had taken his ball during childhood play, found Elizabeth's laxness disturbing, and considered the adult Neil's corruption a direct result of her too-liberal practices. By all accounts the older boys were an unruly bunch whom even their lenient mother called "young savages," but Stanton's oldest was a particular problem. In 1851 Neil joined the children of other reformers at Theodore and Angelina Grimké Weld's school in New Jersey, where the homesick nine-year-old wet his bed and longed for home.[15] He begged his mother to let him and brother Henry return to Seneca Falls. Stanton missed her sons terribly, but she held firm; her list of instructions hints at how much trouble the boys, and Neil in particular, had been at home. "One thing Neilly," she added, "I hope you will try to be more frank. What you do, do openly. Never again deceive, either by word or act." Apparently the child had trouble going "a whole week without one sly or deceitful manifestation."[16] Neil did come out badly by most measures, but the other children seemed to flourish under her regime, rarely complaining openly about her expectations or her theories.

But it was lonely amid the chaos. Henry was hardly around; he never did make it home for any of his children's births. Indeed, it is hard to conjure up much of a mental image of what Henry ("the peppy"?) did at home, except make babies, but this he did with regularity. The Stantons had moved to Seneca Falls with three small boys, having added Henry Brewster Stanton, Jr. (Kit), and Gerrit Smith Stanton (Gat) to the family in Boston. In a century when women, with good reason, faced childbirth with dread, Stanton expressed nothing but praise for her own fortitude. Following Theodore's birth in 1851, she bragged, I was "sick but a few hours, did not lie down half an hour before he was born, but worked round as hard as I could all night to do up the last things I had to do." Twenty-two months later, she bore a "noble girl," twelve-pound Margaret, after only fifteen minutes' labor. Three days later, she was "dressed and about the house as usual." "Am I not a savage almost," she asked Lucretia Mott, calling on the prevalent stereotype of sturdy non-white women. "[F]or what refined, delicate, genteel, civilized woman wd. *get well* in so indecently short a time?" Thrilled to have a daughter (at last!) she exulted, "Rejoice with me all Womankind, for lo! a champion of thy cause is born." Stanton evidently thought she was done with baby-making after number five, but Harriot arrived in 1856 ("a grievous interruption of my plans," she admitted), and Robert Livingston in 1859, when Elizabeth Cady Stanton was forty-three.[17]

Long before her last baby was born, however, "the novelty of housekeeping" had worn off, opportunities to theorize about child raising arose irregularly, and Stanton had grown bored with provincial life. "A mind always in contact with children and servants," she would muse decades later, disregarding the isolation and drudgery experienced by the servants themselves, "whose aspirations and ambitions rise no higher than the roof that shelters it, is necessarily dwarfed in its proportions." Unsure what to do next, she busied herself in "cultivating good feeling" with the nearby "Irish settlement," bullying drunken husbands by "tak[ing] Patrick by the collar" or assisting "poor mothers in the pangs of maternity." In her telling, the story serves mostly to introduce her nearly seamless move from the "ignorance, poverty, and vice" she witnessed in the neighborhood to her own "mental hunger, which, like an empty stomach, is very depressing."[18] She was apparently oblivious to the condescension and intrusiveness this story reflected, nor did she fret over the Irishwomen's absence from the path on which she was about to embark.

What she was not oblivious to was that she was, once again, on the sidelines. Elizabeth Cady Stanton had found in Europe in 1840 that "the world seems to be in a general hubub." By 1848, revolutions were brewing. The new French Republic's final emancipation of the slaves in all French colonies in 1848 emboldened American abolitionists to hope that their movement, too, would soon succeed. Hopes for emancipation from church, state, and custom seemed to be breaking out all over. Just that spring Lucretia Mott, Abby Kelley, and other Garrisonians had called an "Anti-Sabbath Convention," declaring it time to end the "spirit of religious bigotry" throughout the land, while nearby Seneca Indians, in writing a new constitution, were "imitating the movements of France and all Europe, in seeking larger liberty— more independence." And people were growing accustomed to the sound of women's voices. Mott herself had spoken for nearly an hour at the American Anti-Slavery Society meeting that May, and Ernestine Rose had addressed the legislature of New York five times.[19] Finally, that body, which had debated a Married Women's Property Act for a dozen years, passed one into law. It was the best possible time for Elizabeth Cady Stanton to figure out what to do next.

The 1848 convention in Seneca Falls, New York, is widely regarded as the birthplace of the movement for woman's rights in the

United States. Like all origin stories, this oversimplifies both the gathering's distinctiveness and its effects. No one who attended the convention in Seneca Falls was hearing about woman's rights for the first time, nor were they aware that their gathering would go down in history. Newspaper editors, ministers, educators, state legislators, and activists themselves had been debating the issue of woman's rights for years. That conversation had been loudest within the antislavery movement. Sarah and Angelina Grimké had long since drawn the connection between the human rights of the enslaved and those of freeborn women. Lucy Stone, after graduating from Oberlin College, had been speaking publicly "in vindication of the rights of women," as Garrison put it, for nearly a year. Garrison himself was "an able advocate" of the rights of women, and had made his newspaper "the medium of free discussion upon this subject." Even Stanton had, as early as 1841, addressed a temperance society, where she "infused into my speech an Homeopathic dose of woman's rights, as I take good care to do in many private conversations." Countless women experienced the reports of the convention at Seneca Falls as a turning point and an inspiration, but for many it simply gave "form and voice" to long-standing discontents and ideals.[20]

Even among political abolitionists, whose Liberty Party advanced an "extremely limited . . . agenda for gender reform," some sympathy for woman's rights was present all along. Although leading new organizationists such as Henry Stanton were reluctant to alienate ministers by taking a visible stand for female equality, others spoke out publicly. In October 1845, Liberty Party activist Joseph Osborn of Depauville, New York, criticized a major Liberty Party speech for "neglect[ing] . . . some important matters that genuine republicanism must recognize." Prominent among these was "the enfranchisement of females." A petition by six women in rural Jefferson County, New York, to the New York Constitutional Convention a year later hardly made a stir, signaling the ordinariness, in some circles, of the idea of women having "equal, and civil and political rights with men." Indeed, those who gathered in early woman's rights conventions were already deeply engaged in a "shared community of discourse" that sought to define rights, citizenship, and independence for all freeborn Americans.[21] There was, to use a modern phrase, chatter.

But most supporters of woman's rights in these antislavery communities believed that ending slavery was their most urgent responsibility. Elizabeth Cady Stanton played a distinctive part in this conversation, first, because of the intensity with which she experienced these woman's rights stirrings, and second, because she more easily loosed herself from the abolitionist cause to embark on a new crusade. Restless, bored, and longing for action, she somehow knew she would not find a place for herself handing out antislavery petitions, giving temperance speeches, and speaking whenever she could about the issue of woman's rights. Closely associated with the women who were best able to foment another rebellion, but relatively aloof from antislavery itself, she was able and willing to devote her considerable intellectual energy wholeheartedly to a new cause. Perhaps the true significance of the convention at Seneca Falls lies in what Stanton would make of it, how she would use the event to shape her own leadership of the cause that followed.

On Sunday, July 9, a small gathering at Jane and Richard Hunt's house in Waterloo struck what now seems a mighty spark for a woman's rights convention. At the time, it was simply a reunion of a half-dozen friends, all Quakers, who were troubled by events at their recent Yearly Meeting and eager to talk them over with Lucretia Mott, who was visiting from Philadelphia. At Mott's request, Jane Hunt invited her young friend from Seneca Falls to join them, and so Elizabeth Cady Stanton took the train one town over. Stanton may have met some of the women previously (seven years earlier she had referred to meeting "several agreeable friends at Waterloo"), but it was Mott she wanted to see, and pour out her troubles to. It was only by chance that she joined Mott's sister Martha Coffin Wright, Jane Hunt, Mary Ann McClintock, and McClintock's daughter Elizabeth for an afternoon of conversation.[22]

A historian who has looked closely at the events surrounding the convention in Seneca Falls has noted that Stanton "might have felt, at first, like an outsider," but this understates how truly marginal she was to this group.[23] It was London all over again. She was the only one present who was not related to any of the other women; she was the only non-Quaker; even her clothing, and her use of the honorific Mrs., which Quakers avoided, set her apart. She cared little about the internal controversies that absorbed these "earnest, thoughtful women," and she surely made little effort to hide her disinterest. But the group was welcoming and sympathetic, and, in Quaker spirit, willing to listen to "the torrent of my long-accumulating discontent." Hunt family tradition suggests that Stanton's outpourings led Richard Hunt to suggest mildly that the women "do something" rather than simply talk. As Stanton recalled it, her own words were inspiration enough, for it was "with such vehemence and indignation that I stirred myself, as well as the rest of the party, to do and dare anything."[24]

No matter. Having bestirred themselves, the women did what any self-respecting reformers would do: they called a meeting, the first dedicated to "discuss[ing] the social, civil, and religious condition and rights of woman." Eager to have Lucretia and James Mott attend, they decided to hold the conference less than two weeks later, and delivered an announcement to the *Seneca County Courier* the next day; the paper published it on July 11, and other newspapers, including Frederick Douglass's *North Star*, followed suit three days later, on Friday. Stanton and Lizzie McClintock arranged to meet at the McClintocks' house the following Sunday, to "concoct a declaration" appropriate to the occasion. Stanton came prepared with her own first draft, but the women may have scrapped it entirely, for Stanton recalled their shared delight at discovering how well the Declaration of Independence could serve as a model for their own.[25] In writing the Declaration of Sentiments, Elizabeth Cady Stanton and Lizzie McClintock together discovered an aptitude for rhetoric, history, and irony that likely surprised even them.

Elizabeth Cady Stanton's "political friendship" with Elizabeth McClintock (which McClintock's biographer considers "the model for Stanton's and Susan B. Anthony's legendary friendship") was a high point of that exciting summer. But the paths the two women had traveled underscore how unlike her new friends Stanton was. Like many abolitionists in the neighborhood, Lizzie McClintock had been born (in 1821, in Philadelphia) into the reform community. Her parents, Mary Ann and Thomas, were staunch Hicksite Quakers; her father had been prominent in 1827 in organizing a boycott of products made with slave labor, and Mary Ann was among the founders, in 1833, of the Philadelphia Female Anti-Slavery Society. In 1836 the family moved from Philadelphia to Waterloo, where their new drug-store sold a wide range of "free labor" goods and served as a center of news and activism in the community. Among their customers was Edward Bayard, who had developed an interest in homeopathic med-icines, which Thomas McClintock prepared. Few families were better situated, or better networked, than the McClintocks, who warmly welcomed traveling abolitionists and who seemed to be related to, or at least to know, everyone.[26]

In its composed Quaker way, the McClintock home buzzed with conversation, and the connections that linked family, community, reli-gion, and antislavery activism were seamless. Lizzie was only seven-teen when she traveled on her own to Philadelphia to attend the Second Anti-Slavery Convention of American Women, where her "heart leaped and burst within me for joy" at hearing Abby Kelley speak, just before Pennsylvania Hall was destroyed by protesting mobs. Her parents, while understandably concerned for her safety, never questioned her decision to represent them at the convention. Nor did they find young Lizzie's views on woman's rights alarming. Mary Ann McClintock had worked for greater rights for women within their Quaker meeting, and no family would outnumber the McClintocks among the signers of the Seneca Falls Declaration of the Sentiments.[27] Lizzie McClintock had fewer reasons than did Eliz-abeth Cady Stanton to rebel against her family's attitudes toward girls or to resent the religious teachings of her youth. But if she was calmer and less furious than Stanton, she was just as radical in her views; indeed, it was through her conversations with Lizzie that Stanton began to draw conclusions and articulate her demands for woman's rights. Quickly the two became a pair, cooking up plans to write a history of woman's rights, attending—and critiquing—sermons, and challenging local newspapers to debates.

But first there was a convention to be held, a first of its kind. Later Stanton would claim modestly that they had felt "as helpless and hopeless as if they had been suddenly asked to construct a steam engine," but these women had connections, and although Sarah Grimké, Lydia Maria Child, and Maria Weston Chapman declined to come, the two had no trouble persuading Frederick Douglass and other Upstate New York activists to attend.[28] And while it is true that they had no idea how the convention would turn out, they were not quite—or at least not all—novices at holding meetings. Stanton herself was new to leadership, but even she had addressed some one hundred women at a temperance meeting years before. Among those who attended the Seneca Falls convention were some of the most skilled activists of the age, women who knew how to organize meetings, how to advertise them, and how to manage crowds; and although, in a spasm of propriety, they asked James Mott to chair the meeting, they knew perfectly well how to handle points of order, develop resolutions, and petition for change. These antislavery activists were neither the instigators of the meeting nor its guiding philosophers—here Stanton's contribution was essential—but they were not political neophytes by any stretch.

Whatever their experience and their expectations, the organizers had clearly hit a nerve. The call, to their surprise, brought some three hundred women and men, virtually all abolitionists and many of them Quakers, to Seneca Falls. Once they had tackled the unexpected obstacle of the church's locked door—Elizabeth Stanton's young nephew Daniel Eaton, attending the convention with his mother and aunt, climbed through the window to open it—things proceeded smoothly. On July 19, women met alone, making speeches, discussing resolutions, and voting to adopt them; on the second day men, too, crowded into the Wesleyan Chapel. Lucretia Mott, Frederick Douglass, Lizzie McClintock, and Elizabeth Cady Stanton made speeches, while various other McClintocks ushered people to their seats or conducted sessions. There was none of the heckling or disruptions that had long afflicted abolitionist meetings; even when the organizers invited disagreement, "no objections . . . presented themselves."[29]

Most of the names of those who attended the convention in Seneca Falls are unfamiliar today; except for Mott, Frederick Douglass, and Elizabeth Cady Stanton herself, these people did not become national figures. They were grassroots activists, known mostly within abolitionist circles in Upstate New York, and largely acquainted with one another. Indeed, the convention was a decidedly local affair, with families traveling from no more than a day away, staying with friends and relatives, and setting off for home the next afternoon. Stanton herself likely recognized many in the audience as her neighbors. Amy and Isaac Post, and Amy's sister Sarah Hallowell, came from Rochester, some forty miles to the west; so did Catharine Ann Fish Stebbins. Rhoda Palmer, who would live to be 102 and would vote in 1919, came with her father from their farm near Geneva. Amelia Bloomer arrived late on the second day, though Stanton later recalled that she "stood aloof and laughed at us."[30]

But however familiar, even routine, it was for these activists to meet together in a convention, the document they endorsed was stunning, a foundational text in American democratic ideals. "We hold these truths to be self-evident," Stanton read aloud, nervously at first, "that all men and women are created equal." Like Stanton's own thinking, the Declaration of Sentiments was not utterly original, but also like her, it displayed spectacular breadth of thought and imagination. Like Stanton, the Declaration offered ideas in a format that was both familiar and breathtaking, mainstream and radical, and that left many listeners wondering why they had not said these things first or as well.[31]

Adopting the language of the Declaration of Independence was an inspired move; it made the document instantly recognizable and, because of that, repeatable. It also underscored Stanton's and McClintock's conviction that the rights they demanded fit squarely within the nation's traditions of equality and rebellion. That heritage, they insisted, belonged to women as it did to men, and their exclusion from its promises was simply unfinished business. Like the authors of the Declaration of Independence, who blamed King George for their suffering, they chose to go right to the source, as they saw it, of their subordination: the "history of mankind is a history of repeated injuries and usurpations on the part of man toward woman," they wrote, "having in direct object the establishment of an absolute tyranny over her." In this classic feminist statement, the authors' charges ranged widely among economic, educational, religious, and political concerns. "He has compelled her to submit to laws, in the formation of which she had no voice"; "He has made her, if married, in the eye of the law, civilly dead"; "He has taken from her all right in property, even to the wages she earns"; "In the covenant of marriage, she is compelled to promise obedience to her husband"; "He closes against her all the avenues to wealth and distinction, which he considers most honorable to himself"; "He allows her in Church as well as State, but a subordinate position"; "He has created a false public sentiment, by giving to the world a different code of morals for men and women." Yet in spite of its scope, the Declaration, the convention, and Elizabeth Cady Stanton herself became most famous for the document's ninth, and most controversial, resolution: "it is the duty of the women of this country to secure to themselves their sacred right to the elective franchise." Some participants—the record is silent on who or how many—objected to the demand for woman suffrage, but Frederick Douglass's vocal support of the measure swayed the group.

Rhetorical boldness aside, how radical were the demands made at Seneca Falls? Taken individually, they seem rather unobjectionable. After all, vast numbers of Americans already approved of educating girls; many others were in advance of their legislatures in believing that married women should control their own property; and more conservative women's organizations, such as the New York Female Moral Reform Society, had long argued for a single standard of sexual respectability by which to judge people's lapses. None of these alone was so shockingly new. Indeed, parts of the Declaration echoed earlier statements by abolitionist women in support of woman's rights. The eighth resolution—that "woman has too long rested satisfied in the circumscribed limits which corrupt custom and a perverted application of the Scriptures have marked out for her"—virtually quoted a resolution offered by Angelina Grimké to the 1837 Anti-Slavery Convention of American Women in New York. Nor was this the first instance when men had been held accountable for a system of classifying and limiting people by sex. Sarah Grimké had long before blamed men for those laws that "destroy [women's] independence, and crush her individuality" and that were passed because "woman has no political existence" and so was in effect a slave.[32]

Historians, and Stanton herself, have long argued that it was the resolution on behalf of woman suffrage that signaled the radicalism of the convention. Indeed, the demand for suffrage was the only source of real contention, its significance still the subject of much debate. Certainly those who attended the convention found the rest of the Declaration's ideas unobjectionable, and they adopted them unani-

mously. Even Stanton's sister, Harriet Cady Eaton, joined sixty-seven
women and thirty-two men in signing her name. Most of the men,
long accustomed to working alongside women in reform causes,
placed their names next to those of their wives. Not Henry: Uneasy
about his wife's plans to demand suffrage for women—"You will turn
the proceedings into a farce," he is reported to have said—hě spent
the day lecturing in another town.[33] But if the signers noticed that
both Henry Stanton and Martha Coffin Wright's lawyer husband,
David, were absent, they maintained a polite, even Quakerly, silence
on the subject.

However controversial it may have been, the association of
woman's rights with electoral politics had not come out of the blue,
and Henry Stanton had surely played a role in his wife's assertion that
women's right to the vote should be a central demand of the age.
Even with the distractions of children underfoot and the bustle of his
travels, we can well imagine the conversation around the Stantons'
table. Henry, who had long supported an electoral strategy in reform,
talked excitedly about his efforts to gain political office or the joys of
campaigning for antislavery candidates. It could not have strained his
powers of persuasion to convince his wife that politics was the source
of power and change. Indeed, as early as 1842, Elizabeth Stanton had
considered herself part of a "connecting link" between the rival
groups of abolitionists, an "admirer of Garrison" and yet "not yet fully
converted to the doctrine of no human government." "I am," she
declared even then, "in favour of political action, & the organization
of a third party as the most efficient way of calling forth & directing
action."[34] Elizabeth, reminded of her teenage years spent among her
father's law books, easily absorbed Henry's views into her own: politics and law, she was certain, undergirded women's oppression, insti-
tutionalized women's inferiority, and carried enormous potential for
transforming both.

The local Free Soil community in Seneca Falls reinforced Elizabeth Cady Stanton's conviction that politics mattered. Although the
question of women's equality had helped to tear apart the antislavery
movement almost a decade before, there was by now a hum of support among political abolitionists who lived far from Boston's high-
temperature schisms. In Seneca Falls their most visible advocate was

Stanton's neighbor Ansel Bascom, who had in 1843 arranged for prominent Garrisonian Abby Kelley to speak in his own orchard, thus fomenting an "antislavery revival" that established the town as a center of political abolitionism. Bascom believed in extending the practical ideals of equality to women, and he took no great political risk by attending the Seneca Falls convention, his teenage daughter at his side, and speaking about the Married Women's Property Act he had just helped make law. Known as a man who "liked a good argument," he would not have been surprised or offended that woman's rights and political equality would soon be linked in the public mind.[35]

Given all this apparent agreement, Stanton was taken aback that even in the Wesleyan Chapel the question of woman suffrage provoked some dissent. For the rest of her life she would insist that this ambivalence about so obvious a demand merely reflected other people's weakness, their adherence to traditional notions of women's role, and, relatedly, her own foresight. Imagining nineteenth-century women as merely timid, we have implicitly adopted Stanton's view that the demand for the vote was simply too radical for even the most progressive of Americans to swallow.

Certainly the demand for woman suffrage was a startling, even explosive, one, but the truth about its reception in Seneca Falls is more complicated. In demanding women's right to vote, Stanton signaled not that she was more radical, but that she was on a different path, intellectually and politically, from her closest allies; she was also somewhat tone-deaf to their concerns. Unlike most woman's rights advocates, Stanton faced no moral or intellectual obstacles to fusing the demand for woman's rights with political action. In contrast, Lucretia Mott's exclamation, "Lizzy, thee will make us ridiculous," reflected Mott's discomfort with how a convention that included so many Quakers and Garrisonians would be viewed if they made access to electoral politics a central demand. Quaker women such as Mott and Mary Ann McClintock considered voting anathema, an aspect of "the world" that was ever a source of tension among Friends; even after she had joined in demanding the vote for women, Mott would wish publicly "that man, too, would have no participation in a government recognizing the life-taking principle."[36] Among non-Quaker Garrisonians, too, the question of politics still rankled. Voting had been, after all, a source of dissension and hurt for a decade, and an important piece of political abolitionists' disinclination to support woman's rights.

But times were changing. Frederick Douglass, the only man to speak out at Seneca Falls in favor of woman suffrage, had already begun shifting toward a pro-voting position and perhaps indicated this by standing to support Stanton's resolution. Certainly the strong Free Soil presence at the convention signaled that Garrisonians and Quakers no longer exclusively defined the conversation about woman's rights. Even Garrisonians, especially younger ones, were, by the late 1840s, reconsidering the place of electoral politics in the antislavery struggle, and thus votelessness as among the inequities women faced. By adopting the Declaration and all its resolutions, the Seneca Falls convention placed the emerging movement squarely, not to say narrowly, on the political path toward suffrage.

Perhaps it is hard from this distance to understand the symbolic meaning and the practical urgency Elizabeth Cady Stanton attached to suffrage.[37] The right to vote had not always been the core definition of citizenship; the republic's founders saw in the ownership of land and the freedom to establish a household the promise of an independent and virtuous citizenry. By the early nineteenth century, however, land had become less essential to a man's definition of adulthood. Increasingly, credit and trade were central to economic life and the maintenance of a household. These changes would affect men's roles as husbands, workers, and citizens—and by extension the conversation about woman's rights—in two immediate ways: first, by the gradual expansion of suffrage to white men who did not own property, and second, by the battles, state by state, over laws permitting married women to own property and conduct business on their own.

With these changes, the vote increasingly became the primary symbol of citizenship itself. We see this in the antislavery movement's schism over electoral politics, in several northern states' harsh new restrictions on African American men's right to vote, and in political parties' organization of voters in what would come to be known as machines. Talk of rights, power, and liberty infused these settings, linking them, at least rhetorically, to "the popular republican tradition that insisted on equal rights for all, with the franchise the crowning jewel of individual freedom."[38]

The vote, then, was both more and less than a symbol of women's subordination, a sign of their exclusion from the nation's larger concerns, or a visible marker of their relegation to a different, lower, form of belonging. What Stanton displayed so brilliantly in the Declaration of Sentiments was that women's political exclusion was one important indication of how American society defined women entirely as dependent members of families, rather than as individuals in their own right. This definition, and the institutions that rested upon it, crushed, constrained, and belittled women: laws that organized property, marriage, wage earning, and custody of children; prejudices that declared women to be less intelligent, less moral, or less able than men; social customs that insisted that women were unfit for most duties and professions; and religious teachings that emphasized women's subjugation and sinfulness. Stanton exposed pronouncements about women's "nature" as nothing but prejudice that rationalized denying women their rights as individuals; the "pursuit of happiness" itself had been refused them. Given the failed promises of men's protection, women had to demand their own rights, and to do so in a republic required the power to vote for their own representatives. Only with a vote of their own could women confront, and change, those rules at their very source: the law. "Depend upon it, this is the point to attack," she would soon write. It is "the stronghold of the fortress—*the one* woman will find most difficult to take—*the one* man will most reluctantly give up." The long decades of suffrage activism that would lead to women gaining the vote proved her point: "political rights," as she would put it, "involving in their last results equality everywhere, roused all the antagonism of a dominant power, against the self-assertion of a class hitherto subservient."[39]

Stanton might speak of women as "a class," but she devoted her life to abolishing the notion that women were best judged—or, for that matter, represented—as members of a subordinated group (wives, mothers, sisters, and so forth) rather than as individuals. In a letter to the *National Reformer* in September 1848, she and Lizzie McClintock declared that "every *individual* has a sphere"—and indeed hers was a profoundly and radically individualistic philosophy.[40] In this, Stanton's thinking mirrored much of the country's shifting view. By the 1840s the prevailing myth in the northern United States had come to be that of individuals: rising, falling, virtuous, sin-

ful, self-made, and saved. With the glaring exception of chattel slavery, Americans believed that capital accumulation, the rise and fall of
members of various classes, and moral standing itself rested on the
shoulders of each citizen—commonly understood, of course, to be
male. Drawing together philosophical threads from Protestantism,
natural rights philosophy, transcendentalism, and republicanism,
Stanton drew on both radical and traditional ideas to form what was
beginning to look very much like a philosophy of woman's rights that
would place women, too, in this picture, and in so doing widen and
transform its frame.

But for Elizabeth Cady Stanton, the vote was never—not in the
Declaration of Sentiments, not in the decades-long struggle to popu-
larize the idea, and not later, when she criticized the narrowness of
the "suffrage movement"—a sufficient end in itself. Her commitment
to individual rights was never encompassed by the struggle to attain
the vote for women; the breadth of the Declaration of Sentiments is,
in large part, why it remains a strikingly moving piece of American
political rhetoric. Indeed, its demands would stir women to join
the woman's movement for decades to come. Consider its appeal:
women, the document read, had been thought lesser than men, who
had "endeavored . . . to destroy her confidence in her own powers, to
lessen her self-respect, and to make her willing to lead a dependent
and abject life"; girls' intellectual potential was limited, for they had
been "denied . . . the facilities for obtaining a thorough education";
and women's subordination had been reinforced by the Protestant
Church, where ministers had "usurped the prerogative of Jehovah
himself, claiming it as his right to assign her a sphere of action." All of
these charges were laid at men's feet—"Where there is oppression
there is an oppressor," Lucretia Mott would allege—while the duty to
change the situation was women's alone.[41]

What did those who gathered at Seneca Falls *not* demand? For
one thing, they were reluctant to have a woman chair the meeting,
so the ever-gracious James Mott stepped into that role. More important, they did not mention slavery, racism, or the status of black
women—the very issues that had drawn these people to reform in the
first place. The economic, physical, and sexual exploitation of
enslaved women, although ever present in the appeals of abolitionists,

was set aside in favor of a decidedly middle-class version of women's grievances. Although the Declaration condemned men's monopoly of "all the profitable employments," and deplored wage-earning women's "scanty remuneration" in the jobs they were able to hold, there is no other mention of laboring women. Other topics that would soon engross the women's movement barely appeared at Seneca Falls. There was only a brief objection to the laws of marriage, separation, and divorce that gave children to their fathers. Nor did the document discuss dress reform, or women's mental and physical health, or labor organizing, the latter already under way among female textile workers. Men were roundly condemned for denying women their rights, but the economic system, and the benefits middle-class women gained from it, remained blameless. "While its goals were altruistic in the sense that they were designed to achieve equality for women in all social classes," writes one historian, ". . . women's demand for improved educational and economic opportunities and political equality was based unabashedly on the principles of individual self-interest."[42] To the degree that antebellum Americans viewed self-interest itself as a virtue that drove the common good, Stanton's notion of woman's rights as a matter of individual autonomy and fulfillment fit right in.

For all the talk of universal rights and of abolishing artificial distinctions in granting suffrage, no one at the convention seems to have objected to the language of another resolution, which asked for women a right "which is given to the most ignorant and degraded men—both natives and foreigners." Here was the unmistakable stamp of Stanton's elitism. Ever quick to point out the dangers of pernicious comparisons between men's and women's intelligence or judgment as a basis for their rights, she nevertheless incorporated ideas about "worthiness" in defense of her cause.

As Stanton recalled it, the reaction to the convention was as unexpected as it was hostile: "No words could express our astonishment," she declared, "on finding . . . that what seemed to us so timely, so rational, and so sacred, should be a subject for sarcasm and ridicule to the entire press of the nation." But Stanton and McClintock were not that astonished. In the Declaration itself they had predicted that they would face "no small amount of misconception, misrepresentation, and ridicule." Further, the response to the convention at Seneca Falls was far from uniformly negative. Parts of the antislavery press, and especially Frederick Douglass's *North Star*, expressed strong support, though the *Liberator* took a month to print the report of the meeting, and other responses ranged widely.[43] Some Free Soil newspapers, already accustomed to debating woman's rights, exclaimed, "Success to the cause in which they have enlisted!" while others simply reported the event straightforwardly. The *Seneca County Courier* described the "attendance [as] respectable in numbers and highly respectable in character" and reported matter-of-factly on the speeches.[44] Nor did the paper balk at publishing Stanton and McClintock's challenge that "if your columns are open to the women of Seneca county," they would "throw down the glove to any one who will meet us, in fair argument, on the great question of Woman's Rights." Two weeks later, the *Courier* printed the resolutions adopted by the convention, declining further commentary.[45]

But really, how dull these straightforward reports were, and so beside the point. Stanton much preferred a fight. And as word of the convention's demands spread, she got one. "All the journals from Maine to Texas seemed to strive with each other to see which could make our movement appear the most ridiculous," she later recalled. But in advancing a radical cause, no news is decidedly *not* good news. As one historian has noted, "the way that newspaper editors responded was less important than the fact that they responded at all."[46] Throughout the nation, editors could not seem to resist saying something—clever, obtuse, supportive, or absurd—about woman's rights. Stanton knew full well that the articles that opposed her resolutions, and those that called names, gave the little gathering far more visibility than it might otherwise have deserved.

But let us take the frightened opposition seriously and try to envision what was at stake here. What Elizabeth Cady Stanton suggested would, writers claimed, turn the world on its ears, disrupting long- and tightly held assumptions about the differences between the sexes, and challenging the widely shared faith that those differences were essential for society's well-being. Treating women as full and autonomous citizens (or "as men," as many put it) would breed the kind of selfishness that would permit, even encourage, women to leave their homes; it would foster irreligion, divorce, and independence. There would be no end to it, traditionalists asserted whenever people stepped (just a toe and no more, they promised) onto a slippery slope. In this, of course, conservatives were right. To demand full and equal rights for women was to propose a world that no one, then or now, could truly imagine: one that separated sex from reproduction, that saw women in positions of power, that denied biblical teachings about women's subordination to men, and that challenged men's rule of their households.

This is how I think it felt to Stanton's opponents—ordinary Americans, most of them, rather than die-hard conservative ideologues—to hear these scandalous propositions spoken aloud. Consider the hypothetical demand that children be given the vote. The arguments against this would be eerily familiar to every advocate of woman's rights: Children don't reason or have any sense; they are already represented and protected by their parents, to whom they're properly subordinate; they'll vote like their parents; they'll vote against their parents; they'll be coerced by designing politicians; it will be too difficult to control their evil tendencies; it will open the doors to children's making decisions about their own drinking, driving, education, and, most frighteningly, sexuality; they have no sense of the value of property and would misdirect public funds; and anyway, they don't want to vote. Studies would claim that voting would harm children's development, that they would be roughed up at the polls, and that the responsibilities of citizenship would distract from their more important duties in the classroom. Panicky, liberals would ask "which children?" and thus, like Stanton's opponents, miss the principle and the point.

Years later, Stanton claimed that the clamor against the demand for woman suffrage was so intense "in the parlor, press, and pulpit" that "most of the ladies who had attended the convention and signed the declaration, one by one, withdrew their names and influence and joined our persecutors."[47] There is not an iota of evidence for this, though it is easy to picture the conventional Harriet Cady Eaton's "great consternation" at the prospect of their father's opposition. Abolitionist women were used to the charge that they were upsetting God and nature, and surely they were not surprised to read that their new demands would "set the world by the ears." Perhaps some women regretted signing the document, but they left no record of this; none would have joined the opposition. This crowd, long supportive of women's right to education, property, public speaking, and a place in public life, had faced scarier opponents than a few hysterical journalists. And they carried their outspokenness beyond the convention: that autumn, the McClintock family would join with the Congregational (later Progressive) Friends to declare that "the equality of women [will] be recognized" by the meeting, and that "men and women will meet together and transact business jointly."[48] The convention at Seneca Falls had been fun and inspiring, even profound, and had inaugurated a new stage in the conversation over woman's rights, but it was not, to these ultraists, a stroke of lightning, and they were unlikely to temper their radicalism.

For Elizabeth Cady Stanton, however, the convention at Seneca Falls *was* something new under the sun. It represented an outlet for her intellectual energy, new friends, a new passion, the possibility of leadership, "a broader outlook on human life": in other words, a life. Buzzing from the excitement of the convention, she was thrilled that other women wanted to continue the conversation, and soon. Amy Post and other abolitionist women from Rochester announced a follow-up meeting in that city two weeks later. Lizzie McClintock and Elizabeth Cady Stanton eagerly heeded Lucretia Mott's call to attend, though they fretted about the organizers' decision to place a woman in the chair, an uncharacteristic squeak of caution that Stanton soon laughingly regretted as "foolish conduct." Reflecting Rochester's more urban setting, and its organizers' greater alertness to the struggles of laboring women, this gathering focused a more critical eye on women's status as seamstresses, and as domestic servants, whose wages Elizabeth Cady Stanton declared "quite too low for the labor they perform." The movement for woman's rights, barely begun, had already moved beyond its founding moment. If Elizabeth Cady Stanton had hoped to attract attention by calling a convention, her success was immeasurable, for talk of woman's rights was now inescapable.[49]

The promise of future conventions and the challenges of a hostile press offered new life and energy to Elizabeth Cady Stanton, but

Henry's silence hints at trouble to come. Only weeks after the conventions in Seneca Falls and Rochester, Henry wrote an exclamation-point-heavy letter to his "Dear Love" about his own meetings and invitations to speak, and expressed no inkling that she had embarked on a path that would transform their lives. "I attended the Albany County Free Soil Convention to-day, out of town," he burbled. "A good many gentlemen are calling upon me here. I am quite a free soil lion!!!"[50] If Elizabeth's sense of isolation had arisen in part from Henry's absorption in politics, her newfound calling now placed them on parallel tracks, with each absorbed in a separate conversation.

Elizabeth Cady Stanton had fallen hard, and she seems almost immediately to have realized that her new love and the role it offered her were for life; she was likely too busy to mind Henry's disinterest in her activities. Barely home from Rochester, she and Lizzie McClintock set about expanding their influence and spreading the word. They attended, and then challenged in print, sermons that opposed woman's rights; they wrote letters to editors; and Stanton began to give speeches. Perhaps it is here, in her own development, that we find the greatest significance of the convention at Seneca Falls. The gathering itself was not, after all, the first public demand for women's equal rights; it was not even the most radical conference that summer. Nor did it result in a formal organization, much less a full-scale movement for woman's rights. But from that day on we see Elizabeth Cady Stanton, if we can catch a glimpse in the blur, as her contemporaries must have seen her: as a woman on a mission. Overnight, it seemed, Stanton had leapt from contemplating the sources of her personal discontents to articulating a full-blown philosophy of woman's rights. The leap seems almost too abrupt, the result too full-blown, and the words too articulate, except that Stanton had been stewing over these ideas for years.

The words gushed out full force. Even now, when many of her ideas are commonplace, reading in Stanton's earliest writings how women were socialized to be self-sacrificing, kept from exploring their intellectual aspirations, and prohibited from earning a sustenance that might allow them their independence, it is hard to believe that such insights had emerged so quickly. In her "maiden speech" at the Waterloo Quaker Meeting House in the fall of 1848, Stanton offered many of the arguments she would elaborate, the prejudices she would attack, and those she would hold, for decades to come. Funny, ironic, condescending, rambling, and overblown, the speech is classic Stanton. Later addresses would be more polished, as Stanton learned to combine sharp criticism with wit and charm, but many of the ideas seem to have been born whole. That first speech fills more than twenty published pages, covering dozens of sheets in her sprawling handwriting. When she spoke, the audience sat quietly for nearly an hour.[51]

The organization of the speech would become Stanton's signature style. Women themselves must demand their rights, Stanton declared, for "woman alone can understand the height and the depth, the length and the breadth of her own degradation and woe. Man cannot speak for us." Furthermore, the very act of speaking out would challenge and erode the stereotypes that enforced women's silence. Woman's timidity, Stanton insisted, was nothing but evidence of her subordination, for men's "tyranny over her [has been] injurious to himself and benumbing to *her* faculties, that but few can nerve themselves against the storm." (A tricky move, and one Stanton would use to great effect: if you disagree with me, she said in essence, you merely prove how well you have absorbed the lessons of your own degradation.) If all this seemed condescending to women, if actual women balked at being told how crushed and pathetic they were, Stanton had someone to blame: men, and the system of male dominance that it was in their collective and individual interest to uphold. The "Arabian Kerek," the "Mohametan," and the "German" all mistreated their wives, but Stanton aimed her fire closer to home, focusing on "christian countries," whose "advanced state of civilization and refinement" reinforced women's subordination by denying them the vote. Cheerfully, she demolished each assumption about sexual difference that underlay society's view of male superiority and that served to justify inequalities between women and men.

It was prejudice, disdain, and convention that taught men to view women as intellectually inferior, morally weaker, and physically frail, and thus to defend to themselves the denial of women's political and legal rights. In demolishing these claims, Stanton was in her element—she had had a lot of practice proving that she could beat men on their own terms. She employed irony and sarcasm, facts and anecdotes, to great effect, poking at men's vanities and laughing at their pretensions. As for women, far from being naturally inferior, their intellects had been twisted, crushed, and distorted. Both their training as girls and the burdens of the woman's sphere conspired to conquer "whatever yearning her spirit may have felt for a higher existence, whatever capacity she well knew she possessed for more elevated enjoyments." We cannot know whether women will be the intellectual equals of men, she declared, until all doors to education are opened, until women are recognized as "beings of reason," not simply "mere creatures of the affections."[52]

As for morality, men were hardly exemplars deserving of their elevated status. Did the clergy, those who were "so thoroughly ac- quainted with the character of God and of his designs," demonstrate "perfect moral rectitude"? Did men behave themselves at the polls on election day? What kind of moral superiority was displayed in the "perfect rowdyism that now characterizes the debates in our national congress"? And (she could not resist) what about the "lamentable want of principle among our lawyers"? Stanton was happy to concede that men's moral weaknesses were, like women's own failings, the result of "false education," and that men were therefore educable. "We would not have woman less pure," she assured her audience, "but we would have man more so. We would have the same code of morals for both." Stanton also made short work of those who based women's subordination on the Bible. These men, Stanton insisted, following in the tradition of Angelina and Sarah Grimké, "have not rightly read [their] Bible." She urged them to do so.

Stanton would not even "give you an inch lest you claim an ell" on the question of men's physical superiority. Let girls have the same physical education as boys, she proposed, and we will talk about this some more. "We cannot say what the woman might be physically," she suggested, "if the girl were allowed all the freedom of the boy in romping, climbing, swimming, playing hoop and ball." In any case, as Stanton knew full well, brawn had never been the basis for men's political rights or their economic independence in a republic, and it was merely posturing to claim it as one now that women demanded their own.

Stanton's speeches, lawyerly in style, provided an effective rhetorical strategy for women to use when they continued the conversation at home; she anticipated her opponents' objections, inflated them, and punctured them. If people believed that "mingling in such scenes of violence and vulgarity" that occurred at the polls was "unfit for woman," she suggested they be reminded that it was equally "dangerous to her sons and sires." As for performing military service, Stanton simply declared herself opposed to all war, and urged men to show the courage of embarking on moral warfare. The objection that women were already represented in government by their husbands and sons was, to Stanton, so much nonsense. "Let your statute books answer the question," she boomed, referring again to unfair and imbalanced laws. Men's protection was merely "such as the wolf gives the lamb" and had failed to shield married women from abuse and abandonment, desperation and debt; it was not equal rights but legal tyranny. After all, she asked slyly, "how many truly harmonious households have we now?" "The only happy households we now see are those in which Husband and wife share equally in counsel and government," she assured them, a tacit compliment to the Quaker crowd. "There can be no true dignity or independence where there is subordination, no happiness without freedom." This last would be Stanton's mantra, and she would clasp it for life.

Americans had been debating ideas about women's and men's natures and capabilities for years; in Stanton's critique were bits and pieces that they had heard before. But Stanton did not merely challenge the restrictions on women's access to education or employment or assert women's superiority in their own sphere; she also demanded that the social and political hierarchies that these ideas described and reinforced be transformed. She was especially adept at making her opponents' objections look absurd: "We did not as some have supposed . . . propose to petition the legislature to make our Husbands just, generous and courteous," she assured them. Rather, the recent conventions for woman's rights had made rational and just demands on the "government under which we live," asking for rights that were nothing more than the essential liberties claimed by all Americans. Fundamentally, Elizabeth Cady Stanton's very radicalism drew on a decidedly liberal tradition. She believed that only what a later age would call a level playing field could allow us even to imagine each individual's potential; her mission was to survey and expose every hill and fence that elevated men and kept women on the sidelines. After hearing her speak, countless women, and more than a few men, wondered how anyone could ever have thought otherwise.

Of course, not everyone greeted the cause with the vigorous assent its logic so obviously deserved. Men had their prejudices and they made silly arguments, but you could argue with them, as Stanton had all her life. It was the "indifference indeed the contempt with which women themselves regard our movement" that Stanton considered the "most discouraging, the most lamentable" obstacle its advocates faced. If Stanton favored men as worthy opponents in a good fight, women's apparent apathy provoked her to note nastily that women in "the Turkish harem" also "glory in their bondage." Yet she pleaded: "Now is the time, now emphatically, for the women of this country to buckle on the armour that can best resist the weapons of the enemy, ridicule and holy horror."

Actually, ridicule and holy horror were among Stanton's favorite things. For neither astonishment nor novelty nor even the blast of words that came from her pen and her mouth quite capture Stanton's reaction to the epithets and insult that followed the convention: she loved it all. The pleasure of having provoked such tumult, the "spicy discussions," the simple delight in arguing back, shimmers from every report, every letter, of those times. Decades later, someone asked Susan B. Anthony, who met Stanton in 1851, which period in their half-century-long friendship she had enjoyed the most. "The days when the struggle was the hardest and the fight the thickest," she replied without hesitation, "when the whole world was against us and we had to stand the closer to each other."[53] Indeed, the ten years between the Seneca Falls convention of 1848 and the late 1850s, when Stanton's discontent deepened into words, were a romp. There was so much trouble to stir up, and it was all such infuriating fun. It is exhilarating to keep up with Stanton's pace, to follow her reasoning as she excavated evidence of women's subordination. One glimpses it in the glint in her eye, the barely suppressed smirk, in the 1856 photograph of her with her new daughter, Harriot; it is the only picture in which she (or, for that matter, nearly anyone in that first century of photography) looks mischievous.

Elizabeth Cady Stanton brought her vibrant blend of intellect and humor to each and every battle, but she cannot have been the easiest of friends. Lizzie McClintock, for one, may have found it wearing to live up to her friend's standard of intensity, self-righteousness, and outrage. In the summer of 1852, McClintock married Burroughs Phillips and moved to Syracuse, creating a "void in my life," in Stanton's recollection, but the two women may already have drifted apart. As for Elizabeth Cady Stanton, she fired off new ideas every day, sketching out an intellectual path that left little room for people who did not share her passions, who had different reform priorities, or who held her to account for her own inconsistencies. To the chagrin of the Progressive Friends, for instance, she attended the Episcopal church on Sundays ("simply & solely to keep the children still," she insisted defensively). Her friends, she complained, wished "to make me ridiculous whenever they can," but she refused to acknowledge the contradictions in exposing her children to an orthodoxy she had repudiated. Nor did her Quaker Friends always approve of her clothing— Richard Hunt had objected to a "Theatrical" headdress with "a kind of turban & bows"—but Stanton was no more inclined to adopt "Quaker simplicity" in her dress than she was in her combativeness.[54]

Having found her mission, Stanton was too busy to care much what others thought of her. Each day seemed to bring invitations to write articles or to give speeches, and her fame was spreading rapidly. The 1850s were virtually cluttered with babies, friends, ideas, and words, and Stanton kept making more of them all. To an observer, she may still have seemed a dilettante, but the breadth of her analysis soon became a philosopher's strength. She rarely kept her brain still for long enough to tidy up her point, but she flitted from topic to topic to great effect; everything came within her orbit, and no slight, no inequity, no insult was safe from attack. "What are we next to do?" she had asked Amy Post just after the Rochester woman's rights convention, but she barely stopped for breath before proceeding. Alerted to discrimination against women in the New York State Temperance Society, she became president of the newly formed Women's New York State Temperance Society in 1852, where her eagerness to "infuse . . . the radical principle into the proceedings" guaranteed a short tenure. "Women have grievances without number," she declared, and she was determined to expose and challenge every one.[55]

While Stanton thought and wrote and spoke, something that looked very much like a movement was picking up speed, as women organized and publicized meetings in communities throughout the North. In the spring of 1850, women in Salem, Ohio, hosted a convention to "secure to all persons the recognition of Equal Rights, and the extension of the privileges of Government without distinction of sex or color." ("*Never did men so suffer*" as at that meeting, recalled Paulina Wright Davis gleefully, for they had been forbidden to speak and so, "For the first time in the world's history . . . learned how it felt to sit in silence when great questions were pending."[56]) Immediately after, women in New England put out a call for the First National Woman's Rights Convention, to be held in Worcester, Massachusetts, in October. Newspaper reports continued to spread the word. That month, for instance, a young Quaker teacher and reformer named Susan B. Anthony found that "my consciousness was awakened by reading in the *New York Tribune* a full and favorable account of a Woman's Rights Convention held in Worcester, Massachusetts."[57]

Stanton attended neither of these conventions, nor, eight months pregnant, did she go to Syracuse for the Woman's Rights Convention the following winter. Rather, in a pattern she would sustain for decades to come, she signed the call for the convention, followed the proceedings closely, sent a rousing letter to each, and behaved like the presumptive leader of a cause. She had heard, she wrote Lucretia Mott after Syracuse, that "you presided with great dignity—thank you in the name of woman."[58] This single passion, and the hubris to claim to speak "in the name of woman" everywhere, infected everything Stanton did and made every thought she had, every insult she had ever experienced, seem inevitably to lead to this new analysis, this new life.

Through all this, Stanton still had a household to manage, babies to bear and nurse, and children to raise according to her ideas about human nature. She was pleased with the chaos she had wrought and took every opportunity to boast of being what a later generation would call a super-mom. But although she occasionally styled herself as one of the "common place, every day, working characters, who wash and iron, bake and brew, carry water and fat babies up stairs and down, bring potatoes, apples, and pans of milk from the cellar, run our own errands, through mud or snow; shovel paths, and work in the garden," increasingly her mind was elsewhere. Certainly she did not have to do all the work of sustaining her growing household. By 1851 she had hired a young Quaker, Amelia Willard ("one of the best gifts of the gods"), as housekeeper, a job Willard held for three decades. "But for this noble, self-sacrificing woman, much of my public work would have been quite impossible," Stanton admitted, but it reflects well on Stanton that Willard stayed for so long.[59] Indeed, as Stanton entered middle age, the realities of running a large, and ever-expanding, household were increasingly a distraction from her "real" work.

The advantages of having a housekeeper who "could fill any department in domestic life" should be obvious. Even so, Stanton's output was impressive.[60] She sat at her writing table, children underfoot, nearly every day, dashing off letters, appeals, and barbs with humor and insight, in a scrawl that seems to reflect the speed of her thought. Under such pen names as "Sun Flower," she wrote articles for the *Lily*, transforming Amelia Bloomer's new temperance monthly into a forum for advocating woman's rights. In its pages she supported laws permitting wives to divorce drunkards and so "escape from the bonds of an ill assorted marriage"; congratulated the "*magnanimous*!!" legislature (Henry among its members) for expanding married women's property rights; and disparaged women who failed to train their families to "put things in their proper places."[61] She applauded or challenged other advocates of woman's rights as the situation demanded. She spent long hours poring over books and newspapers to locate the causes of and solutions for women's oppression by state, church, custom, men, and themselves. Her life more closely resembled that of a legal scholar than an activist, as she produced petitions, gave speeches, and wrote articles, all of which reflected the high-velocity buzzing of an acute and thorough intellect. The months and years that followed the first woman's rights conventions saw a nearly continuous outpouring of new babies ("a kind of biennial clumsiness," she called it), new ideas, new friends, and a new, not yet fully coherent, vision of the life that Stanton had begun to fashion for herself.[62]

3

"AT THE BOILING POINT"

(1851–1861)

Marriage opened up the world of social reform to Elizabeth Cady Stanton; motherhood provided opportunities to apply her theories of human nature and medical judgment; and activism and writing allowed her to develop her views on women's subordination and their rights. But the thirty-five-year-old Stanton was able to become her generation's leading woman's rights intellectual only because of her new friendship with Susan B. Anthony. It is impossible to read of Stanton and Anthony's chance meeting in May 1851 without envisioning fireworks announcing a lifelong pair. But although the two women later recognized their meeting as life-changing, and Americans have conflated (and confused) their names ever since, the reality was more prosaic. The thirty-year-old Quaker Susan B. Anthony had heard of Elizabeth Cady Stanton, for her mother, father, and sister Mary had attended the woman's rights convention in Rochester in 1848, and had given "the most glowing account of the meeting." Anthony herself sympathized in a general way, as most Quakers and antislavery reformers did, with the advocates of female equality. In the spring of 1851 she was not making a pilgrimage to Seneca Falls on behalf of woman's rights, however, but to hear William Lloyd Garrison and the English abolitionist George Thompson. It was while walking with Amelia Bloomer that Anthony got her first glimpse of Stanton, and it was that brief introduction that Stanton later celebrated in her own account.[1]

The sense of inevitability came later, when Stanton insisted, "How well I remember that day!" At the time, she was too frazzled by "what I had heard, or my coming dinner, or the probable behavior of three mischievous boys," to recognize its significance. "There she stood, with her good, earnest face and genial smile, dressed in gray delaine, hat and all the same color, relieved with pale blue ribbons, the perfection of neatness and sobriety. I liked her thoroughly, and why I did not at once invite her home with me to dinner, I do not know. She accuses me of that neglect, and has never forgiven me."[2] Evidently "neatness and sobriety" were less thrilling to invite home than were Garrison and Thompson.

Anthony, however, was more quickly smitten. She found Stanton's charisma and the quality of her mind, neither of which Stanton ever veiled, thrilling. Stanton took a bit longer to grasp her new friend's powerful appeal. Years later, intending to be complimentary, she would muse that Anthony, with her "conscience tending to morbidity," could have become "a religious fanatic," in different eras "a Stoic; . . . a Calvinist; [or] . . . a Puritan," had she not been born at a time when she could become "by the very laws of her being, . . . a Reformer."[3] The description holds some truth about both women—how typical of Stanton to consider a strict conscience "morbid"! Certainly Anthony could be strident and intense, without the easy and open humor that Stanton used so effectively. But those who knew Anthony well regarded her earnestness fondly and thought her both warm and kind, if somewhat shy. Prickly Anthony could be, and rigid in her devotion to principle, but Stanton quickly became dependent on her friendship, her organizational skills, and her conscience. Anthony in turn had found her soul mate.

The contrasts between the two women would enrich and irritate them for the rest of their lives, and would provide ample opportunity for contemporaries and historians to limit each to her "type." It denigrates neither woman to admit to their differences, in both their strengths and their shortcomings, and to note how complementary they so quickly became. In part their differences were matters of personality, unknowable in origin: Stanton was more intellectually courageous, had a remarkable fluency with writing, and was physically and intellectually exuberant; Anthony had a prodigious talent for organizational detail, strategic planning, and plain old hard work. Stanton was happy to stir some humor into the most important cause; Anthony was more likely to infuse principle and honor. Susan B. Anthony expected a reformer's life to include at least some sacrifice and privation. Elizabeth Cady Stanton, to her friend's chagrin, saw no virtue in hardship; when she married Henry, one historian has quipped, she adopted health reformer Sylvester Graham's rules for spare and healthy living, "except those governing food and sex."[4]

Personality aside, Stanton and Anthony had each come to the cause of woman's rights by a different path—and those paths would shape both their political styles and their strategic choices. Like Lizzie McClintock, Susan B. Anthony was born into reform, and her decision to make it her lifework evoked no opposition from her closest kin; born into a liberal family, she had, she admitted, "no personal grievances." At first, she recalled, "The necessity for the ballot had not appealed to me, as, in those days, Quaker men were not in the habit of voting." Only gradually, "stirred by the terrible injustice which I saw meted out to women on every hand," did she decide to devote herself to the struggle for female equality. Finally, "I became acquainted with Mrs. Stanton, and she soon fired my soul with all her own zeal."[5]

Once converted, Susan B. Anthony became utterly devoted both to Elizabeth Cady Stanton and to the cause of woman suffrage. Like "Mrs. Stanton," she believed there were many sources of women's second-class status, but she did not waver from what she viewed as the one true path to women's equality: the vote. Woman's rights were as personal to Anthony as to Stanton, but with a twist; for Anthony, economic opportunity and true independence required political equality, and the rest would follow. The issues of marriage, divorce, child rearing, and religion, all of which would increasingly absorb Stanton's time and attention, struck her friend as secondary, and certainly irrelevant to her own experience. It was not personal anguish that propelled Anthony into the movement for woman's rights, but the pull that kept her there was greater, for alongside the plump and curly-haired Stanton she found a life that was grounded not in home, husband, or children, but in a cause.

Before Stanton began firing Anthony's soul, however, she noticed her dress. It was more than mere frivolousness that led Stanton to mention the "gray delaine . . . relieved with pale blue ribbons" that

Anthony wore the day of their meeting. That spring Stanton, Lucy Stone, and Amelia Bloomer had traded their cumbersome attire for the "Bloomer costume" and thus made dress reform, by association and almost by accident, a woman's rights demand. The outfit— invented by Stanton's cousin Elizabeth Smith Miller but soon named after Bloomer, who published the patterns in the *Lily*—consisted of a short jacket over baggy ankle-length ("Turkish") pantaloons. The freedom these women experienced will be obvious to every pants-wearing woman. Bloomers freed them from dragging their heavy skirts and underskirts through the mud, allowed housewives to do their work without encumbrance or danger, and declared in a most visual way that women's traditional clothing literally dragged them down.[6]

Health reformers had long pointed out that women's attire, and especially what Catharine Beecher called "the murderous contrivances of the corset-shop," crushed their ribs and distorted their organs.[7] Calls for healthy living were common in reform circles, whether in Sylvester Graham's refusal of meat and caffeine or temperance activists' total abstinence from liquor. And while Quakers had long practiced simplicity in dress, moral reformers urged young women to abandon corsets and avoid the temptations of frills. Just as a small group of feminists more than century later would abandon high heels, makeup, and shaven legs, the women who tried the "Bloomer experiment" did not imagine that they were doing anything so radical when they chose physical mobility over the binding conventions of feminine fashion.

Shortening and splitting a skirt proved to be an entirely different matter, for the sight of women in trousers was profoundly unsettling. That the most visible wearers of bloomers and the advocates of female equality were one and the same simply proved the unnaturalness of both. Advocates of women's equality have always been plagued by opponents' focus on their looks and attire; this was as true for Fanny Wright and Elizabeth Cady Stanton as it is for contemporary female athletes, professionals, and politicians. And indeed, bloomer wearers, during the several years they stuck with the experiment, were greeted with howls of derision: "Heigh ho! the carrion crow / Mrs. Stanton's all the go / Twenty tailors take the stitches / Mrs. Stanton wears the breeches" went one ditty, while editors inevitably sneered about women who wanted to "wear the pants," a metaphor with astonishing staying power.[8] If anyone doubted that women's clothing mattered—reinforcing signs of fashion, consumerism, loveliness, and weakness—the women who donned the bloomer costume could doubt it no longer, as they faced charges of ugliness and unmarriageability. Bloomer wearing was the "bra burning" of the nineteenth century, a convenient epithet used by those who preferred to dismiss and trivialize, rather than debate, feminists' demands.

Elizabeth Cady Stanton's family reacted predictably. Judge Cady was "so distressed about my dress" that he forbade her from entering his house wearing the outfit; equally true to form, she got huffy, announced that "if my friends cannot see me in the short dress, they cannot see me at all," and chopped off swaths of material from all her dresses. She wondered whether "the short dress will cost me the loss of my kin," but in truth she seemed rather cheerful about having caused yet another family crisis. As usual, faced with serious damage to his relationship with his daughter, the judge relented, and Stanton soon exulted that "they are all coming round." "Mama and sister Mag, who are now making me a visit, do not seem to dislike the short dress," Stanton reported to cousin Elizabeth. "Mama even says that when Papa returned from here, he was quite pleased with his visit and his daughter, and declared that he never would have noticed the 'shorts' if he had not heard so much about them." Devoted as ever to custom, the judge's oldest daughters were appalled, and Stanton recalled with glee that "Sister Tryphena actually wept."[9] Stanton would always covet her father's approval and respect (she especially relished their conversations about what he termed her "idiosyncrasies" and what she called "the isms by which I differ from the common herd"), but she did enjoy being the cause of her older sisters' discomfort.[10]

Henry, now serving as a legislator in Albany, was reasonably tolerant of the bloomer outfit, choosing to tease rather than confront his wife. "The worst thing about it would be, I should think, sitting down," he remarked. "Then ladies will expose their legs somewhat above the knees, to the delight of those gentlemen who are curious to know whether their lady friends have round and plump legs, or lean and scrawny ones." Later that spring, engaged in a blisteringly close reelection race, he probably found the whole matter less amusing when "Some good Democrats said they would not vote for a man whose wife wore the Bloomers."[11] This may have been the first time Henry realized how extensive was his wife's growing fame. It may also have been his first inkling that what a later generation would call cultural politics would intersect with, and even threaten, his own (he was sure) weightier partisan concerns.

Some men, such as cousin Libby's husband, Charles Dudley Miller, "never flinched . . . however inartistic their [wives'] costumes might be." Others, such as George Thompson, were merely amused that "with the revolution of public sentiment on the question of Slavery, there will be an upturning on the question of petticoats." No one, male or female, felt as strongly as Gerrit Smith that dress reform was at the very root of women's subordination or were as "amazed, that the intelligent women engaged in the 'Woman's rights movement' see not the relation between their dress and the oppressive evils, which they are striving to throw off." "Were woman to adopt a rational dress . . . how quickly would she rise from her present degrading dependence on man!" Smith was certain. "How quickly would the marriage contract be modified and made to recognize the equal rights of the parties to it! And how quickly would she gain access to the ballot-box."[12] Even his devoted cousin Elizabeth Cady Stanton thought Gerrit Smith took his enthusiasm for dress reform too far.

It was easy enough for Elizabeth and Henry to joke about their friends' legs, and for her to dismiss cousin Gerrit's enthusiasm, but the Stanton boys were mortified. Neil, the oldest, suffered the special embarrassment of a nine-year-old with a weird mother. Elizabeth expressed no sympathy that "You do not wish me to visit you [at school] in a short dress!" It is doubtful the child was assuaged either by her insistence that "I have no other" dress or by the inevitable lesson: "Now why do you wish me to wear what is uncomfortable, inconvenient, and many times dangerous? I'll tell you why. You want me to be like other people. You do not like to have me laughed at." Dead-on, he must have thought—and probably skimmed his mother's instruction to "learn not to care for what foolish people say." Years later Stanton would recall the "humiliation" of their ostracized children as "the bitterest drop in the cup of reformers."[13] She seems not to have considered this when she showed up in public wearing bloomers.

"What incredible freedom I enjoyed for two years!" Stanton recalled of the dress experiment. She felt "as joyous and free as some poor captive who has just cast off his ball and chain." Stanton had donned the outfit for the physical freedom it allowed, not as a statement of principle, but she found herself almost unintentionally formulating a serious analysis of fashion, femininity, and women's health. Still, it was a hard principle to sustain, and she grew "often tired of this fight." "[H]ad I counted the cost of the short dress," she told her cousin, its inventor, ruefully, "I would never have put it on; on, however, I'll never take it off, for now it involves a principle of freedom."[14]

Stanton's "never" lasted until 1854. Women living outside the public spotlight, or who did physical labor in kitchens and on farms, held out longer. Amelia Bloomer wore the outfit for a full eight years, and Elizabeth Smith Miller for seven—in part, Sarah Grimké thought, because her father "thinks the almost existence of the Woman Cause hangs upon her adhering to Bloomerism." Factory workers at the Lowell textile mills wore the outfit as well, at least in part because "the Agent of one of the Corporations in this city, has offered to furnish a handsome dinner for all the girls employed in the same, who . . . shall adopt the Bloomer costume." The *Lily*, passing blithely over the element of coercion in this, "hail[ed] with pleasure the adoption of our costume by the working classes."[15]

But the issue soon seemed more distracting than fruitful. Some women conceded defeat to vanity; Elizabeth Smith Miller finally "quite 'fell from grace,' " she wrote, and found herself "again in the bonds of the old swaddling clothes—a victim to my love of beauty."[16] Others tried desperately to balance comfort, pride, and principle. Lucy Stone scoffed at the "pretence that the Cause will suffer" if reformers wore or, alternately, abandoned, the dress; "it is all fudge for anybody to pretend that any Cause that deserves to live is impeded by the length of your skirt," she insisted to Anthony, for people who wished to insult woman's rights would do so regardless of what women wore. If *she* decided to go back to conventional dress, it would be to escape being "annoyed to death by people who recognize me by my clothes, and when I get a seat in the cars, they will get a seat by me and *bore* me for a whole day with the stupidest stuff in the world." Unable to "decide whether to make it long or short," she left a new dress unhemmed.[17] Upset by Stone's vacillation, Anthony went straight to Stanton. But Stanton, cheerful as ever, did not respond as Anthony had hoped—"lay aside the shorts," Stanton advised Stone, for "what is physical freedom compared with mental bondage?"[18]

Indeed, Stanton was the first in her circle to "capitulate," and she was immediately confident that hers was the right position: having only recently "tried to induce the others to wear the costume," she at once "endeavored to persuade them to abandon it." "Her petticoats have assumed their former length, and her wardrobe cleared of every short skirt," Anthony reported to Lucy Stone mournfully, certain that now that "the dress is not a matter of trouble to [her family], her ultraisms will become more obvious." Having herself suffered "a mental crucifixion" every time she put on the outfit, Anthony was irritated by Stanton's ability to articulate a principle and as lightly to throw it off when it hurt: "Every one who *drops* the dress, makes the task a harder one for the few left," she griped.[19] The reality of dress reform may have been more painful for the "angular" Anthony: "poor Susan," minister and reformer Antoinette Brown Blackwell recalled, "did not look well in bloomers. She was a sort of scape-goat for all of us." Stanton, whose jolliness allowed her to "look well" in nearly anything, casually moved on to a "costume . . . far prettier than the bloomer," whose dress comes "within one inch of my boot tops." Finally Anthony, though she found long skirts "humiliating to my good sense of cleanliness and comfort," gave in as well.[20]

If Elizabeth Cady Stanton saw in women's fashion one small manifestation of their dependence, she consistently acknowledged that politics and the law were the primary sources of their degradation. On February 14, 1854, she spoke at the woman's rights convention in Albany on the legal disabilities of women; the convention had the text printed and sent to state legislators, where it became part of the legislative proceedings. Lawyerlike, and on behalf of "the daughters of the revolutionary heroes of '76," Stanton systematically examined the legal issues facing women in their roles as wives, as widows, and as mothers. She pulled no punches, made no concessions to femininity or tradition: "We are persons," she asserted, "native, free-born citizens; property-holders, tax-payers; yet are we denied the exercise of our right to the elective franchise." She also demanded "that most sacred of all rights, trial by jury of our own peers." And she struck rhetorically at legislators where it hurt, declaring that their attitudes toward women were exactly like those of slaveholders toward their slaves. "Would to God you could know the burning indignation that fills woman's soul when she turns over the pages of your statute books," she declared, "and sees there how like feudal barons you freemen hold your women."

Stanton laced her natural rights argument with her sense of entitlement as a middle-class white woman: "We are moral, virtuous and intelligent, and in all respects quite equal to the proud white man himself, and yet by your laws we are classed with idiots, lunatics and negroes," she maintained, "and though we do not feel honored by the place assigned us, yet, in fact, our legal position is lower than that of either; for the negro can be raised to the dignity of a voter if he possess himself of $250; the lunatic can vote in his moments of sanity, and the idiot, too, if he be a male one, and not more than nine-tenths a fool."[21] The laws placed all women on the same level, she asserted, and declared them inferior to all men, an insult that Stanton took personally indeed. This insistence on the logic of universal womanhood and a world divided exclusively by gender would permeate her thinking in both inspiring and troubling ways in years to come.

If Stanton's views of women's legal standing grew in large part from her experience as a married white middle-class woman, so did her ideas about marriage. It does not take a huge mental leap to recognize the personal sources in Stanton's opposition to the laws and customs that defined women's position as wives and mothers. These were not entirely new insights to her—years earlier she had supported married women's property laws on the grounds that married women were both persons and citizens. But now, surrounded by babies and household responsibilities, and with Henry off in the larger world, Stanton translated her restlessness into a political analysis that "contrast[ed] his freedom with my bondage" and thus, she believed, all women's with all men's. "How sad it makes me feel when I see Henry going about just where and when he pleases," she wrote Anthony. ". . . I am fired anew to open my mouth and pour forth from my own experience the whole, long story of woman's wrongs."[22] That she did more than whine or cave—indeed, that she molded a compelling political analysis that would express countless women's personal discontents in political terms—is no small part of her legacy.

By the 1850s Elizabeth Cady Stanton knew that her marriage would not be a collaborative partnership such as that she admired in Lucretia and James Mott's. Indeed, with Henry earning only $300 as a state senator, two of their sons behaving badly, and the family, as Henry Stanton's biographer puts it, "on the verge of disintegration," Elizabeth Stanton's sense of being cramped only deepened.[23] Only in their ambitiousness and self-confidence, it seemed, were the two truly matched, and with Elizabeth's growing reputation, these traits made for competition more than for harmony. Occasionally she tried to include Henry in her new life, as when she sent him a draft of an article she was writing for the *New York Tribune*. Three weeks later, when he returned it "for revision and correction," Elizabeth was "vexed." "I shall send no more to him for criticism," she informed Anthony; "husbands are too critical. Henceforth, they shall go direct to Greeley, fresh from my brain."[24] By the 1850s, Elizabeth was thinking too quickly for Henry to match her stride. From time to time, she would still ask for, and expect, his political support, but that assistance—indeed, Henry's very presence—was increasingly irrelevant to her expanding public life.

There were few models in the 1850s for a marriage in which the wife's fame eclipsed the husband's. Some leading male reformers married women who served as movement hostesses and caregivers. (Helen Benson Garrison comes to mind.) Lucy Stone and Henry Blackwell's 1855 wedding, in contrast, made famous by their public protest against husbands' "injurious and unnatural superiority" over their wives, commenced one man's lifelong commitment to the woman's rights movement. Certainly in some reform couples—Lydia Maria and David Child, Angelina Grimké and Theodore Weld, Abby Kelley and Stephen Foster—the women had previously secured public acclaim. Far more women, often the wives of politicians or ministers, followed the pattern of Frances Seward, exercising their considerable talents from within, and on behalf of, their husbands' sphere. There were few whose intellectual or political ambitions were realized only after they married and had children. Neither Henry nor Elizabeth Cady Stanton seems to have expected him to smooth her path in any real way, though Susan B. Anthony occasionally griped that he "does not *help* to make it *easy* for her to engage in such work" since he left her "the whole burden of home & children."[25] Finding himself with a wife whose outspokenness, accomplishments, and public acclaim outstripped his own, Henry Stanton probably never quite knew what hit him.

Perhaps not surprisingly, as these two ambitious people each defined a niche in public life, Elizabeth and Henry found themselves engaged in two entirely separate conversations. For Elizabeth, the ideas that were developed in dialogue with Anthony and that then burst from her own pen were what "give soul and zest to my life." Henry was equally absorbed in his speeches and his meetings with famous men at Free Soil and Democratic party conventions. The couple still looked forward to each other's company, although they likely felt the strain of their mutual disappointments—and the burden of having, supporting, and caring for so many children. "Tell your mother that I have seen a throng of handsome ladies, but that I had rather see her than the whole of them," Henry wrote five-year-old daughter Margaret, "but I intend to cut her acquaintance unless she writes me a letter." On Valentine's Day in 1858, the father of six addressed his "dearest love" with a declaration of his "ardent attachment" and the promise that he would soon return home. His intentions were hardly oblique, as he warned her, "So, open wide your arms, for I shall rush into them with all the impulse which love and longing can inspire." That impulse would produce one final baby the following year, but it increasingly came up against Elizabeth's growing desire for freedom of her own.[26]

As a state legislator, Henry Stanton occasionally reported that he had "presented two petitions on woman's rights, one from Waterloo, the other from Seneca Falls" and spoke against those who "tried to throw ridicule upon them," but he was at best a halfhearted "woman's rights man."[27] He supported woman's rights much as Elizabeth Cady Stanton opposed slavery: in the abstract, and with the impatience that came from feeling that other things mattered more. Elizabeth was finding woman's rights endlessly absorbing, but Henry seems barely to have noticed that his wife had become, in Lucretia Mott's words, "wedded to this cause." Although on occasion Elizabeth Stanton admitted that "My views trouble him," Henry seems to have regarded his wife's ideas with mild, if condescending, good humor, only very occasionally, and teasingly, referring to her as "the distinguished advocate of free suffrage for woman." Henry Stanton's attitude is best measured by his silence. Years after his death, when Elizabeth Cady Stanton and woman suffrage itself had become respectable, a younger colleague of Henry's recalled, "I don't remember ever hearing the veteran agitator dwell with particular enthusiasm on that other great cause in which his wife so prominently figured, but have no particular reason for assuming that his heart beat less warmly for the enfranchisement of woman than for the emancipation of the slave."[28] A more anemic assessment of what stirred Henry Brewster Stanton's heart is hard to imagine.

In part Henry Stanton's tepidness reflected his own political ambitions. By the 1850s, he had become so absorbed in political party machinations and ambitions that he lost, and never regained, the sense of direction that had made him a brilliant reformer. New York politics were especially convoluted in these years; political parties were formed, tumbled, broken, and realigned by the national conflict over slavery and its expansion. With the dissolution of the Federalist faction, traditionalists of various kinds—economic activists, reform moralists, and antislavery moderates—established the wobbly coalition called the Whig Party, and had elected William Seward as governor in 1838. Democrats loyal to their party's rhetoric of states' rights and the common man, but also sympathetic to antislavery, became Barnburners, widening the fault line on the issue of slavery and Southern "aggression." That chasm, which would tear apart national church denominations, political parties, and eventually the union itself, was further deepened by the noisy but electorally unsuccessful Liberty Party, which included such prominent abolitionists as James Birney and Henry Brewster Stanton himself. By 1848, with the formation of the Free Soil Party, Stanton was busy working for Martin Van Buren's third-party presidential campaign, spending as much time assuring his friends "that support of Van Buren required no abandonment of principle" as actually stumping for the candidate. It is not surprising to hear Garrisonians such as Lucretia Mott exclaim, "How sorry I am that [Henry Stanton] has thus sold himself!" Soon, however, even the most ardent political abolitionists would view Stanton's adherence to party with dismay: "Poor Stanton!" cried the *National Era*, "how art thou fallen."[29]

But Henry loved this stuff. In this respect he and Elizabeth were remarkably similar; both were far too absorbed in their own passions to care much about criticism, and were content to focus only on the fervor, the battles, and the applause. Thus Henry gushed from Albany about being offered "more than twenty applications to go hither and thither," and brimmed over with name-dropping, including "a special invitation to visit Mr Van Buren." After a speech of his had been printed "at full length in the *Democratic Review*," he boasted to his wife about having thus received a "rare compliment" of the "highest notch." Elizabeth was interested in the goings-on in Albany, and she enjoyed Henry's speeches, but his "inability to be at home" was wearing her patience. "The United States Senator question keeps every democrat in his seat in the Senate," Henry explained to her. "How long it will be pending nobody can tell." Surely Elizabeth knew this; what she wanted to know was why he could not visit his baby son Theodore with the broken collarbone instead of, as Henry reported, "dancing at the Delavan [boarding house] twice a week!" "Last week I danced two nights till about one o'clock," he wrote happily. There is nothing to suggest that Elizabeth kept silent while her husband was having a grand old time in the thick of things. But whatever arguments the couple engaged in remained between them; Elizabeth Stanton would later insist that they experienced no more than "the usual matrimonial friction" in fifty years of marriage. Instead, she turned her resentment of Henry's relative freedom, and his inability to feel as she did about woman's rights, into an analysis of the limitations placed on her sex by the laws and customs of marriage. "Men who can shut themselves up for days with their books and thoughts," she declared to Susan B. Anthony, "know little of what difficulties a woman must surmount."[30]

Decades later, men would recall Henry Stanton's regaling them with stories: "It seemed to me," one remarked, "that he must have known personally every politician, national, State, or local, not only of

New York but also of New England, New Jersey, and Pennsylvania, from the time of De Witt Clinton and Silas Wright down to that of Horatio Seymour and Roscoe Conkling." The truth was, he had become a party hack, having "quickly adapted to the role of regular Democrat, remaining silent on issues that would have seared his soul in the 1830's." Susan B. Anthony, admittedly concerned mostly with the burdens he put on his wife, sniffed that Henry Stanton was off again, "full of *Political Air Castles*." Even his obituary noted bluntly that "the old desire to shine in politics overcame him," making the early 1850s, in the words of his biographer, "a dark chapter in the life of the reformer."[31]

For a brief time, before Elizabeth's career soared and Henry's had not quite soured, the two shared an uneasy place among New York's public figures. In the course of making strange bedfellows, New York's rancorous politics brought to the Whig Party both Gerrit Smith, abolitionist and philanthropist, and Judge Daniel Cady, Federalist conservative. Both his father-in-law and cousin-in-law thus opposed Henry Stanton in his 1851 bid to retain his Senate seat—and, more important, his party's control of the Senate. It was a brutal campaign. As family lore had it, so intense were the hostilities that five-year-old Gat, peering at Theodore being bathed, whispered worriedly, "Mother, is the baby for or against father?"[32] Elizabeth Cady Stanton, now a public figure but somewhat naive politically, declared her neutrality. When she was then seen with Gerrit Smith on his own local election tour, "all the Whigs had it that Mr. Stanton's family and friends were against him, even his wife disapproving of his course." Only later did "the truth" come out: that Elizabeth Stanton "felt no interest whatever in the [Whig-sponsored] canal [financing] question *per se*, but desired Henry's re-election." However much she envied his freedom, Elizabeth Stanton sympathized with her husband's ambitions and recognized his vulnerability: "I rejoice in the victory with my whole soul," she wrote, "for in spite of all my seeming liberality towards his opposers, I would sooner see every relative and friend I have on the face of the earth blown into thin air, and that old ditch running from Buffalo to Albany filled in with mud, than have had Henry mortified by a defeat in this election." Recognizing that she was now subject to scrutiny by the press, Elizabeth abandoned her partisan neutrality and "came out an unterrified Democrat, defending resignation and abhor-ring debt."[33]

Only in 1855, when growing violence in Kansas had convinced many antislavery Democrats that compromise with the South was unlikely, did Henry throw himself into the new Republican Party, and thus land on the same side as most of the Stantons' friends. This came as a relief to his wife, who had accepted his earlier partisan choices as the best hope for his career, which, in any case, never achieved its early promise.[34] And the war, as we will see, saw the col-lapse of any hopes Henry still had of achieving higher office. Two decades into their marriage it must have been clear to everyone which Stanton was the star.

It was Susan B. Anthony, not Henry, who listened to Elizabeth's growing frustrations and encouraged their expression, who answered her frequent plea to "come & stay with me . . . & I will assist you in getting up such a lecture as you desire." But it was not only Anthony's appeal for a particular speech that drew Stanton to her writing desk, for Stanton was driven. "Men and angels give me patience! I am at the boiling point!" she famously wrote her friend in 1852. "If I do not find some day the use of my tongue on this question, I shall die of an intellectual repression, a woman's rights convulsion!" At least part of that convulsion could be relieved by her friend's coming to her rescue: "Oh, Susan! Susan! Susan!" Stanton scrawled. "You must manage to spend a week with me before the Rochester convention, for I am afraid that I cannot attend it; I have so much care with all these boys on my hands." Stanton would come to dislike conventions thoroughly, and would find all sorts of excuses to miss them. But for now she sim-ply felt trapped at home, where she could only hope that "it may be well for me to understand all the trials of woman's lot, that I may more eloquently proclaim them when the time comes."[35]

"While I am about the house," Stanton stated realistically, "sur-rounded by my children, washing dishes, baking, sewing, I can think up many points, but I cannot search books, for my hands, as well as my brains, would be necessary for that work." So, with children wan-dering in and out, books and newspapers piled high, Amelia Willard caring for their material comforts, and Henry on the road, Stanton welcomed Anthony frequently to Seneca Falls, so that together they could formulate a philosophy of women's status and the strategies to gain their rights. Years later, when Stanton pictured "that stately Quaker girl coming across my lawn," she could recall the thrill of knowing "that some happy convocation of the sons of Adam was to be set by the ears, by one of our appeals or resolutions." That experience—the physical conditions of the space that was both Stanton's home and workplace and the exhilarating freedom that came from investigating and challenging the constraints of domesticity itself—influenced Stanton's ideas about marriage even as it highlighted the differences between the friends. Anthony, who was far more astute about her married friend's experience than Stanton was about Anthony's singleness, often grew impatient with her friend's choices. She was not oblivious to the work required of wives and mothers.[36] But Stanton's assumption that her domestic experience was a universal one slighted Anthony's own declaration of single independence. To Anthony, Stanton's immersion in motherhood was a drain on Stanton's time and a distraction from her more urgent work. "I *cant get up a decent document*," Anthony would write desperately, "so for the love of me, & for the saving of the *reputation* of *womanhood*, I beg you with one baby on your knee & another at your feet & four boys whistling buzzing hallooing *Ma Ma* set your self about the work."[37] It is a measure of Anthony's devotion and faith in Stanton's philosophizing that she put up with it at all.

The years until Stanton, who sometimes felt "like a caged lioness," could "be free from household cares, that she may go into the reform work" seemed never-ending. Yet Stanton evidently made little effort to control her seemingly endless fertility. One after another, woman's rights activists were marrying (Lucy Stone in 1855, Antoinette Brown in 1856) and thus choosing, if not "retirement," at least the conflicted obligations that households and children ordained—but none matched Stanton's reproductive output. Anthony, who complained that "those of you who have the *talent* to do honor to poor oh how poor womanhood, have all given yourselves over to *baby* making, & left poor brainless *me* to battle alone," grew increasingly distressed. "I dont really want to be a *downright scolder*," she scolded one friend, as she gave the "*peremptory command*": "*not another baby.*" Stanton counseled her friend to "Let them rest in peace and quietness thinking great thoughts," but Anthony felt abandoned and peeved. Her impatience with Stanton's reproductive excess had long been a source of barbed teasing between them. With two babies to go, Elizabeth Cady Stanton had advised Anthony not to push her too hard: "As soon as you begin to ask too much of me I shall have another baby!" she warned. "Now be careful not to provoke me to that step." For her part, Anthony was sure that Stanton had brought all her burdens on herself; other couples, after all, managed somehow to limit their births or their lovemaking, that "*moments pleasure* to herself or her husband" that only increased her friend's cares. Several years later, declaring that she "would not have one less than seven" children, Stanton referred to "all the abuse that has been heaped upon me for such extravagance [*sic*]." She urged her friends to have "all the children you desire" in spite of "all Susan's admonitions."[38]

Susan B. Anthony's own independence did not mean freedom from responsibility. She carried the burdens both for much of the movement's labors and for her own, and her sister and mother's, support. Her devotion was, by all accounts, bottomless, but her energy was not, and by the late 1850s, having ignored Stanton's urging that "You, too, must rest, Susan; let the world alone awhile," she was exhausted. "I can not get up a particle of enthusiasm or faith in the success, either financial or spiritual, of another series of conventions," Anthony wrote Antoinette Brown Blackwell. "For the past five years I have gone through this routine and something within me keeps praying to be spared from more of it." But she was fiercely proud of her independence, sounding strikingly like Henry Stanton in his 1840 letter that declared himself a man: "I can not bear to make myself dependent upon relatives for the food I eat and the clothes I wear," Anthony declared. "I never have done it and hope I may never have to." So while Anthony traveled and lectured and raised funds, Stanton struggled toward leadership and influence from her base at home, enjoying clippings of her friend's activities, and delighting in Henry's assessment that "You stir up Susan & she stirs the world[.]"[39]

Apart from their different relationships to marriage and motherhood, Stanton and Anthony experienced the politics of the late 1850s differently. For Anthony, as for abolitionists Lydia Maria Child, Abby Kelley Foster, Lucy Stone, and Lucretia Mott, the crises of that decade demanded a renewed moral commitment to ending slavery. Stanton remained somewhat detached from this moment of great urgency for the antislavery cause and the nation itself, asking Anthony, whose two brothers had moved to Kansas to establish a free state, "How do you stand on the Lecompton question? You Garrisonians are such a crochety [sic] set that generally, when all other men see cause for rejoicing, you howl the more grievously. How is it now?" She went on, only half joking, "I desire to know, for as I am one of you, I wish to do what is most becoming to one of the order. Shall I fire off my boys' cannon and a bundle of crackers, or shall I wear sackcloth and ashes?" Anthony, who received this letter during "the hardest three weeks' tour of anti-slavery meetings I have had yet, so cold and disheartening," surely grimaced at Stanton's persistent good cheer and her apparent disregard for the emergency at hand.[40]

But the fall of 1858 was difficult for Elizabeth Cady Stanton, too, as she faced a new and, to her, unexpected limitation. Stanton had always been excessively pleased with her physical abilities, and contemptuous of women whose pregnancies slowed them down; with each birth, she boasted of her strength and sturdiness.[41] But even she had had enough. "Courage Susan," she had written in the summer of 1857, "this is my last baby" and a new beginning: "We shall not be in our prime before fifty & after that we shall be good for twenty years at least." She had underestimated their longevity but also her fecundity, for Harriot was not her last child; a year later, she was pregnant with her seventh baby, and, to her chagrin, exhausted. Typically, she had agreed to address the Boston Fraternity Lecture Course in mid-November—the first woman to speak to that group—without considering this possibility. When she wrote to cancel the engagement, the organizer, Charles Slack, was appalled: "Our whole Course turns upon your appearance now that you have been announced, and it is utterly impossible for us to get a substitute. *Come, therefore,* if you speak to us but 20 minutes." Others implored her not to harm the "cause of woman" by canceling.[42] No one liked her excuse that her trunk had been lost on her way home from Philadelphia, and Stanton looked both foolish and frivolous.

Actually, she had lied. Weeks later, she sheepishly revealed how prideful she was of her public image. "Why did I not fulfill my engagement in Boston?" she wrote to her cousin Elizabeth Smith Miller. "I made the engagement in good faith and prepared myself, expecting fully to be there at the appointed date, which would have been in the fifth month—maternally, not quakerly, speaking—at which time I always have felt well and heroic. But my present experience differed from all its antecedents." Convinced that her childbearing prowess proved her to be a woman who had surmounted the presumed disabilities of her sex, Stanton despised what she viewed as evidence of weakness. Characteristically, however, she expressed only its political ramifications: "I knew if I told Mrs. Severance my dilemma, she would have to repeat it," she explained ruefully, "and as the maternal difficulty has always been one of the arguments against woman entering public life, I did not like the idea that I, who had a hundred times declared that difficulty to be absurd, should illustrate in my own person the contrary thesis. It was all too humiliating to be disclosed."[43] This was Stanton at her egotistical best: mixing pride and principle, declaring her experience a standard for womankind even when she had to fake it, and making it impossible for her friends to stay angry at her for long.

Indeed, Bob's birth that March caused Stanton more suffering than she had known with the previous six. "I have a great boy now three weeks old," she informed Anthony, who devoutly hoped this was the last account of a Stanton baby she would hear. "He weighed at his birth without a particle of clothing 12¼ lb. I never suffered so much before." A week later, she could still "scarcely walk across the room."[44] Finally, she and Anthony, and probably Henry, recognized there would be no more babies. They surely met this moment differently. Anthony had been begging for years for Stanton to be free to leave home, to join her on the road and in the movement. Henry likely felt ambivalent about the remnants of the couple's romantic, and sexual, closeness, although supporting all those children had always been a struggle. Elizabeth, who always wanted it all, was emphatically ready to stop having children, but was hardly eager to launch into the kind of frenetic and selfless life Anthony had planned for her.

Bob's birth preceded a series of losses that year that further strained even Stanton's vigorous spirits. In October 1859, two weeks after John Brown's raid on Harpers Ferry, Judge Daniel Cady died. In early November, Gerrit Smith, who had helped finance Brown's failed uprising, entered the New York State Asylum for the Insane, having suffered a breakdown that Stanton viewed as "worse than death." Stanton, typically, blamed her emotional condition on her "dwarfed and perverted womanhood," but she was simply, and uncharacteristically, sad. Isolated with her babies, reluctant to admit how much she depended on and missed these two men, and desperate to reinvigorate her life with new ideas and new actions, she wrote Anthony plaintively that "it would do me great good to see some reformers just now."[45] Anthony, of course, had a solution for all of Stanton's woes: work for the cause.

Elizabeth Cady Stanton did not droop for long. In February 1860 she addressed a "magnificent audience" at the New York State Legislature's Judiciary Committee hearings in the state capital. Stanton, who no doubt paused to consider the absence of the father who had inadvertently exposed her to the reach and promise of the law, spoke to these men in their own language: "If the object of government is to protect the weak against the strong," she asserted, "how unwise to place the power wholly in the hands of the strong." Yet this was the situation women faced, one that, "in cruelty and tyranny," was worse than slavery, for "woman, from her social position, refinement, and education, is on a more equal ground with the oppressor." Indeed, Stanton declared, "Allow me just here to call the attention of that party now so much interested in the slave of the Carolinas, to the similarity in his condition and that of the mothers, wives, and daughters of the Empire State." She went on to draw comparisons, to anticipate and answer objections, and to declare that women "as a class" were tired of "one kind of protection, that which leaves us everything to do, to dare, and to suffer, and strips us of all means for its accomplishment." The house was packed, Lydia Mott reported, "but so still that not one word was lost."[46] Both the respect with which Stanton's appeal was greeted and the expansion of the Married Women's Property Act that followed told about equally how far the cause, and her own public reputation, had come.

That May, all the national benevolent and reform societies met in New York for anniversary week, and it seemed an auspicious moment to be there. William Lloyd Garrison himself had written Stanton to express "the unanimous desire of the Executive Committee of the American Anti-Slavery Society, that you will be one of the speakers," and she was eager to accept. If Stanton generally found conventions boring and repetitive, that could not be said now, with the antislavery societies torn between crisis and hope, marking both the twenty-five years since Garrison had been arrested to protect him from "the murderous designs of an infuriated mob" and the change in public opinion that had occurred since.[47] Politics were inescapable. Only a few days later, the Republican Party would meet in Chicago and choose Abraham Lincoln, then relatively unknown, as their candidate for president. Already abolitionists were grappling with the party's mixed views on slavery and their own ambivalence about partisan means for change. Garrison himself would engage "in a rigorous but charitable critique" of the candidate, while others, notably Frederick Douglass, withheld their support. "A great many movement men," Garrison's biographer has noted, ". . . held their noses and voted for Lincoln," a stance Henry Stanton found relatively easy to endorse.[48]

Elizabeth Cady Stanton, with Bob a year and a half old and Amelia Willard in charge at home, would plunge even more fully into the fray by the fall, urging the Republican women of Seneca Falls's "Wide Awake Club" to accept "No Compromise with Slaveholders." Declaring herself a "full-blooded Republican," she acknowledged that "Abraham Lincoln has a sound mind in a sound body; his morality is unquestioned; he is temperate in all his habits, and simple in his life and pleasures," but concluded, "and if he were only a good Abolitionist, I could indorse [sic] him with all my heart." That fall, no one even marginally "wide awake" could resist getting fired up by the presidential campaign or the heat of sectional conflict. Even Henry was interested enough in this speech of his wife's that he asked for a copy.[49]

But while everyone else was thoroughly distracted by the growing likelihood of war, and Stanton herself was speaking about antislavery politics, another part of her brain had already moved on. At the Tenth National Woman's Rights Convention, in New York City, a dozen years after she had shocked both radical reformers and conservative editors by demanding woman suffrage at Seneca Falls, Stanton stirred up yet another storm by launching a sweeping attack on women's sub-

ordination to men in the laws and conventions of marriage, motherhood, and divorce.

The woman's rights convention that assembled at Cooper Union
on May 10 opened on an optimistic note. Martha Coffin Wright
began by declaring that "after all that we demand has been granted, as
it will be soon," their opponents will claim that they had "always advocated" woman's rights. The crowd laughed. Indeed, there had been
enormous gains in the decade since the organized movement began.
Susan B. Anthony rose to list a few of them: The New York Legislature had just expanded the 1848 Married Women's Property Act to
include women's right to their wages and their children; Matthew
Vassar had announced his intention to "found a college for girls, equal
in all respects to Yale and Harvard"; women had become doctors and
ministers, and had addressed politicians at all levels of government;
and the movement itself had received significant funds, including a
$5,000 anonymous donation to continue its work. Much that the ear-
liest woman's rights advocates had demanded seemed, at the level of
public opinion, settled. Indeed, so widespread was the support for
woman's rights, Ernestine Rose admitted, that many were asking,
"What is the use of Conventions?" Elizabeth Cady Stanton, who often
asked that question herself, rose to undermine any such complacency
by proposing a new stage in their agitation: divorce reform. "[A]ny
constitution, compact, or covenant between human beings, that failed
to produce or promote human happiness," she resolved, "could not, in
the nature of things, be of any force or authority; and it would be not
only a right, but a duty, to abolish it." "In one swift gesture," one historian writes, "she demoted marriage from a sacred act to a civil function and raised divorce from an offense against God to a civil,
contractual right."[50] The convention erupted.

It is hard now to imagine how radical this was, but the defense of
the sanctity of marriage should sound familiar. Marriage was, with
very few exceptions, considered a permanent arrangement, especially
among the "respectable" middle classes who gathered at woman's
rights conventions. While many woman's rights advocates had long
believed in changing the laws of property, contract, and custody to
resolve some of the inequities women faced, the notion that marriage
itself was merely a contract that could be broken was deeply disturb-

ing. Antoinette Blackwell insisted somewhat frantically that activists hold only to the "true ideal" of marriage; Wendell Phillips argued that the laws of marriage "rest equally upon men and women" and so had no place at their convention. Stanton, however, refused to concede to what she viewed as prejudice and custom, and insisted that the convention take the question a giant step further. "If marriage is a human institution, about which man can legislate," she asserted with cool logic, "it seems but just that he should treat this branch of legislation with the same common-sense that he applies to all others."[51] Even to discuss the subject, whether with hope or trepidation, was to ensure that marriage would never be the same.

Perhaps even Stanton thought the convention's reaction dispropor-tionate to the brazenness of her proposals, for reformers had long suggested that the laws and customs of marriage imposed greater bur-dens on wives than on husbands. The followers of the socialist reformer Robert Owen and other founders of utopian communities had pointed to the economic relations of marriage as the major source of women's powerlessness and dependence, and temperance activists had bemoaned women's inability to leave drunken or abusive hus-bands. Stanton had agreed, telling the New York State Temperance Convention in 1852 that "no woman [should] remain in the relation of wife with the confirmed drunkard." Stanton was, as usual, so thor-oughly convinced by her own arguments that she soon expanded them, and so was often a step or two ahead of her friends. Two years later, in 1854, at the New York State Woman's Rights Convention in Albany, Stanton had described marriage itself as an untenable hybrid, a "half-human, half-divine institution," which instantly transformed the status of independent citizens into wives, and then forbade them from ending the contract itself.[52] With the charge of "free love" hover-ing over the proceedings, legislators and, conspicuously, Stanton's father, Daniel Cady, had been appalled.

Nor was Stanton alone among the leading woman's rights activists in holding these views. In 1853, complaining that conservatives in the temperance movement "wish to stave off the divorce question," Susan B. Anthony had urged Lucy Stone to attend the convention to "dis-cuss it fully & ably." Stone, who agreed with Stanton's position on divorce but was more fearful of the "free love" epithet, preferred that

Stanton speak. Still, she agreed to address the convention "on the right of divorce for drunkenness." Stone's marriage protest in 1855 made public her (and Henry Blackwell's) objection to the lopsided laws of marriage; her bold decision to keep her own name signaled her resistance to the loss of women's individuality in marriage. Several years later, Stone, inspired by having read *Adam Bede* and *Mill on the Floss*, hoped Stanton "would call a convention to discuss divorce, marriage, infanticide, and their kindred subjects," adding "that a wife's right to her own body should be pushed at our next convention." But now, in the spring of 1860, as Stanton planned her assault on marriage and divorce and had "written to Lucy asking her to sustain me if any discussion grows out of the address," Stone blanched. She stayed away from the convention, and so was not forced to choose sides when her sister-in-law, Antoinette Brown Blackwell, rose to declare that the idea that marriage was merely a civil contract was "morally impossible."[53]

It was one thing to disagree—Stanton welcomed a good argument—but she bristled self-righteously at the suggestion that any subject was out of bounds. Wendell Phillips's motion to strike all resolutions about divorce from the convention's records amazed Stanton, who remembered Phillips's faithful defense of woman's rights on the abolitionist platform. She lectured the convention—and Phillips—at some length on the ways that marriage treated women and men unequally, but he seemed unable to hear it; later that summer he remained horrified that Stanton was "lugging onto our platform that noisy alien 'M[arriage] & Divorce.' "[54]

Stanton and Anthony knew full well that highlighting the issue of divorce would take the woman's rights movement in a new direction, one that messily paired state with church, law with custom—and that would invite the charge that they were "free lovers" set on abolishing all regulation of sexual behavior. And although the counterattack was intense, Stanton declared the convention a great success, and noted once again that the very act of raising a subject shifted people's thinking. To Martha Coffin Wright, Stanton exulted "that we have thrown our bombshell into the center of woman's degradation and of course we have raised a rumpus."[55] Stanton knew that many of the views expressed at Seneca Falls had become widely held, even commonplace, among women of her class, however much they still feared public or familial ridicule by speaking out. She was delighted to alarm them anew by challenging women's subordination in relationships that were uncomfortably close to home. "How this marriage question grows on me," she admitted to Anthony as the noise continued. "It lies at the very foundation of all progress. I never read a thing on this subject until I had arrived at my present opinion. My own life, observation, thought, feeling, reason, brought me to the conclusion. So fear not that I shall falter. I shall not grow conservative with age."[56] Anthony was likely less worried about that prospect than about her friend's tendency to become utterly absorbed in a new aspect of the cause.

For Stanton, discovering another position from which to advance woman's rights was thrilling, promising as it did future arguments in the pulpit, the press, and the parlor. Once she had formulated an idea and sent it flying, she tended to get bored, and she was always seeking to add to, or flesh out, her analysis of women's degradation. Each and every time, she was positive that she had found its "one true cause"; this time it was "in man's idea of his sexual rights." She could hardly contain her glee at her own cleverness, writing to Anthony, "Come what will, my whole soul rejoices in the truth that I have uttered. One word of thanks from a suffering woman outweighs with me the howls of all Christendom."[57]

For all her enthusiasm, Stanton's "bombshell" was poorly timed; the rest of the nation was already embroiled in the coming Civil War. But Elizabeth Cady Stanton did not mind, for she looked to the prospect of war as a springboard to women's equal citizenship. While Anthony suffered the discomforts and insecurities of lecturing and travel, Stanton returned home to enjoy the comforts of a house well heated and fully stocked, with a piano, writing desk, and comfortable chair. And if it wasn't yet clear to her how she would remake herself in the relative freedom of middle age, she knew at least that she hated attending conventions and making compromises and that she much preferred the brilliant simplicity of lofty ideals and consistent principles. The push and pull between Stanton and Anthony, between philosophy and organizing, between her needs and those of the movement she had helped found, would go on for another five decades, as

Anthony nagged her to leave her desk and join her on the road, and Stanton pulled back, choosing the life of the mind and the pen. The two women would undergo private strains and disagreements, but would always come back to a new version of their old closeness, reframed by ongoing tensions and debates. "I long to put my arms around you once more and hear you scold me for my sins and short-comings," Stanton once teased. "Your abuse is sweeter to me than anybody else's praise." To an extraordinary degree each was dependent on the other for the prodding and stimulation she needed to live in and for the cause. "O, Susan, you are very dear to me," Elizabeth Cady Stanton admitted. "I should miss you more than any other living being from this earth. You are intertwined with much of my happy and eventful past, and all my future plans are based on you as a coadjutor. Yes, our work is one, we are one in aim and sympathy and we should be together. Come home."[58] And she did.

4

WAR AND RECONSTRUCTION

(1861–1868)

T his war is music in my ears," declared Elizabeth Cady Stanton in
1861; "it is a simultaneous chorus for freedom." Stanton was
forty-five years old when the Civil War began, the mother of
seven children ranging in age from two to nineteen, a woman whose
public reputation was beginning to catch up both to her intellect and
her itch to be closer to the action. At first she remained in Seneca
Falls, while Henry Stanton wrote from Washington, D.C., that "this
union is going to destruction as fast as it can." Whatever the outcome,
whether it was victory over the South or a divided nation, neither Elizabeth nor Henry Stanton doubted that the war, if only it went on long
enough, would end slavery. Henry, for one, began to hope for a dissolution: "When these Southern states have all gone, then we shant
need any ['liberty bills']," he assured his wife. "Half the negroes will
run away, & there will be no fugitive slave law to stop them—for there
will be no slave States in *our* Union."[1] As for Elizabeth, either outcome presaged thrilling possibilities: the emancipation of the slaves,
Elizabeth Cady Stanton believed, would open the way for great ad-
vances in woman's rights.

Others in their circle were less enthralled by the drumbeat of war,
and less certain that war would hasten anyone's emancipation. For
abolitionists, the Civil War presented numerous dilemmas: whether
and how much to support President Abraham Lincoln, who vowed to
preserve the union even if it meant freeing no slaves; whether to
abandon long-held peace principles to endorse military action; and

whether to resist or support their sons' decisions to enter combat. This last, the most personal of choices, was often the most painful. Some pacifists and Quakers simply could not accept their sons' decision to fight, and forbade their underage boys from enlisting. William Lloyd Garrison, who had counseled his friends "to respect the work of [their sons'] conscience," was forced to follow his own advice when his son George enlisted with the Fifty-fifth Massachusetts Regiment; he was no doubt relieved that the next two, William, Jr., and Wendell, stood firm by their antiwar and antigovernment principles. For some, of course, the issue was excruciating. Elizabeth Cady Stanton's youngest sister, Catherine, who had already lost one son at Gettysburg, went "on the rampage" when her son Frank Wilkeson, only sixteen, enlisted. Although she considered reporting his true age to the army, she finally "left him to face his own decisions."[2]

Elizabeth and Henry Stanton faced no qualms about the necessity of war, nor did they seem to fear their sons' military ambitions. Although she considered herself a holder of "peace principles," Stanton now declared fervently that "the age of bullets has come again." Even before the attack on Fort Sumter, there was a martial beat to their correspondence, as when Henry wrote to "Tell Daniel, the Zouave" (the name given to some French infantry units), that if war began he would "look to see his gallant corps rallying among the foremost." ("By the by," he added, in a rare spurt of involvement in the home front, "before the Zouave takes the field, I wish he would write me about how he gets along with Arithmetic, wood-chopping, &c.")[3]

The Stanton boys' wartime experience remains murky. Some evidence suggests that the two oldest enlisted in the Nineteenth Volunteer Infantry, but if so, it is unlikely that they went far or served for long.[4] Certainly Neil had gone someplace, since, not having heard from him by June, his mother was "intensely anxious," and a letter "came to me like a pardon to one condemned." As for Henry (Kit), Stanton's second son, "all his proclivities are to the army," and she took steps to see them advanced. In September of 1861, she asked Secretary of State William Seward (sure he was "too magnanimous to be influenced in this matter by any slight personal differences with my Husband") to recommend the young man, then seventeen, to West Point. Of Kit himself she had nothing but praise: "The boy has the essential elements of a hero," and of course the finest examples at home: "I have endeavored to fire his soul with a holy love for freedom." The appointment did not materialize; one account suggests that Kit "ran away to join the army but was overtaken and brought home," but it may have been Gerrit, the next youngest, who did so. By January, in any case, both Henry, Jr., and Gerrit were under their mother's wing, never "spend[ing] an evening from home & . . . in bed at ten o'clock."⁵ Perhaps the strongest evidence against Stanton's sons' military experience is negative: when other mothers referred to their sons' wartime service as an indication of their own patriotism, Elizabeth Cady Stanton remained silent.

At war's beginning, with the youngest children only two and five and the others in school, an erratic income, and two parents who were often on the road, it is not always clear who was minding the home front. Henry, always a somewhat abstract presence, occasionally inserted himself into domestic matters ("—Boys! Get the leaves & the ice out of the gutters!—Boys! Go to school!—Bobby! Do you want some more money for presents?"), but the war captured his attention more than anything had in years. "Aunt Susan," as the children called Susan B. Anthony, was more regularly in attendance, but even they could tell that she came mostly to free their mother up for what both women viewed as her more important work. "Her advent was not a matter for rejoicing," Harriot recalled of these visits. Indeed, a coolness in later accounts suggests that the children were a bit afraid of her: "Bob to his dying day used to say that Susan was the only woman except his mother, who had ever spanked him," Harriot later wrote. "Even when he had grown old enough, as we all did, to appreciate Miss Anthony's sterling qualities, and her value to the suffrage cause, the spanking episode rankled in his memory."⁶

Elizabeth Cady Stanton had already taken the first steps toward a more independent, less domestically bound life when the war began, but she remained the dominant person in her children's lives, and "a sunny, cheerful, indulgent mother." Simply by the force of her personality, she shaped the household's routines and values even when she went away—"always an acute pain to me," Harriot recalled—and even, or especially, when it was hard to hold her attention. Stanton rarely dwelt on her children's accomplishments and never publicly mentioned their failings or the distance that soon grew between her and two of her adult sons, though she might boast when they showed evidence of having absorbed the family principles. Reading the news one evening about Union troops returning fleeing slaves ("contraband") to their owners, she had asked Henry, Jr., "suppose you had been one of the squad ordered in that duty what would you have done. 'I would have respectfully handed my musket to my superior officer & said, sir shoot me through the heart but send me on no base errand like that.'" It made a mother's heart swell with pride. Still, the children come across as—and likely felt themselves to be—ordinary by comparison to their mother. "Have hope and faith in your seven," Anthony instructed, in about as backhanded a compliment as she could give. "If it should take them all to make their mother, they each will still be above the average."[7]

Finally, in 1862, Elizabeth's yearning for a wider world coincided with Henry's opportunities. Henry Stanton had long ago put the energy he had devoted to antislavery into procuring patronage jobs; his Civil War years tell more about his political advancement—and decline—than about the emancipation of slaves. In August 1861, he accepted a position as deputy collector of the New York Custom House. Elizabeth sold the house and land on Washington Street, and the Stantons arranged the following spring to leave Seneca Falls, where they had lived for fifteen years and which Elizabeth Cady Stanton had stamped with its association with her cause.[8]

If 1840s Boston, with its quaint blend of social stuffiness and intellectual enthusiasm, had been fun, wartime New York was for grown-ups. The entire North was experiencing a wartime boom; New York, with a population of more than eight hundred thousand, and an economy and a political machine that surpassed those of any city in the country, displayed it more dramatically. "Our streets are crowded," wrote the wealthy William E. Dodge in 1863, "hotels full, the railroads, and manufacturers of all kinds except cotton were never doing so well and business generally is active." The gap between rich and poor, always evident in New York, was widening before people's eyes. New millionaires went about ostentatiously spending the riches gained in the wartime economy, as inflation, homelessness, and scarcity plagued the working poor, including many wives and children

of absent soldiers. Political and racial rifts were highlighted by skir-
mishes over African American strikebreakers, the rise of so-called
Peace Democrats, the Emancipation Proclamation, and the draft.[9]
Such a place had plenty of room for Elizabeth Cady Stanton's exuberance, first in Brooklyn, then in town houses at 75 West Forty-fifth
Street and, later, at 464 West Thirty-fourth Street.[10] Eager as ever to
be at the center of things—with Amelia Willard agreeing to come
along to take charge of the household, and Anthony more or less living
with them as well—Stanton packed up her children and girded herself for the chaos of city life.

It was not immediately clear what role the war would demand of
woman's rights activists, and for a while Stanton floundered. Neither
she nor Anthony felt drawn to the sewing, shipping, and nursing that
kept so many Northern women involved, nor were they optimistic
enough about Abraham Lincoln's administration to remain silent.
Even before the war began, Henry had "advise[d] you, & Susan, & all
friends, to keep quiet & let the Revolution go on," but it was hard to
sit by. When the American Anti-Slavery Society decided to cease
holding conventions during the war, Elizabeth Cady Stanton and
other leading woman's rights advocates, in a burst of patriotic optimism, agreed that a similar strategic withdrawal would best advance
the cause of woman's rights, and canceled the May convention.
Anthony, who thought Stanton's view misguided, was largely alone in
finding this position "humiliating, . . . one of expediency not principle." Later, when it became clear that their sacrifice would not be
rewarded with new rights, Stanton declared that canceling their conventions had been a "blunder," and vowed ever after to take "my
beloved Susan's judgment against the world."[11]

On January 1, 1863, President Lincoln's Emancipation Proclamation went into effect, freeing no slaves but signaling at last that the
war might indeed become a war for liberty. "Three cheers for God!"
abolitionist Theodore Tilton exulted, expressing most abolitionists'
feeling that "Even if not all one could wish, it is too much not to be
thankful for."[12] Only now did Stanton and Anthony find their place
in the wartime struggle. Anthony, who had never stopped squirming
against the moratorium on agitation, was eager that finally they could
work to cement the movement's goals.

Elizabeth Cady Stanton had always been clear about what she wanted the Civil War to accomplish: the emancipation of the slaves, she was sure, would pave the way for emancipating women as well. She never wavered in her assumption that the war (that "simultaneous chorus for freedom") would open the door to full citizenship to white women as well as to the enslaved—although few yet imagined that suffrage would become a pivotal demand for either group. In 1863, in a setting awash in rhetoric about black men proving their fitness for citizenship through their military service, she and Anthony set out to establish women's claim to their own rights by demonstrating their faithfulness to the nation's highest ideals. From Washington, Henry Stanton applauded their intentions, warning Anthony that the Emancipation Proclamation "will [not] be of any use if we are beaten." "Susan," he exhorted, "put on your armor and go forth!" After years of resisting the rhetoric of wartime patriotism—and still unwilling to say anything friendly about Lincoln himself—Stanton and Anthony declared themselves "loyal" women and entered the fray.[13]

Fifteen years after the convention at Seneca Falls, Elizabeth Cady Stanton was well placed to assume the leadership of a movement. For one thing, she was in New York, where the Civil War relief organizations were based and where she had a relationship, for good or ill, with the editors of an essentially national press. Horace Greeley, the influential editor of the *Tribune*, may have been tepid in his support of woman's rights, but he played an important role in making the cause, and Stanton, virtually household names by war's end. In addition, Stanton was now firmly partnered with Susan B. Anthony, who implored her to accept the title of president of a new organization while she, as secretary, did most of the work. Signing their names "on behalf of the Woman's Central Committee," an informal cluster of woman's rights and antislavery activists, Stanton and Anthony now issued a call for a new association, along with a lengthy appeal to Northern women by Stanton herself, thus signaling the greatly expanded public influence they brought to bear on their cause.[14]

On May 14, 1863, and over the next two days, a mass gathering of women met in the Church of the Puritans and formed the Women's Loyal National League (a clumsy title that even its founders scrambled). Middle-class Northern women had been hard at work providing relief and support for the troops, but this was something entirely different: an assembly of women who could "philosophize on the principles that underlie national existence," and who were determined to pressure the federal government to make the abolition of slavery its wartime goal.[15] The meeting that founded the Women's Loyal National League drew women from throughout the North and with different views. Not all were radical reformers, and some would never have attended a meeting with the likes of Stanton, Anthony, Stone, and Ernestine Rose under other circumstances. Susan B. Anthony's resolution that "There never can be a true peace in this Republic until the civil and political rights of all citizens of African descent and all women are practically established" raised these women's hackles.[16] Mrs. Hoyt of Wisconsin objected firmly that "we should attend to our own business" rather than support "anti-slavery speeches." Simply supporting "the maintenance of the authority of the Government as it is" should be the league's only goal, she insisted. Seeking to calm the discussion, Sarah Halleck suggested that women stand aside and adopt only the resolution to grant freedom to African Americans, who "have suffered more than the women." ("You are too self-sacrificing," cried a voice from the audience.) Ernestine Rose kindly but firmly "object[ed] to the proposition to throw woman out of the race for freedom," and Angelina Grimké Weld and Lucy Stone persisted as well, defiantly linking the cause of all women and that of the slave. "I want to be identified with the negro," Grimké Weld declared, and Anthony's proposal carried. Mrs. Hoyt remained unassuaged and unsilenced, but was wrong to predict that her own state would reject the plan the league laid out: in the mammoth petition that the women presented to Congress the following year, Wisconsin boasted the ninth-greatest number of signers of all the states.[17]

Opposition from more radical activists was heard as well. Even though "the Anti-Slavery women and the Woman's Rights women . . . called this meeting," the very notion of "loyalty" was a stickler for these abolitionists, who resisted any association with the government in power. Ernestine Rose thought loyalty meant "to be true to one's highest convictions," but everyone knew that that was not its common usage, especially in wartime. Only when Abby Kelley Foster was satisfied that the league supported the government "in so far as it makes the war for freedom," did she enter into the work. But while some lifelong abolitionists (Maria Weston Chapman, for instance) remained unconvinced, abolitionist women throughout the North, who had already begun to petition, were gratified to see their work take root on a larger, and more centralized, scale.[18] For so many women who were impatient with the relief work they had been implicitly assigned, the Women's Loyal National League signaled the end of biding their time and gave them a focus for their wartime activism.

The Women's Loyal National League, under Stanton and Anthony's leadership, stressed the abolition of slavery and strategically quieted their woman's rights goals, thus gaining great praise from the Northern press. "The women of the League have shown practical wisdom in restricting their efforts to one object," declared the *New York Tribune*, which applauded their intention of "obtain[ing] ONE MILLION of names to a petition." Stanton and Anthony set up an office at Cooper Union, Anthony moved into the Stanton town house for the duration, and the work of gathering names on petitions commenced. In February 1864 the Loyal League presented Senator Charles Sumner with some one hundred thousand names, two-thirds of them women, on massive rolled-up petitions; by the next year they had more than doubled that number. With some five thousand members, two paid lecturers, and several thousand women, men, and children gathering names, the organization placed Stanton and Anthony in a new, and newly respectable, light.[19]

The Emancipation Proclamation may have promised that a Northern victory in the Civil War would end human bondage in the United States, but it did not heal divisions among Northerners about emancipation itself. New York City, "the North's most proslavery city," had witnessed especially fierce debates about Lincoln's election and Southern secession, and things would get worse. Only months after an "Emancipation Jubilee" had drawn an excited crowd of African Americans and white abolitionists to Cooper Union, the Republican administration implemented a draft. Already outraged by the very thing that had thrilled abolitionists—so this *was* a war to end slavery after all—many in this overwhelmingly Democratic city opposed the conscription law, which registered men, chose recruits by lottery, and permitted men to pay substitutes $300 to serve in their place. On

July 11, when the lottery began, so did the protests. Within two days, crowds of men and women had gathered from the city's shipyards, manufactories, and foundries. For five steaming hot days, New York witnessed the most intense mob violence and looting in its history, a "pogrom of the desperate against the more desperate," that left at least 119 people dead and thousands homeless.[20]

While it is unlikely that, as one elite New Yorker suggested, "this is an organized insurrection in the interest of the rebellion," the cries of "Jeff Davis!" and "Kill all Niggers!" that rose from the streets inflamed hostility both to the draft and to black New Yorkers. The attack on the Colored Orphan Asylum, from which more than two hundred African American children escaped, further heightened the fears of white abolitionists and Republicans that they would become targets of the mobs. These fears became real for James and Abby Hopper Gibbons, whose daughter reported that "rioters yesterday gutted our house completely" (leaving "broken banisters and doors, burnt panels, and a few half-destroyed pieces of furniture," amid two thousand wrecked books) while Abby was away nursing Union troops. "It is our contribution to the war," James wrote, trying to remain calm and principled. "I am ashamed to have deserved no more."[21]

Black New Yorkers, Gibbons knew, faced far graver threats, as crowds shot, lynched, and burned black men in the street, and looted and destroyed businesses and tenements that catered to black residents. Within days, "rioters had virtually emptied the harbor front of people of color," and thousands of African Americans never returned. It took some six thousand troops to persuade the lingering crowds that the riots had ended. At first, amid the smoke of burning houses and stores, the Democrats seemed to have won, since the draft quota was reduced. But Republican leaders were furious, and defended the city's remaining African American community by providing aid and, finally, by enlisting a black regiment to help win the war.[22]

It was characteristic of Stanton to imagine herself at the center of all things, but in this case she was right. She, Anthony, and the children watched as streams of rioters marched past their home, only a few blocks from the Colored Orphan Asylum and the draft headquarters, both targets of the crowds.[23] One group of rioters, identifying twenty-one-year-old Neil not as an abolitionist (as his mother feared) but as "one of those three-hundred-dollar fellows!" who could pay for a substitute, took ahold of him and yanked him away. "You may imagine what I suffered in seeing him dragged off," his mother wrote her cousin Ann Fitzhugh Smith. Neil had, as his father's biographer wryly put it, "inherited his father's talent for the expedient response, but lacked the Stanton courage" and so bought a round of drinks for the men, toasted Jefferson Davis, and thus appeased their anger. Once things had calmed down, Elizabeth Stanton, grateful and rueful, admitted that although "he undoubtedly saved his life by a bit of deception, . . . it would have been far nobler to have died in defiance of the tyranny of mob law."[24]

White abolitionists responded in various ways to the violence, or the threat of it. James Gibbons gazed at the destruction of his property, considered the "mortal and incurable wounds" of mothers who had lost their sons, and reflected that his family's suffering was "only a scratch." Frances Seward, in her seemingly safe perch in Auburn, New York, passed "a disturbed and fearful week" as rumors flew about a planned uprising by Irish factory workers against the town's small black population. In response, she "furnished William Johnson with a pistol to defend himself if attacked," and informed her son that she wished all the African American men were similarly armed.[25]

Stanton, true to form, proposed to defend her home with words. She coached the children to run to the roof if they were attacked, and then "prepared a speech, determined, if necessary, to go down at once, open the door and make a grand appeal to them as Americans and citizens of a republic."[26] The timely arrival of some soldiers relieved Stanton of having to test her powers of persuasion, but her faith in her own oratory is astounding nonetheless. Quickly substituting bluster with flight, and thus arguably not so unlike the smooth-tongued Neil, she packed her family's bags and hustled with the children to Johnstown, now without her father's presence but still her refuge.

Through all such challenges of wartime, both political and personal, Stanton maintained her resolve not to display emotion in public, and to interpret distressing events in a political frame. That resolve was sorely tested by a scandal and congressional investigation involving Henry and Neil Stanton, causing wife and mother to declare herself newly convinced "how small the sons of Adam are."[27] Indeed, Neil's skirmish with the draft rioters was soon overshadowed by more mundane troubles that he continued to pile up at home—and that had important ramifications for the ongoing balancing act between his parents' ambitions.

Among the perks offered by Henry Stanton's job at the Custom House was the opportunity to spread Republican patronage ever more thinly, which he did by getting Neil a clerkship in the office. There was nothing unusual or, to the Stantons, embarrassing about this practice, which solved the immediate prospects of their baffling eldest son, an "untrustworthy, mendacious and sly boy, indolent and apparently amoral," in one historian's view.[28] But in the fall of 1863, evidence emerged at the Custom House that bonds for the shipment of goods to "neutral places near the rebel ports" had gone missing, perhaps even had landed in the hands of the enemy. Quickly the "abstracted" bonds were traced "to a young man, a clerk in the Custom-house," and Henry Stanton was questioned. So widespread were the rumors that flew around New York's financial and shipping community that the *New York Times* was forced to assure its readers that "The reports that [Henry Stanton] has been arrested, dismissed, &c., are entire fabrications." In an open letter addressed to Secretary of the Treasury Salmon Chase and published in the major newspapers, Henry Stanton pled his defense. "I have endeavored to stand square up to the line of my duty," he declared, but there was no getting around Neil, "one weak boy," as his father admitted. "You will readily understand how deeply wounded I feel," Henry wrote, "and how hard it is thus to speak of my son. But a sense of justice demands it, and I cannot palliate the facts." Henry Stanton was opportunistic and ambitious, and he was likely careless in his management of the Custom House. An embarrassing and inconclusive House committee's investigation, however, found no evidence that he was personally corrupt. Nevertheless, unable to defend himself without further exposing Neil, he resigned his position. As for Neil, apparently his parents' contacts prevented his prosecution, and he was allowed to resign as well. The publicity was excruciating. Certain that there was intrigue and conspiracy afoot, Elizabeth Stanton pulled every string she had with the city's editors to control the fallout, but Henry remained "deeply wounded," and the prideful Elizabeth embarrassed and angry in "this hour of the deepest sorrow of my life."[29]

Facing unemployment and public humiliation at the age of sixty, Henry Stanton must have suddenly seemed—and felt—his full decade older than his wife. Months later expressions of support were still like "balm to his wounded spirit."[30] But his friends and connections came through, and Henry rallied once more. He became a reporter, first for Greeley's *Tribune* and then, in 1868, for Charles Dana's *New York Sun*, writing mostly about the workings of New York politics. Well into old age, he was a ubiquitous presence at the *Sun*, an honored codger and a fount of knowledge. But his hopes for a political career were over.

Neil remained a problem. If the Custom House scandal showed him to be corrupt, the postwar years offered opportunities to prove himself a scoundrel. Reconstruction would find Neil once again in the center of patronage politics, this time in Louisiana, where his father secured him an appointment as supervisor of elections. The agreement that closed this deal was unsavory even for Henry; in exchange for a job for his son, Henry persuaded Charles Dana to stop attacking Republican governor Henry C. Warmoth in the Democratic *Sun*'s editorials.

What Henry Stanton hoped would come from sending his disgraced son to Louisiana (to ensure the fairness of elections, no less) is anyone's guess. Louisiana exemplified both the promise and the violence of the Reconstruction South. Henry Warmoth, an Illinois native who had come to Louisiana with the occupying United States Army in 1864, spearheaded a movement to place the state under federal jurisdiction with legal equality for African American men. Warmoth, "a fun-loving, hell-raising sort" exactly Neil Stanton's age, was an astute political player, who as governor controlled printing contracts, judges, and Custom House officials—and convenient appointments for the wayward sons of Northern political allies. Whatever the proportion of antiracist principles, crude demagoguery, and naked greed, Warmoth's Louisiana was an ideal climate for Neil Stanton, who in his two years in the state, amassed "quite a little fortune" and gave the impression that he had achieved some stature in its government.[31]

As for what Elizabeth Cady Stanton thought of her oldest son's actions, the record offers few clues. Certainly no word of blame or self-reproach has survived in her accounts. Neil himself, the only Stanton child not to attend college and rich enough to be "a gentleman of leisure," remains a mystery, occasionally passing through his mother's stories, smoking with Henry on the "piazza" or listening to his mother read aloud. But that he moved to Iowa, married, had a daughter, divorced, and died in 1891 is absent from her account of her life.[32] Whatever she said about her son's troubles, as well as the letters he wrote her during and after the war, did not survive the later culling of her correspondence. For now, there was a war going on and work to be done, and she plunged in.

In many respects, and in spite of the suspension of woman's rights conventions, the Civil War offered a preview of the tensions, loyalties, and priorities that would shape the postwar movement for woman's rights. Both Stanton and Anthony remained skeptical of Lincoln's antislavery intentions long after the Emancipation Proclamation had taken effect, opposing Lincoln's reelection in 1864 and placing their hopes behind abolitionist John Frémont's candidacy. They were not alone in this. Wendell Phillips, for one, promised Stanton that "I would cut off my right hand before doing any thing to aid A.L.'s election."[33] Those who chose to campaign for Lincoln, such as Henry Blackwell, signaled a level of fealty to the Republican Party that would shape their politics for decades to come. But even the most principled abolitionists could not entirely repress the hope that emancipation might justify the war's devastation.

Certainly their star had risen in the popular press, the Republican Party, and the public eye. It was a giddy experience for once-demonized radicals to be treated as powerful insiders, and to be applauded as the originators of a now widely celebrated idea. With the war's end, Republicans, aware that the Northern victory gave them a mandate to define the rights of the former slaves, declared that they had been abolitionists all along. William Lloyd Garrison himself was invited to the victory celebration at Fort Sumter on April 14, 1865.[34] The assassination of Abraham Lincoln that same day added to the North's grief, but it did not diminish the hope of Radical Republicans, abolitionists, and African Americans that they would be respected participants in the postwar debate over how to remake the nation.

For the generation of African Americans who sought and sometimes gained work, farms, families, literacy, voting rights, and political office, it was an almost painfully hopeful time. The legacy of slavery, the knowledge that Northerners would abandon the freedpeople, and the terrors of white supremacy have obscured the sense of possibility they now experienced. At the time, no African Americans or white abolitionists could have missed it. The "feel of freedom" was palpable, a sharp and partly bitter taste in the air.[35] Certainly Elizabeth Cady Stanton was infected with it, and she bounded toward a postwar world acutely aware that the limits of freedom might grow in ways that few had yet imagined.

With the passage in 1865 of the Thirteenth Amendment ending chattel slavery, William Lloyd Garrison declared, "My vocation, as an Abolitionist, thank God, is ended," and urged that the American Anti-Slavery Society disband. Frederick Douglass disagreed, believing that "Slavery is not abolished until the black man has the ballot." Faced with ongoing violence on the part of white Southerners, political organizing by African Americans throughout the South, and Northern reluctance to do much to protect or advance freedpeople's rights, he joined Republican radicals in declaring voting rights a major goal of Reconstruction. "Without the elective franchise," Douglass had come to believe, "the Negro will still be practically a slave."[36] The security of freedpeople's civil status seemed increasingly to require that black people have and exercise a vote.

Thus, although Northerners disagreed about what former slaves' rights would entail, within two years of the end of the war "politics emerged as the principal focus of black aspirations." Elizabeth Cady Stanton recognized immediately that "by the results of the war, the whole question of suffrage reverts back to Congress and the U.S. Constitution," and supporters of black emancipation and of woman's rights looked to Congress, and especially to the Republican Party, for a meaningful display of gratitude for their loyal service. To Stanton, it was logical, even inevitable, that the same men—friends and allies—who were debating and expanding the rights of former slaves would give their support to the cause of women as well. "Now let us try universal suffrage," she wrote within months of the peace. "We cannot tell its dangers or delights until we make the experiment."[37]

Things did not turn out that way. But Stanton's sense of possibility was not entirely misplaced. Consider just how far the demand for woman suffrage had come. Eighteen years after a small gathering at Seneca Falls declared suffrage a right for women, support for women's political rights was nearly universal among abolitionists, a common topic of conversation in the press, and a matter for serious discussion at state constitutional conventions and Republican Party meetings. When Stephen Foster made an "appeal to the conscience" at the 1866 American Anti-Slavery Society convention, everyone there understood that this included "the ballot for all classes and sexes." Charles Remond, an African American abolitionist, was even more explicit in 1867: "All I ask for myself I claim for my wife and sister," he declared.[38] Many suffrage supporters began to consider victory inevitable, if not imminent: "the day is coming," intoned Henry Ward Beecher in 1865, "when . . . universal suffrage will be the rule and law of the land." For this sentiment there was, the ever-cautious *Times* reported, "moderate applause." The noise came from men, for nineteenth-century women waved handkerchiefs instead, a practice so widespread that one group of women would hold a debate on "women's equal right to applaud." This may have gone to show, as Henry Blackwell remarked years later, "that women will be women everywhere, and will express themselves differently from men, even when it comes to the matter of cheering," but only the most obstinate could fail to notice that assumptions about women's place in political life were changing.[39]

Even the opposition was different now. Nearly all the arguments that would be raised against woman suffrage—that it threatened religion, nature, marital harmony, and female loveliness; that women were already represented; that wives and mothers didn't want or need to vote; and that politics would demean virtuous women—had been made, and, Stanton thought, vanquished. Now she and her allies combated prejudice and partisanship, both of which seemed impervious to rational debate. Inevitably reformers faced questions of strategy and compromise, now that being "right" was no longer enough to move people to join a just cause.

Radicals' and freedpeople's faith in the promises of Reconstruction would soon be replaced by disappointment and betrayal. Plans for giving land to former slaves quickly fell apart, Freedmen's Bureau funds failed to meet the most minimal needs of Southern African Americans, and the mandate for reform was short-lived at best. From Lottsburg, Virginia, abolitionist and teacher Caroline Putnam wailed on the freedpeople's behalf, "How basely we have been betrayed by the *Republicans!*" and wondered "Does nobody care?" As distressing to Putnam as it would soon be to Stanton, antislavery allies seemed to fall into line behind the party in its very moment of compromise and equivocation. It was flattering to be invited to the party, so to speak, and even, as one historian puts it, to "function . . . as the Republican party's left wing."[40] But as radicals and reformers have learned time and again, accepting the invitation was not without risk, and the balancing act between principle and party would grow ever more complex in the years to come.

Republicans had won the war and administered the peace, but they were divided over what to do about the freedpeople themselves. It did not take long for many abolitionists to realize that Republican politicians were more committed to securing the party's continued dominance in the South than they were to achieving humanitarian or revolutionary goals. Nor were Republicans consistent about endorsing black civil rights in the North. Only a half-dozen states in 1865 granted any form of suffrage to black men; between 1863 and 1870, fifteen Northern legislatures defeated proposals to expand black men's voting rights. For some abolitionists, the slight was personal, as when Republicans at their 1866 party convention in Philadelphia balked at welcoming Frederick Douglass, who had been chosen as a delegate from Rochester. Only Theodore Tilton, in the face of his Republican colleagues' "embarrassed pique," took his friend's arm and joined the procession through the city. But the snub hurt, making Douglass feel like "the ugly and deformed child of the family, and to be kept out of sight as much as possible while there was company in the house."[41] It would not be the last, or most personal, insult.

In the postwar climate of hope, partisanship, and betrayal, it grew increasingly apparent that the Republican leadership considered universal rights a burden the party could not bear. Perhaps at first Elizabeth Cady Stanton thought all the references to "black men's" rights were merely rhetorical, or believed that the promise of rewarding those who had supported the Union cause implicitly included women, who had done "their full share in saving the Republic." But her head snapped up when she heard her old friend Wendell Phillips implore abolitionists to labor to guarantee the rights of citizenship to all, regardless of their race. "I hope some day to be bold enough to add 'sex,'" he continued, astonishing Stanton, who remembered his defense of woman's rights a full quarter century earlier in London. "However, my friends, we must take up but one question at a time, and this hour belongs exclusively to the negro." Recognizing the threat, Elizabeth Cady Stanton retorted, "Do you believe the African race is composed entirely of males?" and readied herself for a fight. She was not alone. Reformer Frances Gage was disgusted that the "great advocates of Human Equality" could so quickly "forget that once when they were a weak party and needed all the womanly strength of the nation to help them on, they always united the words 'without regard to sex, race, or color'" in their appeals. Lucy Stone was outraged as well, and exhorted reformers not to "accept the poor half loaf of justice for the Negro, poisoned by its lack of justice for every woman in the land." And African American women, among them writer and political activist Frances Ellen Watkins Harper, argued fervently and consistently that it was they who stood most firmly for the principle of universal rights, declaring that as "much as white women need the ballot, colored women need it more," as she "pleaded for equal rights and equal education for the colored women of the land."[42]

Abolitionism and woman's rights had been intimately associated for more than two decades. "[A]ll who have worked together thus far," Elizabeth Cady Stanton announced, "may still stand side by side in this crisis of our nation's history," and to that end leading male abolitionists—Frederick Douglass, Theodore Tilton, and Wendell Phillips—joined in the call for the Eleventh National Woman's Rights Convention in 1866, the first since the start of the war. There they formed the American Equal Rights Association on a platform of "Equal Rights to All." "[T]he questions" of black men's and all women's rights," proclaimed Henry Ward Beecher, "are one and the same," and participants agreed to "secure Equal Rights to all American Citizens, especially the right of suffrage, irrespective of race, color, or sex."[43] Few imagined the depth of the breach that would occur.

For all the declarations of principled unity, signs of trouble emerged soon enough from the Republican-dominated Congress, which, after considering dozens of drafts, proposed a Fourteenth Amendment to the Constitution that offered equality under the law to all "male citizens." Susan B. Anthony recognized the trap at once, and she was furious. This would be the first time that the word *male* would appear in the nation's founding document; once there, it would be difficult to erase. Stanton, as Anthony's biographer recalled it, was more tempted, "in the presence of brilliant intellect and elegant culture," by arguments she would come to disdain, and so took somewhat longer to react.[44] When she did, her indignation and her absolutism emerged full force. By the time congressional Republicans, with many abolitionists' support, had offered up a Fifteenth Amendment that protected the right of suffrage regardless of race, but not sex, she shared wholeheartedly in Anthony's deep suspicion of anything their erstwhile abolitionist allies and their Radical Republican friends might cook up.

Disappointment, grief, betrayal, resentment, outrage—all played a role in Stanton's fury at anyone who suggested that women stand aside until black men gained the freedoms that they all sought. She had been, she was now certain, entirely correct to maintain her distance from the ruling party, whom she now saw as utterly untrustworthy. Stanton swiftly adopted the role of nonpartisan gadfly. Although she could not vote, no one had said she could not run, so Elizabeth Cady Stanton declared herself a candidate for Congress, the first woman in the United States to do so. "You have no idea of the talk it makes," she wrote gleefully to Wendell Phillips. "My sons . . . said it was the theme yesterday with the lawyers, all looking at the constitution to see if it were possible that the Fathers left such a loop hole through which Eve's daughters could leap into power." (Apparently the discussion moved into the streets when seven-year-old Bob, teased for his mother's actions, "gave another boy a pounding & told them their mothers did not know enough to run for Congress.") She ran on neither party's platform, but "desired an election . . . as a rebuke to the dominant party for its retrogressive legislation in so amending the National Constitution as to make invidious distinctions on the ground of sex."[45] "Mrs. Stanton was not elected," the *New-*

Orleans Weekly Times reported drily, but "two dozen unknown friends" voted for her; Stanton later wished she had gotten their photographs.[46] Still, so prominent was she that even a newspaper as far away as Louisiana saw no need to introduce "Mrs. Stanton" or even to offer her first name; by 1866 its readers presumably knew who she was.

"Some tell us that this is not the time for woman to make the demand; that this is the negro's hour," Elizabeth Cady Stanton declared to a distinguished audience in Brooklyn in 1867. "No, my friends . . . This is the Nation's hour. This is the hour to settle what are the rights of a citizen of the Republic." Stanton's absolutist stance in favor of universal adult suffrage—her insistence that no one's liberation should take priority over another's and her assertion that under no circumstances should woman's rights be traded away—was compelling. Stanton and Anthony declared themselves the true radicals whose "position was unassailable," and who had best learned the lessons of antislavery: "that all compromises with principle are dangerous." Their goal, they insisted, was simple and pure: to ensure that "Women and Negroes will be no longer known in Law or Constitution," but will be "buried in the Citizen."[47] This was powerful stuff, which Stanton expressed as a moral imperative with which no thinking person could disagree.

But thinking people did disagree, both about how to balance principle with postwar realities and how to deal with Stanton's support of that principle on unabashedly racist grounds. Indeed, Stanton's claim to the high ground—it is we, she insisted, who refuse to lift one group's rights above another's—obscured this larger flaw. For Stanton almost immediately answered insult with insult, contrasting the freedmen's "incoming pauperism, ignorance, and degradation, with the wealth, education, and refinement of the women of the republic" when she asked voters for their support. Her language was ugly, conscious, and unforgivable; it exposed a strain in her thinking that was neither trivial nor simply a case of bad temper.[48]

Indeed, Stanton's attacks on immigrants, the working class, and African Americans gained in intensity. Protected by the Thirteenth Amendment, "the black man is declared free," but "as the celestial gate to civil rights is slowly moving on its hinges, it becomes a serious question whether [the 'representative women of the nation'] had better stand aside and see 'Sambo' walk into the kingdom first." Stanton waxed indignant at the dangers women would face if such a step were taken, for she doubted that a black man, once free, would "prove more just and generous than his Saxon compeers." As for black women, Stanton declared firmly if inexplicably, "their emancipation is but another form of slavery," worse than what they had endured under white slaveholders: "it is better," she asserted boldly, "to be the slave of an educated white man, than of a degraded, ignorant black one." Asked straight out whether she were "willing to have the colored man enfranchised before the woman," she answered "no; I would not trust him with all my rights; degraded, oppressed himself, he would be more despotic with the governing power than even our Saxon rulers are."[49]

These were not merely figures of speech, thoughtless slips of the tongue and the pen. Rather, when she evoked these images, Stanton was drawing upon a powerful sense of her own class and cultural superiority. And she seems to have been deaf to how her rhetoric—as well as her assertion, contrary to evidence, that women faced "the hostility everywhere of black men themselves"—both undermined her most principled claims and deepened the coming schism with old colleagues and friends.[50] Nor does she seem to have noticed, or cared, that an appeal to women on racist grounds would have profound implications for the character, reputation, and constituency of the woman's rights movement itself. The harm was deep and hurtful, and it was to a great degree Stanton's doing.

As it had during the crisis of disunion ten years earlier, Kansas provided a dramatic scene for the struggle over universal suffrage. In 1867 the Kansas legislature placed on the ballot two separate referenda, one for black suffrage and one giving women the vote. Lucy Stone and Henry Blackwell, "brimming with optimism and armed with two hundred fifty pounds of suffrage tracts," went to Kansas first, where they stumped the state for passage of both bills. "We came here just in the nick of time," Lucy Stone wrote Stanton from Leavenworth. "Impartial Suffrage, *without regard to color or sex*, will succeed by overwhelming majorities," she telegraphed back east. "Kansas leads the world!" But this was far from the case.[51] As it became clear that the Republican Party would endorse black men's, but not women's, suffrage, Stanton and Anthony joined the campaign for universal rights in Kansas late that summer, prepared to challenge anyone who thought that woman suffrage was expendable.

This was Stanton's first visit west, and her memoir of those three months is dominated by the misery of the food, the bugs, and the wild pigs, all of which ended her idea "that pioneer life was a period of romantic freedom." But the Republican Party was even more infuriating than the bugs, and Stanton and Anthony let it be known that they would befriend any man who made woman suffrage his top priority, who refused, as they saw it, to trade it away as a pawn of partisan bickering. To that end, they accepted the friendship, shared the platform, and took the money of George Francis Train, an openly racist and determinedly eccentric Democratic merchant who "slandered the freedmen whenever he could and anchored his advocacy of woman suffrage to his racism."[52]

Train was a bizarre companion, who drew crowds of curious spectators and lots of press. Prosperous and peculiar, a "somewhat unique specimen of a courtly, elegant gentleman," he was "full of enthusiasm and confident he would be the next President." Upon learning that he was accompanying the leading advocates of woman suffrage on their tour through the state, even lukewarm Republicans were appalled. "All the old friends, with scarce an exception, are sure we are wrong," Anthony noted despairingly in her diary, and she did not exaggerate. Stanton and Anthony, William Lloyd Garrison fumed, "seem to have taken leave of their senses." Although Stanton would refer to her friends' distaste for Train as merely "fastidious," it is hard to disagree with them.[53] It was not, for all their hurt and self-justification, Stanton and Anthony's finest moment. Still, the two women plunged on unrepentently, giving speeches and enjoying the publicity, ever confident that with Train by their side, their commitment to universal suffrage would prevail.

In November 1867, reformers watched bleakly as both woman and black suffrage went down in defeat in Kansas, gaining nearly the same number of votes. Some blamed the addition of woman suffrage to the platform for the loss, some blamed George Francis Train's presence on it, and others held both responsible. This was not how Stanton and Anthony saw it: It was, they declared, "the action of the Republican party [that] had created a hostile feeling between the women and the colored people." Only absolute adherence to the principle of universal rights could have prevented this loss.[54] There was nothing to do but forge ahead, which they did by writing and lecturing against the Fifteenth Amendment, effectively allying with the opponents of black men's suffrage. These decisions—the alliance with Train, the lobbying against expanding the vote to black men, and Stanton's openly racist defense of woman suffrage—served mostly to widen the breach between Stanton and Anthony and most of their oldest friends.

For all the differences among them, it is worth stressing that most abolitionists and woman's rights activists agreed that the right to vote should be granted to both African Americans and to all women. "The right of woman to vote is as sacred in my judgment as that of man," Frederick Douglass insisted in 1868, "and I am quite willing at any time to hold up both hands in favor of this right." And yet just as Douglass had resisted William Lloyd Garrison's absolutism—"He revolted at halfness," he had remarked—so he objected to Elizabeth Cady Stanton's single-minded fervor.[55] But for all the insult and vituperation that lifelong activists faced—and there was more than enough resentment to go around—only Stanton forged a position that "worthiness" or "virtue" should be considered in granting rights. If other leading abolitionists believed that black men were more brutal than white men (and so less fit to govern), they did not say so in public. Frederick Douglass, though provoked, never denigrated women's qualifications, virtue, or intelligence, as Stanton did African Americans'. Indeed, however much he had to grit his teeth, Douglass went some distance to acknowledge Stanton's commitment to human rights: "There is no name greater than that of Elizabeth Cady Stanton in the matter of woman's rights and equal rights," he declared graciously at the May 1869 convention of the American Equal Rights Association. Nevertheless, though he fondly recalled the "refuge" he had always received at Stanton's home "when there were few houses in which the black man could have put his head," his hurt was palpable at her "employment of certain names, such as 'Sambo,' and the gardener, and the bootblack, and the daughters of Jefferson and Washington, and all the rest that I can not coincide with."[56]

Stanton was a master at turning the affront of being considered lesser into a political philosophy, but she expressed no sympathy for Frederick Douglass's mortification at her words. Nor was she correct in her charge that he had abandoned woman's rights; indeed, immediately after the passage of the Fifteenth Amendment, he joined the call for a Sixteenth to enfranchise women. What he argued, and what she seemed unable to hear, was that the crisis faced by his people was simply more extreme: "I do not see how any one can pretend that there is the same urgency in giving the ballot to woman as to the negro," he asserted. Though Stanton refused to acknowledge either his passion or his words, his reasoning was compelling and his evidence chilling: "When women, because they are women, are hunted down through the cities of New York and New Orleans; when they are dragged from their houses and hung upon lamp-posts; when their children are torn from their arms, and their brains dashed out upon the pavement; when they are objects of insult and outrage at every turn; when they are in danger of having their homes burnt down over their heads; when their children are not allowed to enter schools; then they will have an urgency to obtain the ballot equal to our own." All this was agonizing to reformers such as Lucy Stone, who was certain that "We are lost if we turn away from the middle principle and argue for one class." But even she, as devoted as anyone of her generation to both black and woman suffrage, conceded that she would "be thankful in my soul if *any* body can get out of the terrible pit."[57]

A principled consistency on behalf of universal suffrage sounded wonderful on the stump. But the compromise Elizabeth Cady Stanton and Susan B. Anthony so fiercely rejected, and that Lucy Stone and others finally embraced, was deeply rooted in the painful and violent realities of emancipation. Abolitionists who chose to support the Fifteenth Amendment, many of them ardent supporters of woman's rights who joined Stone and Henry Blackwell in forming the American Woman Suffrage Association, made a difficult, sometimes agonizing, moral choice that involved more than "checking [their] brains at the door."[58] They decided that, at that grim and hopeful moment, the African American community urgently needed the vote to defend itself against the violence of white supremacy in the South and their abandonment by the North.

The news coming from the South was horrendous. Whippings,

murders, and lynchings were growing common, especially as former slaves exercised their freedom by leaving plantations to find homes and work elsewhere or by becoming engaged in political life. A new vigilante organization—widely known as the Ku Klux Klan—initiated an era of vigilante terrorism against African Americans and their supporters. On May 1, 1866, a mob in Memphis opened fire on recently disarmed black soldiers, burned Freedmen's Bureau schools, and killed some forty-six African Americans. That same summer, thirty-four black men and women, as well as three white Republicans, were killed in a "wholesale slaughter" in New Orleans, where they had gathered to demand black suffrage.[59] Such accounts convinced many Northern abolitionists and woman's rights activists that African American political power was indeed, as Douglass and others put it, "a question of life and death."[60]

Clara Barton is an unusual source for considering the choice Stanton and her contemporaries confronted; she won fame as a wartime nurse and founder of the International Red Cross, not as an advocate of antislavery or "perfectly equal rights" for women. Yet "no person," Barton insisted, ". . . would or could be more rejoiced than I to see the franchise bestowed upon every person capable of using it without regard to race, color, or sex." "I have been at heart and long before the idea took shape in words a firm and *indignant* supporter of womens [sic] right to all privilege that any rational beings could enjoy." Elizabeth Cady Stanton could have spoken these very words. But Barton had become convinced that granting suffrage to any portion of the African American community was the most urgent demand of the age. "The thousands of hungry Negroes men & women & children at our doors and the thousands upon thousands waiting in fear, trembling and uncertainty all through the South, surrounded by an enemy as implacable as death, and cold as the grave," gnawed at her: "I could not myself, well fed, warmed & clothed with the privilege at least of appealing to the law, if I were in danger . . . give my voice against the franchise of these people."[61] For Stanton, this stance represented cowardice and betrayal; for Barton, it was a moral choice based on the material and political realities of the day.

Stanton's apparent lack of interest in these reports from the South seems callous, but it was not entirely out of character. As she saw it, legal emancipation meant that the "negro question" had "disappeared from view." As one historian notes, Stanton "lived in a mental universe of abstract principles," which she was disinclined to accommodate to what she considered a distant reality. True, she had challenged Wendell Phillips's implication that all freedpeople were male, but, rhetoric aside, the desperation or priorities of African American women failed to divert her from her own analysis. Reading the daily newspapers alongside Stanton's speeches reveals a stubborn, almost willful, indifference to debates within black communities over political representation, marriage, custody, the right to one's wages, and male dominance within families. In the face of these discussions, a small number of woman's rights activists "began to explore what it might mean to put black, not white, women at the center of the movement's concerns." Elizabeth Cady Stanton was not one of them. Instead, she kept her eye firmly on those rights that had been denied her, which she framed in terms of the "broader question" of universal rights.[62] But her adherence to principle was all too frequently followed, and diminished, by an assertion of privilege and self-regard.

To Elizabeth Cady Stanton, the battle over the Fifteenth Amendment was a battle between the sexes, in which all men, black and white, Republican and abolitionist, had joined forces to keep women in their place. Whereas before Reconstruction the vote had been limited on the basis of sex *and* race, universal manhood suffrage imposed upon women an "aristocracy of sex." Those women who endorsed black men's suffrage were therefore either traitors to their sex or simply too weak to argue. How Stanton despaired of "our noblest women, blinded by their past degradation, ignorant of the power and responsibility of the ballot, . . . [who] cry negro first, woman afterward." They had been, she claimed, "educated to self-sacrifice and self-abnegation," and so gave in to demands that they "hold their claims for rights and privileges in abeyance to all orders and classes of men."[63]

On occasion, Stanton hinted that women might govern differently from men, arguing that "the male element, already too much in the ascendant, is a destructive force; stern, selfish, aggrandizing; loving war, violence, conquest, acquisition; breeding discord, disorder, disease, and death." At times when her frustration exploded its bounds, and she reflected on "all the wrongs that have been heaped upon womankind," she felt "ashamed that I am not forever in a condition of chronic wrath, stark mad, skin & bone, my eyes a fountain of tears, my lips overflowing with curses," and the anger grew personal indeed: "Oh! how I do repent me of the male faces I have washed, the mittens I have knit, the pants mended, the cut fingers & broken toes I have bound up, & then to multiply my labors for these white male popin-jays by ten thousand more." In her more common, and calmer, frame of mind, however, she resisted the pull of women's supposed differences from men in the matter of their rights. "The talk about women being so much above men, celestial, ethereal, and all that, is sentimental nonsense," she declared. "She is on the same material plane with man, striving and working to support herself." Women were, she insisted, "National Citizens," and as such they deserved—indeed, required—"National Protection."[64]

But not far under the surface of Stanton's notion of a sex war, and more consistent in her thinking, was her belief that there were better, and worse, "orders of manhood." Men were not, after all, the same. "Just so if woman finds it hard to bear the oppressive laws of a few Saxon Fathers . . . ," she remarked, "what may she not be called to endure when all the lower orders, natives and foreigners, Dutch, Irish, Chinese and African, legislate for her and her daughters?" If by virtue of their sex such men were lifted, politically speaking, to an equal level, "woman touches the lowest depths of her political degradation," for "American women of wealth, education, virtue and refinement" would then be ruled by "the lower orders of Chinese, Africans, Germans and Irish, with their low ideas of womanhood."[65]

"The true statesmen for this hour," Elizabeth Cady Stanton wrote the editor of the *National Anti-Slavery Standard* just after the war, "are they who teach most clearly the lesson of individual rights." On the face of this, most of her coworkers would agree. And yet Stanton's own radical individualism prevented her from viewing suffrage in any light other than as an individual possession, its use a matter of individual conscience and self-protection. In the face of the collective violence, poverty, turmoil, and distress that haunted the South, Stanton's view obscured the evidence that within African American communities, the vote itself was both more and less than a personal possession. There it served as a source of community authority and a guarantee against reenslavement, and as such it took on "a sacred and collective character."[66] This collective was decidedly not all male, for black political culture in the post-emancipation South involved women in mass meetings and church assemblies, as well as in more formal state constitutional conventions. Women, one historian has suggested, also played an essential role as "enforcers," mobilizing men to vote and employing sanctions against those who strayed from the Republican fold. Even as some women organized crowds to punish such partisan "traitors," others, including large numbers of female domestic servants, attended political gatherings; many expected to be heard in debate and even to vote, usually to weigh in against the more "conservative faction." Lively debates over women's participation at the Colored National Labor Union convention and the National Convention of Colored Men reflected and deepened the support for woman's rights within the African American community, as did Southern legislatures' and church assemblies' endorsement of woman suffrage. Some delegates to constitutional conventions declared woman suffrage "an inherent right," and spoke out against including the word *male* in the new state constitutions they were designing.[67] African American women, like white women, were formally disenfranchised, but they were vocal in their expectation that black men would use "their" vote for the good of the community at large.

Elizabeth Cady Stanton had long ago embarked on an intellectual path that led from the Founding Fathers' notions of republican government to her deep indignation at women's exclusion from that government and from there to the demand for woman's rights as individual citizens. "The right of suffrage," she would always insist, "is simply the right to govern one's self." But the purpose of the vote, its uses in a representative political system, and its role in redistributing resources and rights were both more and less than an abstract matter of individual self-ownership. Stanton did not consider that the very meaning of the vote might be modified by community traditions she tended to scorn, or that abstractions about individual rights might not be the only way to understand the power of representative government. During the crisis of Reconstruction, Stanton's commitment to that particular republican vision, while it offered a thrillingly single-minded analysis of male dominance, limited her view of the widest possibilities for social transformation. With the rupture among woman's rights leaders, Stanton was now free to pursue whatever principles she wished, unburdened by the tethers of compromise and coalition, and unrestrained by whatever competing principles might arise. She and Anthony were also, increasingly, very much alone.[68]

Mere mention of the Reconstruction-era schism and of the choices Elizabeth Cady Stanton made could raise the ire of activists, and their children, for decades to come; it still rankles historians. Modern feminists have often applauded Stanton and Anthony for standing firm against the selling-out of woman's rights, against the insult of being told by men and parties to postpone their demands for another day. Many have agreed with Stanton that her support of woman's rights, even when it became a statement of women *first*, was a principled defense against those who had abandoned women in the name of wartime necessity. Some have explained Stanton's racist remarks as expressions of temporary fury or have noted that while memory of her words "arouses discomfort today, [such comments] were commonplace not only for someone of her background and education but also among a broad spectrum of society," and have chosen not to ask whether such rhetoric undermined her standing as the staunch upholder of universal rights. For those who read the story this way, people such as Lucy Stone were simply more conservative, or less committed to woman's rights, and weak in finding it "unbearable to go against the men beside whom they had labored so long."[69] But if Elizabeth Cady Stanton was not more racist than most white Northerners of her day, it is worth recalling that she did not consider herself a member of that mainstream; she thought of herself, instead, as a reformer of the radical school, a member of the antislavery community, and a student of Mott, Grimké, Douglass, and Garrison. The views she expressed in the name of principle were, within that community, intolerable.

More than personal enmity or rhetorical strategy was at stake here. Elizabeth Cady Stanton's positions on the relative worthiness of black men and white women as citizens did not remain within the confines of an activist community where, conceivably, they might do personal, more than philosophical, harm. Instead, her choice of all-too-familiar racist language had broad and lasting consequences, both theoretical and strategic, for the movement she helped lead. By claiming that some American citizens were more worthy of rights than others, Stanton helped lay the groundwork for a defense of woman's rights based on race, respectability, religion, and class that would be hard to shake. Surely Stanton and Anthony understood this when they reported on the formation of a "White Woman's Suffrage Association" in Washington, D.C., or admitted that the proposed Fifteenth Amendment "rouses woman's prejudices against the negro" while increasing "his contempt and hostility towards her as an equal."[70] Furthermore, this appeal to prejudice, whether it was an intentional strategy or not, worked. One woman wrote Stanton and Anthony's newspaper, *The Revolution*, to declare that she had "never thought, or cared, about voting till the negroes began to vote," but now "felt my self-respect rise." She went on: "If educated women are not as fit to decide who shall be the rulers of this country, as 'field hands,' then where's the use of culture, or any brain at all? One might as well have been 'born on the plantation.' "[71]

Elizabeth Cady Stanton had been arguing for years that it was women's lack of self-respect that caused them to defer their demands, even though (she now claimed) "the influence and vote of an educated woman are of more value to a government than those of an ignorant man."[72] Now, in the heated atmosphere of Reconstruction politics, that logic's disagreeable corollary came into prominence, and it would stick to the suffrage movement like tar: white women's self-respect, as this letter writer suggested, could be heightened by comparison with people of "lesser" races. Pleased by evidence that women were developing their self-esteem and so would demand their rights, Stanton seems not to have worried that advocating woman's rights on this basis, and severing the movement's ties to its abolitionist and antiracist roots, might damage the cause's claims to universal justice. Nor did she express any concern that her use of racist language to denigrate black men, along with her implicit embrace of a politics of white racial pride, might diminish the movement's appeal to African American women themselves. Whether or not she meant to endorse an explicitly racist tactic to draw new groups of white women into the cause is impossible to know; that she published the letter, entitling it "A Washington Convert," suggests that she was willing to take the risk.

Judge Daniel Cady (Elizabeth Cady Stanton, *Eighty Years and More* [New York: T. Fisher Unwin, 1898])

Margaret Livingston Cady (Elizabeth Cady Stanton, *Eighty Years and More*)

Elizabeth Cady at age twenty
(Seneca Falls Historical Society)

Henry Brewster Stanton (Elizabeth Cady Stanton, *Eighty Years and More*)

Elizabeth Cady Stanton with Henry, Jr. (Kit), in 1854 (Elizabeth Cady Stanton, *Eighty Years and More*)

Elizabeth Cady Stanton with Harriot in 1856 (Library of Congress)

Woodcut of Elizabeth Cady Stanton
in bloomers (Elizabeth Cady Stanton,
Eighty Years and More)

The "Bloomer costume" (from N. Currier,
Currier & Ives, 1851; Library of Congress)

Lucretia Coffin Mott (Elizabeth Cady Stanton, Susan B. Anthony, Matilda Joslyn Gage, *History of Woman Suffrage*, vol. 1, 1848–1861 [New York: Fowler and Wells, 1881])

Susan B. Anthony in 1868 (Ida Husted Harper, *The Life and Work of Susan B. Anthony*, vol. 1 [Indianapolis: The Bowen-Merrill Company, 1899])

Lucy Stone, with daughter Alice Stone Blackwell, in 1858 (Blackwell family papers; Library of Congress)

Frederick Douglass (ca. 1865–1880) (Brady-Handy Photograph Collection; Library of Congress)

Martha Coffin Wright (Elizabeth Cady Stanton, Susan B. Anthony, Matilda Joslyn Cage, *History of Woman Suffrage*, vol. 1, 1848–1861)

Isabella Beecher Hooker (The Harriet Beecher Stowe Center, Hartford, CT)

Victoria Woodhull (The Woman Suffrage Collection of Khyber Oser)

Matilda Joslyn Gage (Elizabeth Cady Stanton, Susan B. Anthony, Matilda Joslyn Gage, *History of Woman Suffrage*, vol. 1, 1848–1861)

Three generations of Stanton women: Elizabeth Cady Stanton, Harriot Stanton Blach, and Nora Blatch (Bryn Mawr College Collection)

Elizabeth Cady Stanton's eightieth birthday, with Margaret Stanton Lawrence and Robert Stanton (Elizabeth Cady Stanton, *Eighty Years and More*)

Susan B. Anthony and Elizabeth Cady
Stanton in the 1890s (Library of Congress)

Advertisement for Fairbanks Fairy
Soap, *Ladies' Home Journal* (Sept.
1899)

Elizabeth Cady Stanton at home (Photograph Collection, Miriam and Ira D. Wallach Division of Art, Prints, and Photographs, The New York Public Library, Astor, Lenox, and Tilden Foundations)

5

REVOLUTION AND THE ROAD

(1868–1880)

As every student of American history knows, Reconstruction
ended in 1877, when the last federal troops left the South,
Rutherford Hayes assumed the presidency, and the Republican Party left African Americans in the hands of Southern redeemers.
But to Elizabeth Cady Stanton, the time to move on had come years
before, when African Americans had been emancipated from slavery
itself. "[T]he curtain has fallen on the last act," she wrote in 1868,
". . . the lights are extinguished, and the audience gone to their
homes."[1] Stanton's hopes for Reconstruction, with its optimism and
its betrayal, effectively ended in March of 1870, when the Fifteenth
Amendment, guaranteeing all men the right to vote, became part of
the United States Constitution.

There were surely lessons to be learned from all this, though the
effort to find them in Stanton's own self-reflection is frustrated by her
determination to appear resolute. But perhaps this is the place to
pause, as Stanton must have, to assess the nature of her leadership, to
imagine how she must have grappled to define her future. It is not
easy to calculate her stature, especially since her most visible role, as
president of the National Woman Suffrage Association, was, to her,
more a burden than a measure of accomplishment. She already knew,
even as she helped Susan B. Anthony launch and lead the association,
that she much preferred being an absolutist to a strategist, that her
strength and her passion lay in gathering people around her and offering them radical ideas in her most thrilling prose. Although free of the

cares that had earlier tied her to home, Stanton was as unwilling as ever to be constrained by the demands of an organization. The challenge now lay in expanding her cachet as the public philosopher of woman's rights to new audiences in a context permeated by disappointment, abandonment, racism, and betrayal. Whatever moments of self-doubt there were—and how could there not have been some, given the outcry against her by people she had once so admired— were carefully hidden by a posture of embattled righteousness.

Certainly Stanton's spine was stiffened by the controversies, and she plunged into the future with characteristic steadfastness, even obduracy. Her positions, she declared from every possible post, had always been the correct ones; nor did she spend much time regretting lost friendships and alliances. To be sure, there were moments when she seemed unable to anchor herself firmly in a postwar role, but she always, at least in public, hoisted herself back up and plunged into whatever battle was at hand. The state of the world discouraged her, but she remained emboldened by her own boldness, charmed by her own exuberance, and determined to take on new projects—a newspaper, a national organization, and a career on the lyceum circuit—with a display of great cheer. Elizabeth Cady Stanton was nothing if not determined, and she took it upon herself as a self-declared leader of women to remake her life. With her desire for independence intensified, her arrogance intact, and her certainty on display, she seemed to stride past the failures of Reconstruction certain of her particular analysis of woman's rights, of other women's timidity, and of her own brave steadfastness.

And yet, while she relished her intellectual freedom from prewar coalitions, the 1870s were a difficult time. Even her determined optimism showed signs of slipping when she admitted in 1870, "My life since we left Kansas is to me like a long sad dream." Two years later she was so "demoralized . . . that I have been entirely indifferent to the 'political situation.' " Years later she and Anthony, referring to themselves in the third person, would admit that "at times a sense of utter loneliness and desertion made the bravest of them doubt the possibility of maintaining the struggle or making themselves fairly understood."[2] It would take the better part of the decade for Stanton to carve out a place in American public life that best suited her talents and met her needs, and there would be significant strains and missteps along the way.

If there was a blessing for Stanton in the tumult of the postwar years, it was in fulfilling "my dream for years" of founding and editing a newspaper, *The Revolution*, which received funding from George Francis Train.[3] While Susan B. Anthony set up shop in the Women's Bureau, near Gramercy Park, and dealt with business matters, and Minister Parker Pillsbury did much of the editorial labor, Stanton finally had a springboard from which to launch her missives, a place to express her most radical thoughts without constraint. From the first issue in January 1868, the paper covered a distinctive, even eccentric, range of subjects, including Stanton's reports from Kansas, a speech of Lucy Stone's, and Train's platform for "educated suffrage" and "an American system of finance," and included an advertisement for "Henry B. Stanton and Henry Stanton, Counsellors at Law, No. 170 Broadway." Female reporters considered the paper's offices "editorial bliss," and described in lavish detail the pleasant and decidedly un-scary women who ran it.[4]

The paper's masthead ("Men Their Rights and Nothing More—Women Their Rights and Nothing Less") was deceptively modest, for soon Stanton was writing on any topic that bubbled from her brain, including economic and labor policies, Tammany Hall corruption, dis-putes about the Fifteenth Amendment, far-off suffrage agitation, the condition of prisons, and her own visits among friends and reform-ers—all within a frame designed to expound Stanton's philosophy of women's legal, political, sexual, marital, and religious status and rights. Subscribers from as far away as California found *The Revolu-tion* a lively and challenging forum for debate, and the newspaper cir-culated among the immigrant and ethnic press as well. One writer warned against allowing "the Jews and the Chinese" into the country, noting "that great harm accrues to us from the vast accession of vora-cious, knavish, cunning traders, especially Jews," and cautioning read-ers that "As a race, . . . they are a useless portion of society." The article made its way to the *Jewish Messenger*, whose editor pleaded with *The Revolution* to "let the Jews alone." Perhaps the article was "a little absurd," the latter paper's editors admitted, but they took the opportunity to chastise the Jewish press for being "a thousand times more severe on the Jewish women" than *The Revolution* was on them.[5]

Now that Stanton had her own battleground, she could decide the rules of engagement. When other reformers harangued *The Revolution* for refusing to endorse black male suffrage or for supporting liberalized divorce laws, Stanton published their attacks—followed, of course, by her rebuttal. The paper welcomed hostile words, knowing that criticism offered more publicity than being ignored. Pillsbury and Stanton delightedly reprinted reviews that looked forward to "keen criticisms, . . . knife-blade repartees, [and] lacerating sarcasms" from her pen or that called the paper "spicy, readable, and revolutionary."[6]

The Revolution never lacked for "spicy" topics. The postwar decade saw more than its share of scandal and corruption, and stories of murder, adultery, and betrayal were all passed through a woman's-rights lens. The case of Hester Vaughn, a teenage girl found destitute alongside her dead newborn baby, whom authorities claimed she had killed, filled page after page. To *The Revolution*, the case served as a warning to all women of their helplessness in a society that denied them their right to vote.[7] Less famous cases taught similar lessons. In Johnstown, Stanton reported, a "horrible murder" had taken place when "A husband, heated with whiskey and passion, in the presence of five little children, kicked and pounded his wife to death!" Since "the parties were servants in our household years ago," Stanton expressed great sympathy toward everyone involved, and concluded, "Better far that men and women should be divorced, when antagonistic, than to be held together by church and state, until by violence they sunder the ties they cannot bear."[8]

An 1869 murder brought these issues into even greater prominence when actress Abby Sage's lover, well-known *Tribune* reporter Albert Richardson, was shot by Sage's ex-husband Daniel McFarland. Newspapers quickly chose sides. While the *Tribune* expressed outrage at the murder, its competitors saw "better circulation gains in trumpeting the cause of McFarland." But to Stanton the principle at stake was clear: she "rejoice[d] over every slave that escapes from a discordant marriage." To *The Revolution*, the case, and McFarland's acquittal, offered further proof that women needed "an entire revision of the laws of New York on marriage and divorce," as well as inclusion on juries and the independence not to marry at all. "With the education and elevation of women," Stanton declared, "we shall have a mighty sundering of the unholy ties that hold men and women together who loathe and despise each other."[9]

Maybe woman suffrage would not end murder, adultery, and mayhem, but Stanton and Anthony were confident that it held the solution to poverty and greed. In contrast to Lucy Stone and Henry Blackwell's *Woman's Journal*, richly funded by Boston businessmen, who paid its editor, Mary Livermore, a handsome salary, *The Revolution* advocated a pro-labor position, linking organizing and suffrage as a path to all workers' self-respect and independence.[10] Such a stance, not coincidentally, offered the possibility of gaining new allies for the woman's rights cause; as an added benefit, potential pro-labor allies tended to be Democrats, further inflaming their Republican friends. Still, their rhetoric was lofty, and set the stage for working-class women to demand the vote as a matter of right, of respect, and of need. "Give woman the ballot, you dignify her and exalt her, make her labor valuable, and increase the price of your own," they exhorted workingmen's organizations. The editors joined with female printers—among the highest paid and best skilled of laboring women—to launch a Working Women's Association in 1868, using *The Revolution* to declare that "with the right of suffrage to all comes an end to the dynasty of capital over labor." True, Stanton's understanding of that "dynasty," as well as her relationships with working-class women themselves, remained largely theoretical. Perhaps Stanton's privileged background hampered her efforts to build a cross-class coalition for woman's rights or to recognize that, although the women expressed a shared outrage at union men's prejudices against female workers, their priorities differed. Stanton and Anthony considered suffrage the pivot around which to demand female equality in the trades; they were taken aback by printer Augusta Lewis's hesitation to "mix up political questions" into the association, and by her assertion that working women only "wished to get paid fairly for their work." Yet despite Stanton's limitations, for a brief and dramatic time in the late 1860s, she joined Anthony in appealing to male labor leaders and female wage earners to stand with them in the struggle for woman's rights.[11]

Helping to found and lead the National Woman Suffrage Association added little to Stanton's pleasure or her sense of purpose, though she assumed the title of president as her due. Susan B. Anthony discovered that she enjoyed the maneuvering and negotiating with "*seceders* & *neutrals*" (unpleasant epithets in the postwar North) that founding the association entailed; she looked forward to spending each winter in Washington, D.C., where the women lobbied for a Sixteenth Amendment to the Constitution.[12] But Stanton considered associations dull and dispiriting, and found that the political skills required to build them tended to repress her most soaring ideas. She wanted to be at home, to think and write without the bickering and constraints that characterized organizational life; above all, she hated being "in a position where any set of people have the right to say, 'For the sake of the cause don't do this or that.' "[13]

She did try, at least once, to soften her appeals to satisfy others' sense of the cause's best interests. Isabella Beecher Hooker, a younger sister of Henry Ward Beecher and Harriet Beecher Stowe, was new to the cause of woman's rights and was full of plans to make it respectable. "She is precisely like every new convert," Susan B. Anthony sniffed, certain that "each of the Apostles in turn, as he came into the ranks, tho't he [could] improve upon Christ's methods." Hooker boldly sent her new friends "a letter of instructions re dress, manners, and general display of all the Christian graces," as Stanton sneeringly put it. Stanton responded by giving what she called "the most inoffensive speech I could produce . . . I believe I succeeded in charming everyone but myself and Susan who said it was the weakest speech I ever made. I told her that was what it was intended to be." Now more than ever she hoped "that my Convention days were over."[14]

Elizabeth Cady Stanton was simply never going to be an organization woman. With the National Woman Suffrage Association barely launched, she begged off attending the convention. "I stand ready to pay anybody you can get to go to Washington in my stead," she promised Susan B. Anthony in late 1869. "I had rather give you five hundred dollars than go to Washington." Thus began Stanton's parry in a battle that would go on, unresolved and unabated, for another four decades. Anthony would make demands on her—please, she would

beg, attend this convention, write that paper, stick to suffrage, *focus*—
and Stanton would demur, declaring that she had to be at home, or on
the road, or simply (surely Susan knew this already) that she hated
conventions. In the face of Anthony's emotional arm-twisting, Stanton
agreed to "stand by you to the end," but their views of what this
entailed never quite meshed. "If you will promise solemnly to let me
free in May, I will wear the yoke a few months longer, bravely and
patiently . . . But if your life depends on me, I will be your stay and
staff to the end."[15] Anthony remained grimly determined not to be
swayed by her friend's excuses or her promises of eternal love. She
would arrive at Stanton's home on her way to Washington, and more
or less bodily take Stanton along with her. Sometimes Stanton tried to
circumvent Anthony's pull: "If you would now take this whole movement under your wing I would gladly contribute generously to
the publication of tracts," she promised the eager Isabella Beecher
Hooker. Hooker replied that *she* would be happy to accept the bribe,
but "Susan looked disgusted" and insisted that Stanton come to the
capital at least to address the congressional committee. "Susan's
affection," Stanton grumbled, "leads her quite often to overestimate
my importance."[16]

Stanton was not alone in her hostility to "our dragging, vapid conventions and meetings."[17] Martha Coffin Wright had "long tho't that
an occasional one, when the exigencies of the cause seemed to
demand it, would have more spirit & life, and perhaps do more good
than the frequent ones we have had." "They were needed," she admitted, "until every possible argument was advanced, & the only thing
that can be said now, in favor of them, is that there are still so many
people to whom the whole subject is new."[18] But Susan B. Anthony
considered annual meetings and speeches to congressional committees a solemn obligation and an effective strategy, and Stanton's resistance was exasperating indeed.

As woman suffrage lurched toward respectability, and grassroots
organizations flourished, Stanton grew bored; she was also, as ever,
unwilling to be handled. "We have made the thing popular, and now
let Mrs. Hooker run the machine if she chooses," she declared firmly,
"but she will not run me." But she was neither lazy nor tired, nor had
she decided to retreat from the fray. Rather, Stanton had come to real-

ize that "So long as people will pay me $75 or 100 every night, to speak on my own hook, there is no need of my talking in Conventions." "I have done working for nothing," she announced firmly. "I think I have done my share of that business, in the last twenty years."[19]

Indeed, finances became a central focus of the 1870s. Money plagued *The Revolution* from the first; not long after supplying the initial funds, Train had absconded to Europe, where he ended up in an Irish jail. The editors did not miss his written contributions, but they did miss his money, and the newspaper's shaky finances put into relief the women's own. Within two years it was apparent that the paper could not support itself. In 1870 they admitted defeat and sold *The Revolution* to Theodore Tilton and Laura Bullard, leaving Anthony personally responsible for a crushing $10,000 debt.[20] Stanton suffered from the loss of control; remember, she told Anthony pointedly, "you did not sell my pen in your transfer of the *Revolution*. I am not to be bought to write at anybody's dictation." Stanton urged Anthony to look after her own comforts, too: "Do not make any more plans for me, but take care of yourself," she begged, apparently oblivious to how she had added to her friend's financial cares. "Pray let conventions and Associations go, and do some work for a living, that you may not forever appear in the attitude of a pauper."[21]

Stanton's and Anthony's attitudes toward wealth and comfort remained decidedly different. Anthony's household, which included her mother (until her death in 1880) and her sister, Mary, was entirely her financial responsibility. Once Anthony purchased their home on Madison Street in Rochester, Mary kept house while Susan earned their living as a reformer. Like Stanton, Anthony returned from the rigors of the road to a hot fire, clean clothes, companionship, and a meal. But having been raised in Quaker austerity, dedicated to a particular ideal of the reformer's lot, and anxious to preserve her independence, she scorned material opulence. Neither woman lacked the basics of a middle-class lifestyle, but Anthony's wants were basic indeed. Stanton, in contrast, accustomed to wealth, openly relished, and felt entitled to, luxuries she could not quite afford.

Stanton's finances were never as fragile as Anthony's, but they remained tenuous. Expenses were mounting with two sons finishing law school, Theodore and, soon, Robert at Cornell University, and the two girls about to attend Vassar. College was cheap by today's standards—in 1865 Vassar cost $350 per year, and in 1872 Cornell was somewhat less—but this was serious money under the circumstances.[22] Henry contributed to the household's maintenance, but it could not have been much, especially following the loss of the Custom House job. Harriot would later recall that her wish to leave Vassar for the coeducational Cornell was "checkmated by my aunt, Harriet Cady Eaton, who was putting me through college." Indeed, as in the early days of Henry and Elizabeth's marriage, much of the family's material comfort came from Daniel Cady's wealth, its reach pervasive long after his death. But even their inheritance of money and land from the judge could not support the family in their customary fashion.[23] Once she realized she could earn it, money became inextricably tied up with Elizabeth Cady Stanton's activism, with her children's education, and with her wish to remake, perhaps to reestablish, her domestic life.

For a while Elizabeth tried to include Henry in her vision for starting anew, but their relationship had steadily soured. From 1866 to 1873, when she was often away from home, only one letter between them has been found (and that one edited posthumously by their children). Writing from Kansas, Elizabeth declared, "This is the country for us to move to." A house could be built for $3,000, and ponies were so cheap "that all our children could ride and breathe, and learn to do big things." Referring obliquely to Henry's need to "feel like a new being," she promised, with a hint of the old admiration for his talents, "You could be a leader here as there is not a man in the state that can make a really good speech."[24]

Kansas had special meaning to abolitionists, many of whom, including Susan B. Anthony, had either considered moving there or had family members who had laid down roots and risen to prominence.[25] But it was not for the Stantons. Instead, Elizabeth Cady Stanton purchased "a new house in the country" and moved the household to Tenafly, New Jersey, which would be her home until 1887. Ever ready to put a positive, and political, spin on her decisions, Stanton good-naturedly described the move as strategic. "Having secured to the women of the Empire State nearly all their personal and property rights," she wrote in *The Revolution*, "we shall now make New Jersey the field of our future missionary labors."[26]

For a time, Stanton kept open the possibility of starting fresh; it was Henry, she suggested, who was uninterested in this. In 1871 she contemplated moving to Ann Arbor, Michigan, but was unable to uproot "a certain venerable gentleman, chained to two thousand musty old statute books and the dingy courts of the metropolis," who, unlike her, was "not so easily transplanted." By the following year, when she wrote Ezra Cornell inquiring into the benefits of moving to Ithaca, New York, she left Henry out as a factor to be considered.[27]

Buying the Tenafly house seemed to confirm that Elizabeth and Henry would not reestablish their marriage in any significant way. Henry rented rooms in New York, where he continued to write editorial pieces for the *Sun* and shared a law office with whichever of their sons was then practicing in the city (though Margaret later quipped that they had "more causes than effects"). The men crossed over to New Jersey only on weekends. With Amelia Willard still in charge of domestic matters, the house was very much Elizabeth's: "in the midst of an enclosure of three acres, and from garret to cellar, from kitchen to drawing-room . . . a model of neatness." By the fall of 1874 the only children at home were Neil, back from Louisiana, and Bob, who had recently suffered a crippling accident. (The good news, his mother wrote a friend, was that this most uncomplaining of children "can almost run on crutches.") Hattie and Maggie were "doing finely" at Vassar, and Theodore was studying in Paris. By the summer of 1877, Stanton reported, it was competent Harriot who "held the purse" in the household, "and it is astonishing how triumphantly we have come through thus far."[28] Although the Stantons were not separated in the modern sense, Tenafly signaled the distance they had traveled on separate paths.

But much as Stanton relished the comforts of her new home, retiring to think and write would have to wait, for as long as there was tuition to pay, she saw little respite from travel. These were the years of lyceums in the United States, when "by far the most lucrative and most abundant job prospects existed on the lecture circuit." Indeed, Anthony was amazed to discover that being a reformer now promised a decent living, as "profit and emolument" had replaced "ridicule &

scorn" for those who could draw a crowd. Much as we might prefer to think that reformers, radicals, and other revered figures worked for justice alone, lecturing meant hard cash. So, in 1869, in the midst of editorial and organizational labors, Stanton signed up with the James Redpath Lyceum Bureau. She would spend the next dozen years on and off the road, where financial calculations, as well as political ones, shaped her decisions about where to speak, how often, and on what topics. Martha Coffin Wright "rejoiced that you & Susan have found a way to influence public opinion free from [organizations'] trammels," and Stanton could hardly agree more.[29]

Stanton's itinerary through the 1870s was daunting. Indeed, her own recollection of those years reads more like a travel account (as when she assured her readers "that such enterprising travelers as Miss Anthony and myself visited all the wonders, saw the geysers, big trees, the Yosemite Valley, and the immense mountain ranges") than a serious career move.[30] In 1871, to take but one example, she and Anthony spent three months traversing Ohio, Nebraska, Wyoming, and Colorado before reaching California (where, an amused and somewhat smug Anthony reported, though "perfectly confident that she would have no trouble," Stanton had a terrible time hoisting herself on and off a horse[31]). From there, Anthony, who would travel a "full 13,000 miles" that year, went on to Oregon, while Stanton returned east just in time for her mother's death. Other years saw her on a similarly grueling schedule, traveling from town to town, speaking almost daily to large halls, and charging at first "$75 or $100 except when I lectured on Sunday, or to women alone, for the latter $50, Sunday $10." Talk, Stanton soon realized, was far from cheap, and she quickly raised her fee. Sometimes she earned a great deal; in one summer month in Michigan in 1874, she pulled in approximately $600, and one historian has estimated her annual income at well over $100,000 in today's terms. She was proud of both her earnings and her effect on her audiences, writing to Gerrit Smith that first January that she had "made $2000 above all expenses since the middle of November beside stirring up the women generally to *rebellion*."[32]

Earning a significant income justified the travel, but conditions were rough. From Iowa, Stanton reported a drunken conductor, a late train, and a thirty-mile route "through mud and swollen streams." As always, she found a woman's rights moral in her travails, for "such are the results of [men's] own management. Women have not one word to say about railroads, stages, bridges. When we have, oh, what order and harmony will reign!" And much as she enjoyed the time spent with Susan B. Anthony or local activists or, in Iowa, her son Gat, who had settled there to farm, Stanton was often lonely.[33] Sometimes, amid the discomforts, she found it hard to convince herself, as well as her daughter Maggie, that "above all pecuniary consideration, I feel I am doing an immense amount of good in rousing women to thought and inspiring them with new hope and self respect . . . [and] making the path smoother for you and Hattie and all the other dear girls."[34]

The year 1872 was a particularly distressing one for Stanton, saturated with politics, accusations that she had embraced free love (the current "word of momentous import, with which to hound the lovers of truth and progress"), and tensions that strained Stanton's most intimate friendship. Through it all, she viewed it as her mission to locate hypocrisy—not difficult to find, in that Gilded Age—and turn it into a principle that would further support her positions on woman's rights.[35]

The year opened in the middle of a scandal that seemed to involve nearly everyone Elizabeth Cady Stanton knew. Victoria Woodhull, a flamboyant reformer, spiritualist, and the bearer of a mysterious sexual past, had arrived in New York after the Civil War and, aided by the wealthy Cornelius Vanderbilt, gone into business as a stockbroker. In 1870, with her sister, she made a splash with *Woodhull & Claflin's Weekly*, a magazine discussing politics, finance, woman's rights, and free love, and published the first American edition of Karl Marx's *Communist Manifesto*. Stepping briskly onto the woman suffrage platform, Woodhull addressed both the National Woman Suffrage Association and a congressional committee in 1871: "We are plotting revolution," she declared, to the dismay of many. But Stanton and Anthony were enthralled. "Go ahead! bright, glorious, young, and strong spirit," Anthony wrote her exultantly. True, Woodhull's much-rumored sexual indiscretions raised the hackles of the more conventional women who were entering the cause, some of whom refused to sit next to her on the stage. But Stanton, disdaining the prudery of such self-righteous reformers, considered it a "great impertinence in

any of us to pry into her affairs." "We have had women enough sacri-
ficed to this sentimental, hypocritical, prating about purity," she pro-
nounced to Lucretia Mott, as she urged her to "stand by womanhood"
and, especially, her dazzling new friend.[36]

But even Stanton, for all her bravado, was a bit wary of Woodhull's
weekly. In a rare cautious moment, she hoped that Woodhull "would
be careful that nothing very outrageous goes in it."[37] It was Stanton's
own fault that this hope would be dashed, for she provided her new
associate with the means to cast herself as a central player in a
national scandal. In a quiet moment Stanton had confided to Woodhull that Reverend Henry Ward Beecher, a pillar of mainstream
Protestant respectability, had been having an affair with Elizabeth
Tilton, Theodore Tilton's wife.

Victoria Woodhull, resentful of attacks on her own romantic past,
published the story, thus, she claimed, exposing the hypocrisy of a
community that protected the "king of free love" while it punished
women for their sins. Rumors about Henry Ward Beecher's infideli-
ties were nothing new, but this new evidence—Stanton and Susan B.
Anthony, it appeared, had separately heard the story from Theodore
and Elizabeth Tilton themselves, and had witnessed a dramatic scene
between the couple—was unavoidable. The publicity, Woodhull happily reported, as well as her own arrest for sending "obscene materials" through the U.S. mail, "burst like a bomb-shell into the ranks of
the moralistic social camp." Anthony was mortified by her role in the
story, and was in any case unwilling to let the movement be distracted
by matters of sex; she refused to comment. But Stanton, with whom,
in one memoirist's words, "a secret was not safe an hour," agreed to
discuss her and Anthony's role in leaking the scandal.[38] The outcry
was enormous, not least among the Beecher clan, who were furious
both at Woodhull's charges against their brother and at their younger
sister Isabella's continued association with the radicals who had
exposed him. A dramatic investigation by Beecher's Plymouth Church
and a civil trial, complete with charges and countercharges of slander
and adultery, held the newspaper-reading public entranced.

More than a sordid sexual scandal was at stake here; there were,
as is so often the case, politics involved. Victoria Woodhull had discovered the movement for woman's rights only after she had declared

herself a candidate for president. She had established a third party (it
went by several names, including the Equal Rights Party and the People's Party, but the Victoria League was probably the most accurate)
and launched her campaign. Susan B. Anthony was frantic when
Stanton declared her support for Woodhull's wild gesture, and insisted that "my name must not be used to call any such meeting" for a
third party. Stanton put her friend's name on the announcement of a
"People's Convention" nevertheless, thus putting Anthony in a *"foolish
muddle."*[39]

Not that there were much better choices for the supporters of
woman suffrage that election year. The Republican Party platform
declared that "the honest demand of any class of citizens for additional rights should be treated with respectful consideration," but it
was the tiniest of crumbs—a *"splinter"* rather than a plank, Stanton
astutely noted.[40] Nor were the candidates any better, since both the
incumbent, Republican Ulysses Grant, and his rival, editor Horace
Greeley, were staunch opponents of woman suffrage. On the one
hand, Martha Coffin Wright fretted, there was "a party that only *pre-
tends* to be friendly while secretly despising the aid it solicits" and on
the other "the one whose contempt is open & indisguised." Like
Wright's family, Stanton's household was "quite divided." Henry Stanton and four of their sons supported Greeley, Henry's old friend and
employer; Anthony, who considered Greeley nothing but "our persistent and uncompromising enemy," endorsed Grant; and Elizabeth
Cady Stanton, though it was "rather an awkward attitude for me" in
light of those endorsements, stood by Victoria Woodhull for president.[41]

"It wd. be amusing to watch the various political complications,"
Martha Coffin Wright admitted, "if one had not quite so deep an
interest in them." Indeed, leaders of the movement for woman suffrage had a deeper and more personal stake in the presidential election of 1872 than they ever had before. Woodhull's arrival on the
suffrage scene coincided with, and made far more popular, a "New
Departure" in suffrage politics: the idea, proposed by Missouri lawyer
Francis Minor and explicated by his wife, Virginia Minor, that since
the Fourteenth Amendment's equal protection did not explicitly *pro-
hibit* women from voting, individual states could not prevent them, as

citizens of the United States, from doing so.[42] For several years now, scattered groups of women, black and white, both lifelong activists and those recently emancipated from slavery, had ventured to vote, and some had been arrested for their efforts. But so focused had Stanton been on the addition of the word *male* to the Constitution that she had failed to notice either their action or the loophole and strategy it suggested. Once alerted to the implications of the Minors' analysis, she called on women to take, rather than simply plead for, the vote. Susan B. Anthony, with her sisters and neighbors, answered that call herself. "Well I have been & gone & done it!!—positively voted the Republican ticket," she wrote Stanton excitedly.[43] She and the others were duly arrested and charged with "knowingly, wrong-fully, and unlawfully" casting a vote.[44]

Anthony's trial quickly became a cause célèbre, her refusal to pay the fine a model of civil disobedience. Still, combined with the sexual and strategic messes of that year, the whole incident further irritated relations between the friends. It had been two decades since they had begun to trade stories of outrage and indigation, and Anthony fully expected Stanton to share her fury at her treatment by the court. Instead, Stanton commented, rather meanly, that "one more act of puny injustice in line with all that has been done, does not add a feather's weight to my chronic state of rebellion." (She "fails to com-prehend the situation, altogether," griped Anthony.[45]) In the mean-time, hundreds of women throughout the North and West strode to the polls. Several of them would take their cases all the way to the Supreme Court, which ruled in *Minor v. Happersett*, in 1875, that the Fourteenth and Fifteenth amendments to the constitution did not guarantee women the right to vote.

Stanton's and Anthony's differences over the 1872 presidential election was but one sign of the divergence in their reform priorities. Anthony had decided that pressuring politicians and their established parties was the only route to gaining woman suffrage, which she had come to see as her central mission. In contrast, Stanton, who dis-missed as hypocrites the men who led those parties and the reformers who remained loyal to them, was certain that an exclusive focus on one goal would hasten their movement's growing conservatism. As they traveled through the West, Anthony spoke about "Work, Wages and the Ballot" and "Women Already Voters," while Stanton orated to "grand meetings" on "Our Young Girls," "Coeducation," "The Antagonism of Sex," "The Bible and Woman," "The True Republic," and, famously, marriage and divorce.[46] "Women respond to this divorce speech as they never did to suffrage," she reported to Anthony. "Oh, how the women flock to me with their sorrows." Indeed, Anthony reported in her diary, some twelve hundred people had attended Stanton's talk on marriage in San Francisco and "the people seem to accept every word." Stanton never abandoned her belief that the denial of the vote to women was the crucial defect in American democracy, the fundamental flaw in the nation's "claim to have a republican form of government."[47] But faced with evidence that the once-dangerous demand for woman suffrage could become watered down as it entered the mainstream, Stanton struggled to keep an expansive woman's rights agenda before as many women as possible, even as many of her demands began to look alarmingly safe.

And flock they did. In the places where Stanton and Anthony traveled in the 1870s, many of their views, including their demand for suffrage for women, were surprisingly popular. In 1872, amid election battles and organizational chaos, Stanton noted wryly to Anthony that "We shall not be spoiled with flattery that is sure." But for all their emphasis on "the ridicule, persecution, denunciation, detraction, the unmixed bitterness of our cup," Elizabeth Cady Stanton had become immensely popular, an eminent lady who drew hundreds to halls across a wide swath of the United States.[48]

Indeed, newspaper accounts of Stanton and Anthony's lecture tours throughout the West and Midwest read like receptions given more often to rock stars than to radicals. "Mrs. Stanton," one Kansan recalled, "was the object of admiration and honor everywhere." "Of all the women who have appeared before the public as lecturers, and especially those who have made the treatment of the different phases of the woman question a specialty, we know of none so worthy to be heard as Mrs. E. Cady Stanton," declared the *Wisconsin Daily Journal* in Madison, which considered itself "among her warmest admirers, at the same time that we dissent from some of her opinions." In her black silk dress with the matching lace shawl, Stanton made the most of the apparent contradiction between her stereotypically grandmotherly looks and her radical speech. As early as 1867 (when she was just over fifty), she was already being introduced as "an elderly lady of a noble and gracious presence, with a profusion of curling flaxen hair"; several years later reporters were struck by her "cheery, motherly face so beaming with intelligence and benevolence and so sweetly framed in snowy locks tastefully arranged," and such gushing only increased. The *San Francisco Chronicle* published drawings and biographical sketches of the suffrage pair, describing Stanton as "STOUT AND FLORID, The picture of perfect health and entire good humor, and were we to sum up her appearance in a word, it would be 'jolly.' " No article failed to mention "Her hair, which is of silken fineness, is as white as snow, and was tastefully arranged in curling bands," and of which Elizabeth Cady Stanton herself was inordinately proud.[49]

She was also proud of her self-declared role in "helping to rouse the apathetic and lethargic to wakefulness and action."[50] And there is no denying that she helped to keep things stirred up wherever she went. But in the West at least, people were thoroughly roused already. The cause of woman suffrage was generally respectable in the 1870s West, far from the radical demand of a few outsiders. When Mary Livermore, a fairly recent, and more conventional, convert to the cause, hit the circuit, she found that lectures on suffrage alone "do not pay—in fact, when free . . . will not command an audience."[51] Livermore exaggerated—lectures on woman suffrage certainly paid when Stanton or Anthony delivered them—but the point remained that in the "Wild" West, woman suffrage was no longer controversial. It is hard to measure just how mainstream the question of woman suffrage had become. Few states and territories (only Wyoming in 1869 and Utah in 1870) had actually passed full woman suffrage, though some localities had passed partial suffrage, with no noticeable upheaval in domestic relations or election day behavior. Still, as a historian of voting rights has noted, this "limited roster of successes . . . does not do justice to the strength of the movement" or the pervasiveness of its support.[52] In legislatures throughout the land, lawmakers echoed Stanton's arguments about women's individuality, their rights as taxpayers, and the mandate for equality under a republican government, as well as arguments, increasingly popular, that women's essential differences from men would serve the nation well. Certainly not everyone considered woman suffrage a matter of common sense. But only with growing successes in passing suffrage laws did an organized opposition (called "antis") emerge on a national level.

The very idea of woman's rights achieved the success it did in part because Elizabeth Cady Stanton and Susan B. Anthony were so adept at garnering publicity. In 1876 the nation celebrated the centennial of the Declaration of Independence with an exposition in Philadelphia that ignored women's struggle to gain their rights. Anthony, as ever a whirlwind of organizational energy, rented office space near Broad and Chestnut streets in Philadelphia and printed stationery from the "Centennial Headquarters" of the National Woman Suffrage Association; she and Stanton appealed for signatories on their new "Woman's Declaration of Independence"; and with Matilda Joslyn Gage began distributing literature and giving lectures that decried the "one discordant note" in a nation "buoyant with patriotism." On the Fourth of July, with Gage and several other supporters, Anthony strode onto the platform, presented the astonished men with the "Declaration of Rights of the Women of the United States," and left, handing out copies as they departed. A "very discourteous interruption," the *New York Tribune* deemed it, though the *St. Louis Dispatch* considered it "safe to say, . . . another centennial will see woman in the halls of legislation throughout the land." "The thing is coming," Republican and woman's rights supporter John M. Broomall had told the Pennsylvania Constitutional Convention two years earlier. "It is only a question of time."[53] Even in Philadelphia there was a growing acceptance of the idea that women would one day vote.

Stanton may have looked soft and fluffy, but she had not even begun to lose her edge. Nor was she easy to live with, or to love, or to criticize. While she insisted that she had a "general regard for all womanhood," she was far more supportive of women such as Victoria Woodhull, whose sexual reputations were under attack, than of more conventional women, whom she held in some contempt.[54] Typically she portrayed women reluctant to support woman's rights as weak-kneed and frightened of the criticisms of men. She told and retold the story of a dinner party in Albany years before when William Seward teased her and Judge Elisha Hurlbut about their support for woman's rights, while the two, "with wit and sarcasm . . . fought the Senator inch by inch until he had a very narrow platform to stand on." After the women adjourned into the parlor, as was the custom, Frances Seward thanked Stanton for her words and assured her that she had remained silent only because she was a "born coward" who dreaded "Mr. Seward's ridicule." The other women, none of whom had spoken out on Stanton's behalf, agreed. But support for woman's rights was, among the women of Stanton's acquaintance, more widespread than such anecdotes imply.[55] And in any case, Frances Seward was no coward. She was her husband's close and often critical adviser—whether he was serving as governor, senator, or secretary of state—and an adept politician, a passionate abolitionist, and a close friend of Martha Coffin Wright. Stanton shaped that story in the way she understood best: to reflect on her own radicalism and boldness, in contrast to that of other women. She was even harsher toward women whom she deemed "sick unto death with propriety," and she did not grow more tolerant with age.[56]

After their disagreement over the wartime suspension of conventions, and for reasons both personal and strategic, Elizabeth Cady Stanton and Susan B. Anthony worked hard to present an image of perfect harmony. It was not easy. Stanton's charisma and charm were undeniable, but they could exhaust even her most beloved companion. "I miss Mrs. Stanton," Anthony wrote her sister after Stanton had left her in California, "still I cannot but enjoy the feeling that the people call on *me*" in the absence of the "brilliant scintillations as they emanate from her never exhausted magazine." Nothing could be done about it, Anthony admitted, for Stanton was simply a force of nature: "whoever goes into a parlor or before an audience with that woman does it at the cost of a fearful overshadowing, a price which I have paid for the last ten years." Anthony quickly composed herself—she had made these sacrifices "cheerfully," she added, "because I felt our cause was most profited by her being seen and heard, and my best work was making the way clear for her"—but the sense of being outshone by "that woman" stung.[57]

Indeed, the strains of political differences and shattered alliances were showing even between these committed friends and allies. Stanton continued to sign her letters to Anthony, as to no one else, "With love as ever and ever till death us do part," and declared that "our hearts are eternally wedded together," but their perfect unity had been shaken. Even references to "love unchanged, undimmed by time and friction," attest to the pressure their friendship had endured. "How I wish I could see you," Stanton wrote soon after Grant's reelection and a day after Greeley's sudden death, "even if to fight all the time." Though Stanton would casually inform a friend that "Susan & I are one & that one is Susan," and their relationship remained the central one in both their lives, they would end this trying decade frazzled from travel and financial cares, torn between acclaim and controversy, and with their fierce and mutual loyalty somewhat ragged for wear.[58]

Despite the applause and the money, Stanton hated being on the road. "I am fearfully tired of this endless travel, on, on, on," she confessed to her son Theodore in 1880. Pictures of Stanton in these years show her in her armchair, the mischievous glint subdued. It is tempting to imagine her, in her growing corpulence, as an ordinary mortal who had chosen a well-deserved retirement. But Stanton was eager to preempt any suggestion that she had lost her exceptional stamina, and so assured her son, "It is the wonder of everybody how at my age, I stand it."[59]

After a decade of political strife, grueling travel, difficult relationships, and plain hard work, Stanton welcomed retirement from the lyceum circuit so that she could gather her energy to take on new projects with all the passion that befitted a sixty-five-year-old woman with a penchant for battle. Over the next twenty years, Elizabeth Cady Stanton would challenge American society, as well as her closest friends, with her most self-reflective and controversial works. With Susan B. Anthony and Matilda Joslyn Gage, she would edit the three-volume *History of Woman Suffrage*, and thus establish their version of the woman's rights movement for years to come. She would write *The Woman's Bible*, evoking controversy and censure within the movement she had helped found. She would speak on "The Solitude of Self," an address she considered her finest work. And, as befitted a movement founder and leader, she would write her memoir, *Eighty Years and More*, sculpting the image she liked best: chubby, cheerful, and with abundant curls, and never, not once, shy about saying what was on her ever-adventuring mind.

6

MAKING A PLACE IN HISTORY

(1880–1902)

"The best is yet to be," Elizabeth Cady Stanton wrote, quoting Robert Browning as she began to keep a diary on November 12, 1880, her sixty-fifth birthday. With an unswerving faith in the positions she had staked out and the missiles she had not yet launched, Stanton kept her eye fixed firmly on the future. Still, seeking a balance between accomplishment and legacy was inevitable: the following day, as if to remind her of time's passing, she learned of Lucretia Mott's death. Stanton "vowed again, as I have so many times, that I shall in the future try to imitate her noble example." Mott being something of a saint, this would not be easy, but certainly Stanton wished to be remembered in an attractive light, even if it meant bending the truth, as when she referred to herself as a "moderate eater."[1] Bossy and self-confident as always, and more determined than ever to establish herself as the originator of the very idea of woman's rights, she set out to shape her legacy on matters both ridiculous and sublime.

For years, Stanton and Susan B. Anthony had dreamed of writing a history of their movement, both to record the facts of their cause and to memorialize their own leadership for future generations. They had already signed an agreement with Matilda Joslyn Gage, a founding member of the National Woman Suffrage Association and editor of the suffrage newspaper *National Citizen and Ballot Box*, who would join them as coeditor. Finally, with lecturing behind her, Stanton was eager to begin the work. With a new generation joining the cause, Stanton and Anthony planned to offer lessons about the past and arguments for the future in a volume that would be both popular and instructive. "It will not be a stiff, formal, mannish work," Stanton told one interviewer, "but a lively, chatty collaboration of our reminiscences." The women imagined that the project would fill a tidy volume, and would serve as a "precious heritage," as the editors modestly put it, "to coming generations." The entire *History of Woman Suffrage*, their own three massive volumes and three more published later, remains the major, if not the definitive, collection of primary source materials on the nineteenth-century movement.[2]

"The prolonged slavery of woman is the darkest page in human history," the volume began, and from there portrayed a dramatic and mythic story of struggle and resistance, with the 1840 London convention, New York State, Seneca Falls, and Elizabeth Cady Stanton herself at the very center of the action. Both more and less than an "authentic and exhaustive account of the movement for the enfranchisement of woman," as the *New York Sun* declared it, or "a disorderly repository of facts," as *The Nation*'s reviewer sniffed, the *History of Woman Suffrage* told a particular, politically motivated story of the woman's movement and its leaders. In that story, Stanton alone articulated the demand for woman suffrage, and Anthony led the charge; there was only one major organization (theirs); and the differences of principle that led to division brooked no debate. As one historian has argued, Stanton and Anthony "took control of movement memory in order to consolidate their power," and the book does read as a celebration and vindication of women who had seen and followed the light of woman's rights. And yet, for all the dramatic struggles and "multifarious persecutions" they depict, these volumes describe progress as inevitable, if only women followed their call to carry on the work in the image of Stanton and Anthony themselves.[3]

The process of compiling these documents, essays, and engravings, like the woman's movement itself, quickly sprawled out of its creators' control. Though the first volume took only half a year to complete, the project dominated their lives for the better part of a decade. Sometimes Stanton and Anthony managed to devote months to the work, when the house in Tenafly became "more like a school than a place for vacation recreation." At other times they sat in their separate homes and tried to make sense of the piles of paper they had accumulated. Susan B. Anthony had saved a great deal. Gage, too, was a saver of papers, who also, in Stanton's words, "had a knack of rummaging through old libraries, bringing more startling facts to light than any woman I ever knew."[4] Elizabeth Cady Stanton, in contrast, tended to throw things away, to the intense irritation of her coeditors.[5] In late 1880, Anthony shipped boxes of material to Tenafly, Gage sat in her home in Upstate New York looking through her own books and papers, Stanton took up her pen, and they settled in to finish the first volume, a story of the origins of the movement for woman's rights, now increasingly defined, even by the authors, by the demand for suffrage itself.

Although Stanton moaned about the tedium of reviewing "such endless detail!" she loved sifting through her memories, reconsidering her ideas, shaping the story, and establishing as historical truth her own positions on "universal rights." For a change, it was Anthony who complained that she "hated this kind of work," and Stanton who dragged her away from meetings and lectures to finish it up.[6] The friends' different personalities and skills also became a source of tension. No one had ever accused Elizabeth Cady Stanton of being methodical, and Anthony had no patience for her friend's inattention to detail. Stanton's attitude toward dates was casual at best: "She can tangle up chronology to beat any other one who puts pen to paper," Anthony grumbled, and, not surprisingly, the History project only heightened Stanton's tendency to philosophical speculation and rhetorical flight.[7] Anthony simply could not abide sitting still for this, and frequently left the others to do their compiling while she returned to what she considered her more important activist labors.

There were times, however, when even Anthony considered the time spent on the project "delightful." Just being together in Tenafly, now with "such perfect quiet," without children underfoot, was its own freedom. The room they worked in was large and sunny, with a well-kept fire and drawers stocked with documents and engravings, and Amelia Willard around to cook. They "start off pretty well in the morning," Stanton's daughter Margaret reported, "fresh and amiable." Inevitably they would disagree over some point of philosophy or chronology, and "suddenly the whole sky is overspread with threatening clouds, and from the adjoining room I hear a hot dispute about something . . . Sometimes these disputes run so high that down go the pens, one sails out of one door and one out of the other, walking in opposite directions around the estate, and just as I have made up my mind that this beautiful friendship of forty years has at last terminated, I see them walking down the hill, arm in arm." For most of a decade, every spare moment, every week that was free from speaking engagements, they devoted to the *History*. Even Margaret, who rarely complained, likened the work to a "favorite adopted child, that filled [the children's] places in a mother's heart."[8]

The volume of work itself was mind-boggling. For every item collected, every reminiscence solicited, there were letters to write, queries to answer, promises to make. "Everybody amplifies," Stanton complained, which required her to suggest politely that "it is better for you to rewrite & condense" since "We are already swamped with material." Anthony was in charge of the volume's steel engravings, while Stanton begged people for their memories, their parents' stories, their state's laws concerning women, and their documents—and then liberally applied her scissors and pen to whatever she felt needed editing. We are "buried in manuscripts," Stanton admitted, as they sorted through packages of crumbling correspondence that old friends had sent. Even Anthony had to be begged to "sit right down and write everything you can remember of yourself, and write objectively just as you would of another person." As for herself, Stanton was simply not organized or focused enough to do any of the work alone. "The moment you left me last summer, I packed the whole thing away and have never put pen to paper since," she admitted. "I cannot work on the big job alone."[9]

While some people wrote too much, others refused to participate at all. Stanton pleaded with Lucy Stone to write a brief memoir of her movement labors, but years of hostilities between the two camps of woman's rights leaders had hardened Stone to Stanton's appeal, and she refused to "have any hand" in the project, since "I do not think it *can* be written by any one who is alive to-day." Aside from their proximity to the events themselves, there were problems of bias: "Your 'wing' surely are not competent to write the history of 'our wing,' nor should we be of yours, even if we thought best to take the time while the war goes on." (Lucy "thinks it desecration of her immaculate being to be even mentioned by such profane lips as ours," sniffed Stanton.[10])

By the summer of 1881, with Stanton weak from "a three-month siege of intermittent fever," she and Anthony decided that Harriot Stanton should complete the editorial work on the second volume. Hattie had graduated from Vassar in 1878, where she was voted by her classmates most likely to be the country's first female president, and was living in Germany, grappling from a distance with her complicated relationship both to woman's rights and to her daunting mother. She responded to the summons home with an irritated sigh ("It was quite definitely stated that I would be expected by February 1882," she recalled tersely), but without open rebellion. The work on the *History* "proved heavier than I had anticipated" and she was dismayed that there was no plan for covering Stone and Blackwell's rival American Woman Suffrage Association. Finally, "the cruel conclusion" was that Harriot should write that chapter. The whole affair left a bad taste for Harriot, first because her name appeared only as the compiler of the one-hundred-plus-page section, but perhaps more because she resented the workload Anthony expected of her mother, which she always framed in terms of the movement's best interests. This time, she won the skirmish: in May 1882, Harriot Stanton experienced "the joy of eloping with my mother" to France. It was the first time Elizabeth Cady Stanton had been abroad since her honeymoon in 1840, and she relished the chance to be, she admitted, "beyond the reach and sound of my beloved Susan and the woman suffrage movement."[11]

How different this experience was and how Stanton must have reflected on the decades that had passed since her last visit. As if they needed a reminder of those changes, she and Harriot carried a carton of copies of the *History of Woman Suffrage* for distribution to libraries. First they visited Theodore Stanton and his wife, Marguerite Berry, in France, where Stanton met her first grandchild, Elizabeth Cady Stanton II (Lizette). The Stanton women then spent a few recuperative months in a convent in the south of France, where Elizabeth Stanton enjoyed the irony of spending time in "these holy precincts" with "some of the most radical and liberal-minded residents" of the area.[12] Then to England, to catch up with old reform acquaintances and to plan for Harriot's marriage to an Englishman, Harry Blatch. Marriage was for Harriot, as it had been for her mother, a defining step in her evolution as a woman's rights activist. Harry Blatch was a kind, well-meaning, not terribly well-educated businessman who promised Harriot both comfortable support and the freedom to develop whatever career she chose. But whereas her brother Theodore's marriage to a foreigner had not altered his status as an American citizen, by marrying an Englishman, Harriot would lose her citizenship. It was perhaps the first time that Hattie, born into the cause of woman's rights and educated to be an independent "new woman," recognized that the law circumscribed her rights simply because of her sex.

It had seemed to Stanton that the children of reformers "seldom follow in the footsteps of their parents," that none "has ever . . . echoed our demands."[13] Indeed, most of the Stanton children stayed away from the political side of the family business, and to varying degrees remained outside their formidable mother's orbit. Gerrit Smith Stanton (Gat), after graduating from Columbia College Law School, moved to Iowa, where he opened a stock ranch on land that had once been owned by his grandfather, Judge Cady. He hung Elizabeth Cady Stanton's and Susan B. Anthony's lithographs above his sofa, reminding neighbors (and constituents, when he was mayor of Woodbine, Iowa) who his mother was. Filial loyalty, however, did not extend to sympathy with her activism. In his opinion (he'd been only three at the time), "The Seneca Falls convention woke up all the cranks, long haired individuals, ismists, both male and female in the State of New York and all roads led to Seneca Falls and the Stanton mansion."[14] Henry, Jr., remained closer to his father, but after some "very gross" newspaper attacks against his mother, Stanton forecast that "The next sensation will probably be a cowhiding of Greeley by Kit . . . [who was] . . . getting so stirred up that I can hardly hold him still." Robert, the youngest of Stanton's children, who had, in his mother's view, "grown very large, & wise," could also get "quite stirred up with the fray" her writings provoked, though he urged her not to "mind what these jackasses say."[15] Stanton's daughter Maggie, whom her sister, Harriot, considered "an example of patience and good spirit and an even temper," married Frank Lawrence in 1878, lived in Idaho until his death in 1890, and returned to New York City, where she finished school and became the "physical director" at Teachers College. Although only a "lukewarm suffrage saint," Maggie was fervently loyal to her mother; she and Bob, who never married, shared an apartment with her in the final years of her life.[16]

But Stanton was only partly right that reformers' children eschewed their causes. Both Harriot and Theodore were busy inventing careers that followed directly from their mother's concerns, though they moved an ocean away to do it. Theodore was, his mother wrote unblushingly, "as near perfection as a young man can be," a foreign correspondent who wrote frequently about woman's rights, and the author of *The Woman Question in Europe*.[17] But it was Harriot who was drawn to activism. She joined the British woman's suffrage movement, where she learned a political style that would shape her approach to suffrage when she returned to the United States.

Much as she enjoyed her adult children's company and delighted in being her grandchildren's "Queen Mother," Elizabeth Cady Stanton was now a notable public figure in Europe, and so each visit included work to be done, speeches to give, and reports to write for the American press. She was thrilled when Susan B. Anthony joined her there in 1883—"I don't see why I can't have a little fun the same as any one else," Anthony was reported to have said—and together they explored Europe's major cities and were welcomed as visiting dignitaries by those whom the British called suffragettes. Stanton, who "rejoice[d] every day that I was born in America," got impatient with what she viewed as British stuffiness and despaired at "the hopeless slavery of the working classes." But she loved foreign cities' odd delights, finding Paris a great place for its public restrooms. "No one here disciplines the bladder," she informed Bob merrily. ". . . With seats & such conveniences I am quite at ease in all our peregrinations."[18]

But for all the pleasures of foreign travel, the speeches about the American movement, and the transatlantic contacts she made, Anthony itched to go home and "besiege Congress . . . for a sixteenth amendment." It was harder for Stanton to pull herself away from Europe, from Hattie's company, and from her granddaughter, Nora, and only Anthony's pestering got her, time after time, to return home. Thus in 1888, after another eighteen months' stay in Europe, Stanton returned to the United States reluctantly, just barely in time for the first International Council of Women that she and Anthony had orchestrated, and only after Anthony had written a letter that "will start every white hair on her head." "She will never be forgiven by me, or any of our Association, if she fails to come!" Anthony warned bluntly, so Stanton relented, once again.[19]

The International Council of Women was not the first instance of transatlantic cooperation among the advocates of woman's rights, whose rhetoric had resounded across the ocean and been greeted with amazed familiarity on all sides. But this "web of feminist connections" had grown thin in the post-revolutionary 1850s; while the American movement flourished as a philosophical and political affair, European radicals either were jailed, went into exile, or were otherwise kept from public agitation.[20] By the 1880s, middle-class woman's rights activists had reemerged within Europe's political mainstream. They welcomed Stanton and Anthony to their platforms, and now joined them in the capital of the United States to celebrate the respectability and stature of the international cause of woman's rights.

With the National Woman Suffrage Association at the helm, dozens of organizations, from the Woman's Christian Temperance Union to women's clubs, labor unions, and professional groups, not all of them pro-suffrage, joined, with forty-nine delegates from Western Europe, Canada, and India, to celebrate the accomplishments of women. It was a gala event, as its daily coverage in the *Washington Post* attests. President Grover Cleveland greeted the visiting delegates, and senators held receptions in their honor. Lucy Stone and the American Woman Suffrage Association played a visible role, signaling that the divisions between the two organizations might soon be healed. Still, there were lingering grudges, and each celebration of a watershed moment was open to conflicting interpretations. Anthony, now practiced at shaping the public's perception of the woman's rights movement, used the meeting to commemorate the fortieth anniversary of the convention at Seneca Falls. Confoundedly, Lucy Stone planned to address the Council on "Pioneer day" on "The Advance of the last fifty years," although, Anthony grumbled, "just why she puts it 50—instead of 40—I do not know."[21]

Elizabeth Cady Stanton, the movement's most prominent public intellectual, spoke that week at the Council, at an Easter Day sympo-

sium, at the celebration of "Pioneer" women, and to the Senate Select
Committee on Woman Suffrage. Women, Stanton declared, whether
"housed in golden cages with every want supplied, or wandering in
the dreary deserts of life," shared a common bond, but she meant, as
she always had, much more than their inability to vote. "[T]he humil-
iations of spirit are as real as the visible badges of servitude," she proclaimed. With their spirits thus squelched, "women have been the
mere echoes of men," and yet Stanton's generation had provided
younger women with advantages that should lead to "speedy con-
quests." But Stanton also warned her audience against angering
women so much that they "strike hands with Nihilists, Socialists,
Communists, and Anarchists, in defense of the most enlarged liberties of the people."[22] We who advocate woman's rights, she seemed to
suggest, are the safer choice in a Gilded Age of troubling unrest; just
look around at the group assembled here, well educated and well
coifed. Over the next two decades, with immigration on the rise,
black men once again disenfranchised, and working-class activists
clamoring for economic and political power, Stanton's own sense of
class superiority would ever more openly shape her notion of the dangers faced by a democracy.

Stanton's radical insight that women, as individuals capable of
moral choice and intellectual distinction, deserved the rights granted
to citizens of the United States, had always been infused with the
entitlement she felt as an educated white native-born American. Ever
since her girlhood in her father's law office, Stanton's outrage had
been nourished by her bone-deep conviction that she was an heir to
the United States' most egalitarian traditions, a citizen whose rights
had been arbitarily denied on the basis of sex. The contrast with less
"worthy" Americans was sometimes explicit, fading in and out of her
speeches and writing as her own irritation waxed and waned. In her
very first speech after Seneca Falls she had been aware that "We need
not prove ourselves equal to Daniel Webster to enjoy this privilege" of
voting, yet even then she resented that "the most ignorant Irishman in
the ditch has all the civil rights [Webster] has." "All men in this country have the same rights however they may differ in mind, body, or
estate," she claimed, and even when, years later, published versions of
this speech changed that phrase to "all white men," her intention was

clear.[23] It was her identity as a "true" American, one descended from the nation's very founders, that had helped fuel her indignation about black male suffrage after the war; it now led her to endorse a law to limit suffrage to those she deemed worthy of the privilege.

Years before, Stanton had argued convincingly that sex had no more place in assigning rights than did class, race, or religion. But even then, she had sometimes signaled her willingness to sacrifice other people's rights in defense of her own. George Francis Train's demand for "Educated Suffrage, Irrespective of Sex or Color" had been prominently posted on The Revolution's front page, and Stanton had conceded that "if we are to have further class legislation," we should "take the educated classes first." "[E]ducated women first, ignorant men afterward," she had proclaimed in 1868, and ten years later, "after much thought," supported a proposal that "those who vote, after 1880, must read and write the English language."[24] An educational qualification "in no way conflicts with the popular theory that suffrage is a natural right [because it] does not *abolish* the suffrage for any class," Stanton declared, but it was a hard argument to defend; years later Anthony regretted that her friend had become "very *strenuous about 'Educated Suffrage.'* " But Stanton's sense of insult had never faded, and she now declared that raising foreigners "above the most intelligent, highly-educated women—native-born Americans," was "the most bitter drop in the cup of grief, that we are compelled to swallow."[25]

Elizabeth Cady Stanton was a force to be reckoned with, and it took guts to challenge her directly. Anthony considered the question of educated suffrage "a *side issue*," but she loyally delivered Stanton's speeches. (In an odd twist of logic, Stanton saw her friend's opposition as more evidence that she had grown "more conservative as she grows popular."[26]) Significantly, the most powerful public dissent came from two people who had been influenced by, in one case, European radicalism and, in the other, American antiracism: Harriot Stanton Blatch and William Lloyd Garrison, Jr., now the editor of The Nation.

In 1894, Harriot Stanton Blatch sat down to read a debate about educated suffrage between her mother and their old friend, William Lloyd Garrison, Jr. What she saw made her furious and, even worse, embarrassed. Her response to "My Honored Mother" cannot have been an easy letter to write, and she published it in, of all places, Henry Blackwell's *Woman's Journal*. But Harriot pulled no punches: she was horrified by her mother's defense of educated suffrage on the grounds that "if a person can *read and write*, he is 'enlightened' and 'educated,' and if he cannot read and write, he is 'ignorant.'" Surely Stanton knew that someone "who could satisfy a board of examiners of his collegiate accomplishments, is lamentably ignorant; while many a man, without a sign of the 3 Rs about him, is gifted with the sterling commonsense and abiding honesty which the school of life's experiences teaches." But "you go still further," Harriot wrote with some bitterness, "and call every American citizen who was born in Europe, and who cannot read or write the *English* language, an 'ignorant foreigner.'" With such epithets Stanton dismissed people's education in their own tongue and ignored the needs of the poorest and most vulnerable, namely working-class women. However trying it may sometimes have been to have Elizabeth Cady Stanton as a mother, it was only now that Harriot was actually ashamed of her. Only the comfort that "I could claim Mr. Garrison as one of my personal friends, at least," saved her from even greater humiliation.[27]

Stanton jumped into this public dispute with great cheer, confident that she had put her daughter and Garrison "in a corner," but just as sure that they "will wiggle out." Garrison's notion that educated suffrage was no different from a literacy requirement for former slaves was nonsense, Stanton declared, for when "there were no free schools, and [slaves] had been forbidden to read and write," such a restriction "would have been the height of injustice." Back then, she stated blandly, the enfranchisement of black men "like the greenback, was a war measure, an imperative necessity," casually omitting to mention that she had rejected this argument at the time. Conceding that she supported "the large class of honest, industrious, intelligent, moral men and women who have borne an honorable and important part in building up this nation," Stanton persisted in writing about "the perils of immigration." "I am opposed to the admission of another man, either foreign or native, to the polling-booth, until woman, the greatest factor in civilization, is first enfranchised," she informed her daughter. Stanton also insisted that "foreigners are opposed to the enfranchisement of women," just as she had asserted years before, and with as little evidence, that African American men were arrayed against her.[28] In the end, her support for educated suffrage, like her willingness to embrace suffrage activists on racist terms, may have served only to convince immigrants, African Americans, and working-class activists that the movement for woman suffrage, whatever its rhetoric, was primarily concerned with gaining rights for white middle-class women. It was an image that would be difficult to erase, and one that was not entirely false.

For all her breadth and brilliance, Elizabeth Cady Stanton tended to dismiss demands for freedom that did not fit into her own framework for understanding rights. In her support of American imperialist adventures, for example, she joined many other woman suffrage supporters (but not, notably, Anthony) in viewing "voting . . . less [as] a right of citizenship than of civilization." During the war with Spain she informed William Lloyd Garrison, Jr., that Cuba would be better off under American rule. "What would this continent have been if left to the Indians?" she asked. "Would they ever have attained our present civilization?" Furthermore, she mused, "How much further advanced the Chinese would have been developed had Anglo-Saxon blood been infused there." Garrison's response was immediate and withering: "Regarding imperialism," he wrote, "I wonder that you do not see how applicable your reasoning regarding inferior races is to the negro and the woman question . . . In our present attitude we will stand in history pilloried with the slave-trader, the destroyer of the Indian and the persecutor of the Chinese."[29]

So far as racial justice was concerned, Stanton remained determinedly liberal, as her era understood the word. Though "no one asks that ignorant laborers, of whatever color, be admitted into the higher classes," she supported the legal equality and education that would help them improve their lot. Thus Stanton declared a woman suffrage convention in Grand Rapids, Michigan, "grievously compromised" for rejecting a "resolution of protest against the treatment of the colored race in parts of the South, practically requiring the reestablishment of separate cars for whites and blacks." But she showed greater alacrity in judging others than herself. She found a "cause for reflection" in "a pleasant evening at Mrs. [Frances Garrison] Villard's," where the guests listened to "African and Indian students from Hampton Institute" sing. Imagine, she wrote, "Representatives of these two subordinated races standing side by side to amuse the arrogant dominant race." "Well, my conscience was clear," she declared firmly, if a bit defensively, "for my very first efforts in reform were for the negro."[30]

Although she remained convinced of the profound injustice of denying the vote to women, Stanton stuck to her refusal to limit herself exclusively to that goal. Indeed, as the organized movement for woman's rights focused on gaining actual legislative victories, it seemed increasingly a drag on her time and patience. For one thing, Stanton had laid out every argument she could think of: "I have said all I have to say on the subject of suffrage," she announced. For another, her dislike of organizational life had only hardened with age. Susan B. Anthony, who now saw the achievement of suffrage as a matter of organizational muscle, devoted herself to merging the two suffrage associations, and she expected Stanton to help. Old grievances remained, but they were now more personal than strategic. Stanton felt that "we shall always have trouble with Blackwell & Lucy," who persisted in "contradicting what I say," and she griped for years about Alice Stone Blackwell's tendency to "deny all my *truths of history*" in defense of her parents' party line.[31] Still, it seemed time to bury old resentments in the larger interest of the cause. Younger women, after all, did not care about the ancient battles of Reconstruction that had created the schism in the first place. And with campaigns for partial suffrage effectively enfranchising women in almost two dozen states and territories in school board and other local elections, a consolidated organization would lead a sprawling national movement to its final victory.

Perhaps Stanton was correct that she had "been in favor of union from the beginning," but it hardly mattered; she had long abandoned much hope that the suffrage organizations would advance a broad agenda for woman's rights. "Our cause has become too popular, our numbers too large for me as a leader," she wrote woman's rights activist and minister Olympia Brown with the merger imminent. ". . . Lucy & Susan alike see suffrage only. They do not see women's religious & social bondage, neither do the young women in either association, hence they may as well combine for they have one mind & one purpose." Still, she gave in to Susan B. Anthony's pleading to accept the presidency of the newly merged National American Woman Suffrage Association at its first convention, scheduled to coincide with a gala celebration of Anthony's seventieth birthday. Anthony knew that Stanton would never toe a party line; she was not surprised when Stanton used the platform to advocate yet again for the broadest possible agenda. Stanton then got on a ship and sailed to Europe, leaving Anthony to wonder what she would stir up next. "My feeling," Stanton had declared with neither understatement nor undue modesty, "is to tone up rather than down."[32]

Tone up she did. The power of Stanton's mind, her extraordinary way with words, and her uncanny ability to have the newspapers report her every utterance made her as dangerous as she was thrilling. It was Anthony who had to face, time and again, the infuriating fact that Stanton's words would "be *charged upon me & all the woman suffrage women of the entire nation!*" Take the public outrage at Frederick Douglass's 1884 marriage to Helen Pitts, a white woman. Elizabeth Cady Stanton composed a warm congratulatory letter to her old friend that reaffirmed her belief in individual rights. "If a good man from Maryland sees fit to marry a disfranchised woman from New York," she declared, ". . . full liberty of choice in such relations should be conceded." When Anthony caught wind of Stanton's intention to make the letter public, she exploded. Do not, Anthony wrote, "put your foot into the *Douglass* question, of *the intermarriage of the races!* It *has no place on our platform.*" Anthony was already beside herself that "The papers all stated that the *woman was a suffragist!*" although (she had checked) "Her name is not on our books." "I beg *you*," she entreated, "not to congratulate him by letter! He has by this act compromised every movement in which he shall be brought to the front!" More pleading followed, until, "Lovingly & Fearfully yours," she signed off. Stanton, for once, relented, though only briefly. Several months later she explained to Douglass that she had long intended to "ridicul[e] this ridiculous prejudice of color," and enclosed the original letter. Ever gracious, Douglass responded that even "without one word from you on the subject," he had assumed that she would "vote against the clamor raised against my marriage to a white woman."[33]

Knowing that Frederick Douglass had found a partner who shared his interests and his causes must have added to Stanton's growing sense of solitude, for her own marriage had never become the passionate partnership she observed in others. And yet she still admired other people's capacity for romance. "I have just finished George Eliot's Life, and what an existence in rich experiences, crowned with such love to the end," she wrote Elizabeth Smith Miller at seventy. "What blessedness. How few mortals ever taste the joy of a deep soul-love . . . The older I grow the deeper my sorrow that I have no son of Adam to reverance and worship as a God." She also remained open about women's, and implicitly her own, sexual pleasures. In 1883 she sat down to read *Leaves of Grass*, and although she misunderstood Whitman's interest in women's sexuality, she offered a view of her own. "Walt Whitman seems to understand everything in nature but woman," she complained to her diary. "In 'There is a Woman Waiting for Me,' he speaks as if the female must be forced to the creative act, apparently ignorant of the great natural fact that a healthy woman has as much passion as a man."[34]

Henry Stanton had faded in and out of his wife's story in stages. Of his final decade or so there is little said, and biographers differ about whether the two were separated or "came to terms."[35] Evidently Isabella Beecher Hooker had years earlier thought the Stantons' "domestic relations not altogether happy," but Elizabeth retorted defensively that Henry was "a highly cultivated liberal man," with whom she could still laugh, although "our theology is as wide apart as the north and south pole so we never talk on those points where we both feel most." She then went on to list all the things—walking, food, and oratory topped the list—that they enjoyed in each other's company, admitting only that "we should be nearer and dearer" if he were as philosophically accepting as she of their differences.[36]

But Henry Stanton appears as only a minor character, an erratic and vague presence, in his wife's stories; even Harriot barely mentioned him in her own memoir, whose index lists his name only twice.[37] Sometimes a young reporter would be disappointed not to meet the famous woman's husband, "since our universal experience has been that wherever you find a brave, cheerful, progressive wife, you will also find a noble, helpful, unselfish husband."[38] Elizabeth Cady Stanton must have grimaced when she read this; she expressed mostly mild amusement and controlled impatience toward this man who had grown old and faded by her side. She noted loyally that "Mr. Stanton's 'Random Recollections' have been published and well received," and sent the *Sun*'s "three column notice" of the book to Theodore in Paris; she may not have sent the *Times*'s description of it as "amusing gossip."[39] But she could not have been pleased that the book's only mention of her was as the daughter of Judge Daniel Cady. Evidently the Stantons had a chat about this; the third edition listed various women who served in the antislavery cause and then referred awkwardly to "The celebrity . . . of two women" whose fame "in another department" had obscured the "distinguished service they rendered to the slave." By now, though Elizabeth admitted that Henry was "uniformly in good spirits," the Stantons' daily lives overlapped barely more than their reminiscences did. "As no ladies were invited," she did not attend his eightieth birthday gala, and "can only judge from the reports in the daily papers and what I could glean from the honored guest himself" how it went; tellingly, whether Henry was invited to the fêtes in honor of his famous wife's birthdays is unknown.[40]

For the most part, Henry Stanton withdrew into his own sphere, a world composed largely of men, including his lawyer sons. He never did visit his children overseas, and met his European grandchildren only once, in 1886, when Theodore and Harriot and their children came for a visit. Two years earlier, Stanton had postponed traveling to Europe because "Henry is so old now, that I feel my first duty is to make a home for him," but this time, when Hattie and Nora sailed back home, Elizabeth Cady Stanton joined them on board. Thus she was in Europe in January 1887 when word came that Henry had died; appropriately, he had caught a cold from "standing outdoors to watch the election returns."[41] "Death!" Elizabeth Cady Stanton exclaimed at the news, more shocked than devastated: "Then well up regrets for every unkind, ungracious word spoken, for every act of coldness and neglect. Ah! if we could only remember in life to be gentle and forbearing with each other . . . our memories of the past would be more pleasant and profitable." She returned home a full year after his death, busy as ever, and a year later had not found time to go through his papers. Oddly, Henry Stanton left no will; his estate, his son

Henry, Jr., attested, totaled no more than eleven hundred dollars, and so was easily settled. Although Alma Lutz, with Harriot Stanton Blatch's collaboration, testified to Elizabeth's and Henry's "deep and true" affection for one another, and spoke of Elizabeth's "bravely adjusting herself to life" without him, she seems barely to have missed a beat. Henry, after all, had not challenged her mind or her independence for years.[42]

Indeed, the widowed Stanton remained utterly herself: flirtatious, charming, and intimidating. She cheerfully embraced the nickname "Queen Mother" that her granddaughter Nora had given her, and allowed reporters to describe her as a comforting maternal figure who "makes cake and other little dainties for the table." Perhaps few shared Lucy Stone's "inveterate dislike of Mrs. Stanton," but even her admirers found her daunting. Mary Livermore admitted, "you have such a frankness in expressing yourself that I am afraid of you," and another suffragist declined to argue with Stanton, "for, however good natured, and humorous, and delightful she is as a friend, I own to a little fear of her sharp points." Apparently oblivious to such fears, Stanton considered herself "good natured, generous, & always well & happy."[43] Men seem to have been especially susceptible to her charms. Frederick Douglass visited Elizabeth Cady Stanton in Paris in 1886, where he found his old friend with "no snobbery about her" and "more radical than ever." Once, in 1897, the journalist John Swinton wrote to tell her that he had dreamed of her: She was standing "upon a huge rock, in a boundless desert, discoursing upon righteousness and the judgment to come."[44] Mostly she remained smitten with herself: delighted by her own wit and her "chronic condition of rebellion." "If I had not naturally a sunny temperment & good health," she reflected, "I should have been the princess of feminine devils." Even in the midst of the most tedious work or visiting in the small world of Johnstown, Stanton could always "amus[e] myself shocking people with all manner of heresies, political, religious, social."[45]

At times Susan B. Anthony's focus on gaining woman suffrage left her unprepared for the heresies Stanton might choose to address. In 1892 Anthony dragged her friend one last time to speak to congressional committees and the woman suffrage convention in Washington, D.C. There Stanton delivered what she considered her most significant speech, the "Solitude of Self." "The point I wish plainly to bring before you, . . ." Stanton intoned, "is the individuality of each human soul; our Protestant idea, the right of individual conscience and judgement [sic]; our republican idea, individual citizenship." Women's self-sovereignty, not the "incidental relations of life" as wife, mother, and daughter, was what finally mattered. Laws, wages, even the vote could not prepare women for the "awful solitude" of their own salvation. "The strongest reason why we ask for woman a voice in the government under which she lives; in the religion she is asked to believe; equality in social life, where she is the chief factor; a place in the trades and professions, where she may earn her bread, is because of her birthright to self-sovereignty; because, as an individual, she must rely on herself." "Who, I ask you, can take, dare take on himself the rights, the duties, the responsibilities of another human soul?"[46]

The "Solitude of Self" was not the rousing call to action that Anthony and the rest of Stanton's audience of activists and politicians expected to hear. It was depressing, even bleak, an existential declaration of people's utter isolation. Indeed, responses to the speech varied. Anna Howard Shaw, a rising young suffrage leader, called the speech "an English classic." Lucy Stone considered the speech so important that she published the entire thing in the *Woman's Journal*, in the space where she would ordinarily have printed her own address. Anthony at first thought it Stanton's "poorest" speech, though eventually, Stanton crowed, she deemed it "the best thing I ever wrote"; Anthony's initial reaction, Stanton complacently asserted, was simply because the speech "did not sing the refrain suffrage every line." The fourth volume of the *History of Woman Suffrage* notes that the speech was considered by many a "masterpiece," and excerpted it at length. Without doubt the speech's greatest fan was Stanton herself, who thought it "has more pathos in it than all the Journal tracts together."[47]

Whatever its virtues as a philosophical tract on woman's rights, the "Solitude of Self" was as close as Elizabeth Cady Stanton would come to reflecting on her own sense of personal and political isolation. Every individual, Stanton suggested, is responsible for her own salvation, and ultimately only individual salvation matters. At seventy-six, Stanton felt entirely accountable for her own spiritual and intellectual path, and there is an air of regret and resignation as well as pride in her words. The organized movement for woman suffrage, now led by her closest friend and ally, would not, she knew, provide the forum for her most expansive and radical views. Stanton was probably not surprised—years earlier she had warned, "Ah, beware, Susan, lest as you become 'respectable,' you become conservative"—but she felt sad nonetheless. The vote, Stanton still believed, was an essential cause and symbol of women's subordination, and although Harriot came to wonder whether "you and Susan would vote now even if you had a chance to," Stanton remained adamant that she would indeed. But the suffrage organizations themselves no longer expressed a broad and radical vision of how full citizenship could transform women's status. A preeminent historian of the woman suffrage movement has noted that suffrage has wrongly been "regarded as an isolated institutional reform" rather than as the movement for "radical change" in women's lives that Elizabeth Cady Stanton envisioned.[48] Stanton might have used precisely these words as a challenge to the movement she had helped build.

New heresies were more than ever called for, for suffrage was becoming wildly popular in certain circles, "the fashionable fad." "You have no idea how stirred up our people are," Stanton reported to Theodore in 1894 as New York prepared to hold another constitutional convention. "Susan has spoken in every county in the state. There are parlor meetings all over the city; two or three a day in each district; they are held in large fashionable houses, in churches, halls, school-rooms; men and women speaking for and against." Stanton herself had become "the heroine of the evening" at mass meetings where "the hall rang with cheers," but she had no intention of mellowing her indignation to fit the part.[49]

Stanton now aimed her indignation at organized Christianity, which she had long viewed as a dangerous source of women's subordination. Whatever actual religious beliefs Stanton had personally she held lightly, identifying more with freethinkers and congenital doubters than with people of faith. Occasionally she developed an intellectual fascination for theology, or got caught up in the contemporary rage for phrenology, spiritualism, or reincarnation, but the evidence of any deep spiritual conviction on her part is slim; sometimes the search for it misses Stanton's sense of humor and irony. She claimed, for instance, that theosophist Annie Besant's belief in reincarnation appealed to her because it allowed her to hope that "all those wicked Democrats in Congress who have opposed woman suffrage will return to earth as women." Similarly, although the ever-curious Stanton inquired into the various fads of the day, she preferred her friends to remain "safely anchored on the rock of common sense." When both she and Anthony tried to understand what the spiritualist fuss was about, Anthony concluded wryly that they were fated to be "of 'the earth-earthy' " rather than having strong spiritual leanings, and so they resigned themselves to it. Indeed, Stanton was far more impressed with another intellectual innovation: "admit Darwin's theory of evolution," she wrote Elizabeth Smith Miller in 1887, "and the whole orthodox system topples to the ground."[50]

Elizabeth Cady Stanton's hostility to organized, orthodox religion was of long standing, and it was a familiar critique among activists of her generation.[51] Years earlier, when the newly formed Women's Loyal National League vowed to "educate the nation into the true idea of a Christian Republic," Stanton had caused "Considerable preliminary debate" when she tried, and failed, to omit the word *Christian*. To her, "A book that curses woman in her maternity, degrades her in marriage, makes her the author of sin, & a mere afterthought in creation & baptizes all this as the word of God cannot be said to be a great blessing to the sex."[52] Who among her close friends would disagree? But now, emboldened by philosophical debates about religion and science by European positivists and secularists, and fearful of the rising evangelical movement's influence on American political culture, Stanton had grown ever more distrustful. So much did she fear "the rank and file of womankind [who] are bound in the fetters of the middle ages" that she began to "feel more anxious about *how the women would vote*, than in hastening the day when they should vote." Indeed, she told Clara Colby, editor of the *Woman's Tribune*, she would prefer to "live under a government of man along with religious liberty than under a mixed government without it."[53]

It was in this context that Stanton embarked upon a reinterpretation of biblical texts that would shed new light on women's role and status. The plan was gutsy, even for Stanton, involving work more often undertaken by formally trained scholars than by an activist housewife with a breathtaking grasp of history, rhetoric, logic, and her own abilities. With a rare twinge of humility, she acknowledged that she lacked some of the skills for the work—she especially needed women scholars of Hebrew and Greek—and she sought out a committee that could produce a *Woman's Bible* that would "bring within the smallest compass all the texts that refer to the status of woman under the Jewish and Christian dispensations."[54]

Gathering such a committee turned out to be harder than Stanton thought. Some women felt that the project threatened their own religious faith, a response Stanton expected and dismissed. Still others, though generally supportive, felt inadequate to the task or were simply too busy working for woman suffrage.[55] Antoinette Brown Blackwell, an old friend and a minister with expertise in biblical criticism, had projects in mind that were "a thousand fold more important than yours." And quite a few close friends thought the whole task a misuse of Stanton's time and energy. Religious liberals and Quakers such as Elizabeth Smith Miller thought the project "quite needless." Whether or not the Bible "approves the doctrine of equal rights for man and woman" hardly mattered, Miller wrote her cousin firmly. Anthony, too, thought that most people "are above the need of your book," now that "Even the liberalized orthodox ministers are coming to our aid." Anthony was, she assured her friend, delighted to see "the old superstitions and bigotries . . . crumbling on every side," but she felt no compulsion "to tear to tatters the lingering skeletons." Anthony never did become reconciled to Stanton's priorities; several years later, outraged about yet another indignity imposed on African Americans in the Jim Crow South, she implored Stanton to pay attention to "this barbarism [that] does not grow out of ancient Jewish Bibles—but out of our own sordid meanness!!" Other women who agreed that "much in the Bible does distinctly approve of women being considered inferior to men" considered the point too obvious to discuss: "It is what one might indeed logically expect in a book compiled by men," wrote one correspondent. Stanton was sure that her project would have international appeal, but friends in Europe doubted that "your Bible revision idea will excite much interest in France," and expressed some surprise that "great minds like yours can give time to it."[56]

Susan B. Anthony, always alert to her friend's impact on the cause of woman suffrage, objected on both intellectual and strategic grounds. "You say 'women must be emancipated from their superstitions before enfranchisement will be of any benefit,'" Anthony said, "and I say just the reverse, that women must be enfranchised before they can be emancipated from their superstitions." Anthony's own feet were firmly planted on the earth, where, she was certain, all women's would be if they had their rights, "instead of living in the air with Jesus and the angels." Anthony knew she could not dissuade Stanton from writing the book, but she refused to let her name be added to the committee. She "simply [didn't] want the enemy to be diverted from *my* practical ballot fight."[57]

To Stanton, all this back-and-forth only reflected people's, even Susan's, failure to recognize her radical vision. "Let us remember that all reforms are interdependent, and that whatever is done to establish one principle on a solid basis, strengthens all," she wrote. "Reformers who are always compromising, have not yet grasped the idea that truth is the only safe ground to stand upon. The object of an individual life is not to carry one fragmentary measure in human progress, but to utter the highest truth." Once again, the sweep of Stanton's analysis was surpassed only by her self-regard, which was breathtaking. Although Anthony admitted that her friend was "doing good . . . [by] making Rome Howl," hearing Stanton refer blithely to woman suffrage as a "fragmentary measure" must have made her howl as well.[58]

The first volume of *The Woman's Bible* was published in 1895, the year Stanton turned eighty. "More polemical than scholarly," claims a leading historian, "the *Woman's Bible* was at once a Bible commentary, a spiritual guidebook, and a political treatise."[59] In it, Stanton and her colleagues offer a somewhat disjointed set of reinterpretations, retellings, and reactions to the Bible's treatment of women. On the surface, it provides a searing critique of biblical teachings and the hold they purportedly had on women. But the book is also, ironically, pervaded by an implicit preference for Protestantism over other religions, for Stanton looked forward to a day when "robust Saxon sense has flung away Jewish superstition and Eastern prejudice." Indeed, Stanton was, a woman's rights delegate from Iowa remarked, "a little hard on Judaism." But she had long ago arrived at her answer to this one; no more needed to be said than that Orthodox Jewish men prayed, "We thank thee, oh Lord that we were not born women," and she dismissed any suggestion that she was "a Jew-hater." "[O]n the contrary," she had, untruthfully, written years earlier, "some of my dearest friends are Hebrews," and she remained oblivious to the complex Jewish community and traditions, both religious and secular, in her midst.[60]

The impact of *The Woman's Bible* was less in the field of biblical criticism than in the suffrage movement itself, where the book at once touched a nerve. Even Anthony was unprepared for how bad the storm would be, or how much it would imperil Stanton's reputation. Conservative Protestant ministers immediately declared the book proof that woman suffrage was a heretical cause. At once, more conventional woman's rights supporters, especially those who saw woman suffrage as a means to abolish liquor and sin, or to establish a greater "female" morality in politics, grew alarmed and defensive. They decided to protect their association from the threat. Anthony herself might have viewed the Bible project as simply a massive distraction, but it was she who was left to defend Stanton against the firestorm she had provoked.

In public, at least, the danger remained hidden in the fall of 1895, when thousands gathered at New York's Metropolitan Opera House to celebrate Elizabeth Cady Stanton's eightieth birthday: it was the "Event of the Century," one newspaper said.[61] But only a few months later, the National American Woman Suffrage Association moved to censure the author of *The Woman's Bible* for damaging the movement she had helped found. Stanton's opponents included the movement's new leaders and strategists—Anna Howard Shaw, Carrie Chapman Catt, and Anthony's close associate Rachel Foster Avery—who declared that "our Association has been . . . much hindered by the general misconception of the relation of the organization to the so-called 'Woman's Bible' " and sought to disengage from all controversy over its positions.[62]

For once, Stanton, reduced to sending Clara Colby a steady stream of scribbled notes, regretted not attending the convention, as she begged her friends to "Do your best not to allow the association as such to take any action on The Woman's Bible" that would merely "cater to the religious bigotry of the age." But the woman suffrage platform was simply not broad or radical enough to include a discussion that "belittled the grandeur of the Scriptures and jarred painfully upon the feelings of all devout Christians." Both Stanton's letter writing and Anthony's lobbying were futile, and the convention resolved, by a vote of fifty-three to forty-one, to have "no official connection with the so-called 'Woman's Bible,' or any theological publication." This was precisely what Stanton had feared in an organization whose goals were so narrowly framed. Still, it hurt, not least because the resolution against her "would be a stain on Susan's honesty that would never be forgotten." "If I were Susan," Stanton insisted, "I would resign rather than endure any such proceeding. I have just written her a strong letter."[63]

All of this distressed Susan B. Anthony terribly. The three weeks of fighting within the association had caused her "agony of soul, with scarcely a night of sleep." She struggled between resigning the presidency and remaining to protect "the rights of the minority," and decided, to Stanton's chagrin, to remain at her post. "No, my dear," she wrote in response to Stanton's "strong letter," "instead of my resigning and leaving those half-fledged chickens without any mother, I think it my duty and the duty of yourself and all the liberals to be at the next convention and try to reverse this miserable, narrow action."[64]

Usually impervious to personal attack, Stanton was disappointed, shocked that Anthony would remain in an association that had publicly condemned her work. But she recovered her composure quickly, enjoyed the support of old friends such as Theodore Tilton, and reminded herself that she relished debate and publicity more than popularity.[65] Like all book bannings, the controversy over The Woman's Bible generated sales. "Whenever there is a lull in the sale of the Woman's Bible, some convention denounces it or some library throws it out," Stanton wrote her son Theodore wryly. "So the bigots promote the sale every time . . . The western papers have given columns to the discussion of removing it from the libraries. It is," she concluded contentedly, "a tempest in a tea-pot."[66]

Susan B. Anthony had grown weary of supporting, prodding, protecting, and excusing her intellectually reckless friend, and it must have been tempting to submit to the pressure to abandon her. Although Anthony still considered her friend the only woman whose "half-century's magnificent utterances for woman's emancipation" were worth hearing, adoring Elizabeth Cady Stanton was hard work. And if Stanton remained Anthony's most intense and complicated love, she was also responsible for great disappointment. In 1891, following the death of Stanton's son Neil and a long (and final) trip to Europe, Anthony pleaded with her friend to come live with her permanently. Instead, Stanton chose to settle with two of her children, Maggie and Bob, in New York City. Anthony tried desperately to portray her longing as for the good of the cause, but Stanton's decision had struck up "an inner wail in my soul, that by your fastening yourself in New York City I couldn't help you carry out the dream of my life—which is that you should take all of your speeches and articles, carefully dissect them, and put your best utterances on each point into one essay or lecture." Perhaps by way of apology, Stanton spent a long visit in Rochester that fall, where she and Anthony had the artist Adelaide Johnson sculpt a bust of them (Stanton hated hers, for "the curls looked just like bananas"), published pronouncements, and held receptions. For Anthony, the strain Stanton had put on their friendship was inseparable from the challenges she posed for the cause itself.[67]

But their devotion was remarkable nevertheless. Stanton remained as much in awe of Anthony's "rejoicing in more grand campaigns" as Anthony was of Stanton's intellect and her writing. "Susan is still on the war-path," Stanton informed Hattie in 1892. "All through this hot weather, she has been following the political conventions. I wrote the addresses to all and she read them and signed them as President of the Association. By resigning the office, I hoped to have done with all State Papers. But Susan keeps me at it." They had survived decades of joint projects and battles over policy and principle, and "jogged along pretty well for forty years or more," Stanton wrote Anthony, and she thought that perhaps "you and I deserve some credit for sticking together through all adverse winds, with so few ripples on the surface."[68] Throughout the uproar over *The Woman's Bible*, therefore, Anthony remained unflinchingly loyal. She had always insisted that it was "Mrs. Stanton" who had led the way, and though they disagreed heartily about strategies, priorities, and coalitions, she would not abandon her now.

If there was one thing that Susan B. Anthony and Elizabeth Cady Stanton agreed on, it was that Stanton had hardly changed. Love being blind, Anthony assured Ellen Wright Garrison in 1899 that Stanton was "just as bright and full of life as she was forty years ago." Certainly Elizabeth Cady Stanton epitomized the saying that the older people get, the more they get like themselves. She remained defiant, condescending, and proud; she would give old age no assistance in catching up to her. Undoubtedly there was more of the woman who had long ago been described as having "very solid proportions."[69] Anthony, slim and fit as ever, sometimes referred humorously to the difficulties Stanton faced because of her portliness, but as Stanton entered her seventies, her weight became a serious matter: "I have one melancholy fact to state which I do with sorrow and humiliation," she wrote Elizabeth Smith Miller. "I was weighed yesterday and brought the scales down at 240."[70] Still, Stanton, though "lumbering," remained delighted with her own good health, bragging to a medical journal, "My teeth are all sound, my hair luxuriant, my hearing perfect, and my eyes still able to read the fine print of the *New York Sun* with spectacles." And one can almost hear her giggle across the century when she consoled cousin Elizabeth about her own ailments: "I really wish I could share my health and flesh with some of our loved ones of the present generation," she wrote smugly.[71]

Stanton remained determinedly sensual in her desires and her demeanor, "a ripe grape," as Theodore Tilton had once called her, who "carries a whole summer's sunshine in her blood." Ever ready to turn her pleasures into virtues, Stanton boasted often about her "genius for sleep." "The insane asylums," she declared confidently, "are full of people whose sweet morning slumbers have been rudely broken by some ignorant theorist." Nor was Stanton shy about her comforts and her appetites. On one trip to Glasgow, others stayed in the "Temperance Hotel," but her hosts apparently "thought my temperance opinions were not sufficiently strong to lead me to prefer a small hotel built on sound principles to a good one on [a] more worldly basis." This was, she remarked, "a rational conclusion for which I am truly thankful."[72] Her vanity remained intact as well.[73] Elizabeth Cady Stanton never lost her stubborn belief that she had been spared the weaknesses of ordinary mortals, or that her achievements were due entirely to "the self-assertiveness and determination of my character." Through her eighties, she cheerfully wrote Harriot and Theodore about her many "pronunciamentos, so you may see that I am still trying to reform the world with my pen," and boasted of what she had earned.[74] Her days were full and productive, even when she could no longer see well: "The daily *Tribune* and four weekly papers are read to me regularly, to all of which I send short articles," she informed Harriot. "But all this does not prevent me from working in two good naps every day." In public, she continued to insist that "old age [is] the heyday of life—the grandest season that time allots to mortals." Nor did her humor falter, even when it concerned a physical indignity that happened to come her way. Caught in a rainstorm one day with her cousin and guests, Stanton's picnicking party had to walk: "Can you imagine me on the highway, hobbling alone with a cane, dripping wet, my thin garments all clinging to my robust person?" she asked Theodore in her next letter. "How humiliating for 'the champion of her sex!'"[75]

But though her mind remained sharp, and her ego intact, Stanton increasingly needed assistance to see, to write, and to walk. Susan B. Anthony refused to accept this, and she berated her friend about getting up and doing more. The 1898 convention in Washington, which commemorated the fiftieth anniversary of Seneca Falls, and which Anthony insisted was *the most* important convention yet, sorely tried Anthony's skills at seducing Stanton away from home; it also underscored her refusal to give up. "Now my dear," Anthony begged (though who would believe her?), "this is positively the last time I am ever going to put you on the rack and torture you to make the speech or the speeches of your life." But Anthony's pleading confronted Stanton's growing immobility, her dimming eyesight, and the barrier of Maggie and Bob's care and caution. Anthony stubbornly held to the view that Stanton was just being lazy and that Maggie exaggerated in her "discouraging presentation of her mother's condition." Anthony's friends thought "I should give up all hope of getting Mrs. Stanton to Washington," but "All that [Elizabeth Stanton] says about dreading the journey has been just as true of her on every occasion for the last forty years, as to-day." However mightily she tried to deny Stanton's growing infirmity, Anthony could hardly deny that she might one day face a far deeper loss: "I have a feeling that every pen-scratch I receive from her may possibly be the last," she admitted. "Therefore I keep them all as sacred as so many nuggets of gold." Stanton's absence at the convention that year would turn out to be only one sign of the frailty of the older generation of activists; Frances Willard, who brought to the suffrage movement the support of the enormous Woman's Christian Temperance Union, died during the week.[76]

There were many deaths, of course: Martha Coffin Wright in 1875, her sister Lucretia Mott in 1880, William Lloyd Garrison in 1879, Wendell Phillips and Sarah Pugh in 1884. By the 1890s the remaining "pioneers" of the antislavery and woman's rights move- ments seemed always to be writing obituaries. Even when she was not present at national conventions, Stanton wrote, and Anthony read, numerous such tributes: in 1893 to John Greenleaf Whittier and Ernestine Rose; and the following year, to Lucy Stone, "one of the most effective speakers and earnest pioneers of our movement." Hav- ing outlived her rival, Stanton could not stop herself from recalling their "earnest debate on the comparative degradation of the educated women of the North and the ignorant slaves of the South." "Like all those baptized into the anti-slavery reform," Stanton explained, appar- ently forgetting that she considered herself one of that sect, Lucy "felt the slaves' wrongs more deeply than her own," whereas she "saw and felt the wrongs of women more deeply than any other class."[77]

Frederick Douglass's tribute to Lucy Stone pointedly struck a dif- ferent note. Rather than resurrect old schisms directly, Douglass con- fronted the woman's rights audience with the racial injustice that still plagued the nation. This was not a parlor debate limited to "the early days," Douglass insisted. "While I sincerely admire her work for woman's suffrage," Douglass declared, "you will pardon me if my trib- ute to her is mainly due for what she was and what she did for the cause of the slave in the dark hours of his need."[78] Exactly one year later, after attending a meeting of the National Council of Women, Douglass, too, would be dead. "He was the only man I ever knew who understood the degradation of disfranchisement for woman," Eliza- beth Cady Stanton mourned.[79]

But tribute writing was dull and depressing, and it tried Stanton's patience to be nice; she much preferred firing missiles to "dwelling on [people's] graces, virtues, and heroic deeds." When Anthony begged for some eulogistic comments for the 1896 convention, Stanton complained that she hated becoming "a sort of spiritual undertaker for the pioneers of the woman suffrage movement" and wished that "some of our younger coadjutors [would] do the bubbling."[80] Still, all that memorializing reminded Stanton that there was one person whose "spiritual undertaker" she was anxious to be. So amid speeches and letters and a never-ending stream of articles, she wrote the story of her life.

Eighty Years and More, which appeared in installments in Clara Colby's *Woman's Tribune* and was finally published in 1898, is pure Stanton, for good and ill. Like all memoirs, it relies heavily on individual memory, and Stanton was notoriously loose with facts; but the book represents a remarkable effort to shape the historical meaning of the cause of woman's rights through Stanton's personal tale. It is here that she tells the story of a smart, independent girl who had been insulted by her father's preference for boys and who had turned the affront into a philosophy of woman's rights. It is here too that she conflates her own initiation into woman's rights with the emergence of the idea itself, apparently forgetting Lucretia Mott's warning that woman's rights activism had begun several years before she arrived on the scene. *Eighty Years and More* presents Elizabeth Cady Stanton as largely harmless, benign, and motherly. "She did not," admits one historian, "depict incidents in which she might appear to be radical, arrogant, heretical, demanding, self-centered, or difficult to live with," all of which she surely was, as well as elitist, stubborn, uncompromising, and smug. She presents her life as "a series of minor challenges" that she faced alone, and that she overcame through the power of her own mind.[81] She thus locates in her own personal story the story of all women's obstacles, limitations, and ambitions. It is a profoundly American epic tale of one girl's struggle to remake herself into a person worthy of the rights she demanded for all women.

Bob Stanton had borrowed $1,000 to publish *Eighty Years and More*. His mother welcomed the book proudly and hawked it widely. She shamelessly asked "all my rich friends to take five or ten copies, to distribute among their impecunious friends & neighbors, that the

Book may reach as many women as possible." The reformer Emily Howland received Stanton's plea in February, and evidently agreed to do as she asked: a 2006 listing in a rare books website offered a copy of *Eighty Years* with the following inscription: "Lydia King / from her friend / Emily Howland. / Sherwood / May 23, 1898." To some of her correspondents Stanton offered guidance about which section of the book might offer "some hints" for their own work.[82]

Nor was Stanton shy about soliciting reviews—or offering editors helpful advice about what to say. "My publisher sent you to day 'Eighty Years & More' my reminiscences just issued," she wrote William Lloyd Garrison, Jr. "I write to ask you to review it for the Nation in as complimentary a manner as your literary conscience will permit. Your Father & family are mentioned as they deserve." But for sheer brazenness, the review in the New York *Journalist* won the day. Even its author admitted that "An editor's request that I review my own book was quite startling." Still, "After my first surprise," Stanton continued, "the idea struck me as a good one. Who could so well review a book as the one who knew all about its conception, birth and introduction to the world of letters?" She went on, largely tongue in cheek, to discuss the book's strengths, conceding, quite rightly, that "The first chapters are the best in the book."[83]

Stanton did not remain satisfied reflecting on the past. With her mind racing from topic to topic, she wrote with passion about urban filth, the "jackasses" in the legislature, the Spanish-American War, injustices toward women in Hawaii, women's right to ride bicycles, strikes in Chicago, capital punishment, prisons, public reading rooms, books she had read, and recipes she had tried. She undertook a lonely campaign against "Some of our conservative churchmen . . . [who wished] to enforce a more rigid observance of sabbatical ordinances": "They are opposed to opening the libraries, picture galleries, museums and concert halls, on the only day when the laboring masses have an opportunity to visit them," she wrote, furious as ever. Newspapers were always happy to publish, and pay for, her words.[84]

There were moments of absurdity, too. In an 1896 advertisement, Elizabeth Cady Stanton endorsed Paine's Celery Compound, a restorative for elderly women, widely sold in its amber bottles. "This Great American Recommends Paine's Celery Compound to Those

Who Suffer From Nervous Ills," the ad declared, although it is impossible to imagine Stanton having, much less admitting to, any such ailment. "Fairbank's Fairy Soap" used her famous image as well, with her assurance that "It leaves the skin soft and velvety, and I particularly like it because it is as free from odor as the air and sunshine. I abhor a perfumed woman." Then there was the little fire in the apartment on West Sixty-first Street where Stanton lived with Maggie and Bob. For Stanton, there was only one possible lesson in both the shoddy construction of the flooring and in the fire department's reluctant response: "[W]omen," she assured a reporter, "could have done better than that." "Many wrongs I see yet to be righted," she remarked to an old friend in 1895. "My last undertaking is to clean up the Continent."[85]

Not surprisingly, Stanton viewed the accomplishments and priorities of younger women—the first "postfeminist" generation—with mixed feelings. While Stanton and Anthony applauded—and, with some justification, took credit for—the opportunities available to Stanton's daughters and Anthony's "suffrage nieces," both women fretted over the younger generation's indifference, and sometimes hostility, to the cause of woman's rights. An anti-suffrage petition by fifty women in Massachusetts had irritated her to no end, Stanton informed Anthony. "The one who headed the petition was a graduate of Wellesley College; just think of it," she sniffed. "After entering in and reaping the advantage of our agitation, she turns and kicks down the ladder by which she climbed."[86]

Although she insisted that "I do not cultivate any feelings of revenge or hostility," more personal resentments sometimes leaked out.[87] She had made her choices, and they had been impolitic ones, but it hurt that younger women worshipped Susan B. Anthony, and not her, as the symbolic founder of the cause. Anthony's supporters had often given her gifts of cash; at her seventy-fifth birthday dinner, led by her "loving and loved first adopted niece, Rachel Foster Avery," they presented the suffrage leader with an $800 annuity. Stanton loyally insisted that "Dear Susan deserves all she has received," but it rankled. "If my Suffrage coadjutors had ever treated me with the boundless generosity they have my friend Susan," she wrote another associate, "I could have scattered my writings abundantly from Maine to Louisiana. They have given Susan thousands of dollars, jewels, laces, silks and satins, and me, criticisms and denunciations for my radical ideas."[88] Being oppositional by conviction and temperament, it turned out, was a mixed bag.

In spite of herself, by the fall of 1902, Stanton's health had failed badly, and Harriot and Nora arrived from Europe "glad to be with mother again," Hattie reported, since she "needs Maggy or me to be near her constantly." Harriot pressed Anthony gently to "be in New York at the time of the 87*th* birthday as I'm sure there wont be another." Even then, Stanton refused to quiet down. True, she had to dictate her letters now, but this only increased the pace of her advice and observations. Late that September she approached Ida Husted Harper, who was already overwhelmed with writing Anthony's biography and editing the *History of Woman Suffrage*, about taking on a volume of her speeches and miscellaneous writings. "[Y]ou are just the one," she wrote, "to give the finishing touch to *my* literary efforts." She went on chattily, warning Harper of the dangers of overexertion—for Anthony. "She & [President Theodore] Roosevelt are the nearest examples of perpetual motion that we have yet had illustrated by any man & woman," Stanton scolded, "and now Roosevelt is flat on his back for his many indiscretions." "If," she continued with the hubris of someone who believed firmly in her own good health, "when Roosevelt's leg first pained him, he had stopped careening about, and rested under his own roof, he might now be enjoying perfect health." "The fact is," she concluded, without a touch of irony, "he is vain of seeming so strong and active and I am afraid there is a touch of the same feeling in Susan."[89]

President Roosevelt may have been "flat on his back," but that did not prevent Elizabeth Cady Stanton from appealing to him from her own bed. She had already noted that he and Abraham Lincoln were "the only heads of the nation who have ever declared themselves openly in favor of woman suffrage," and now, smoothly glossing over her own dislike for Lincoln, she urged that "what President Lincoln did for the colored race, President Roosevelt should do for the thirty-five million educated, law-abiding, tax-paying women in the United States." She then wrote two letters, one each to the president and his wife, Edith, urging Roosevelt to speak out for woman suffrage in his message to Congress.[90] With Maggie, Harriot, and Bob around to care for her physical needs, and so much trouble left to make, Stanton did not waste time musing about her own mortality. Most likely she never believed in it.

Certainly Susan B. Anthony didn't. The telegram arrived at Anthony's house on October 26, 1902: "Mother passed away today," Harriot had written. Anthony was flat out astounded by the news, and she scrawled on the message, "First *Telegram* of Mrs. Stanton's death—or indication of her illness!!" Probably her death took Stanton as much by surprise, for Theodore mourned "that mother herself had to go *in spite of herself.*" Later that day another telegram arrived in Rochester: "Private funeral for you & ourselves only, Wednesday eleven."[91]

Elizabeth Cady Stanton took up a lot of space, physically, intellectually, and emotionally, in life, and she remained a presence in death as well. First, there was the matter of her brain, which the freethinker and suffragist Helen Gardener claimed Stanton had agreed to give to Cornell University. Harriot was outraged, refusing to consider that her mother might so "pain those nearest to her and whom she loved," but she was wrong. Fifteen years earlier, Gardener had asked Stanton to "arrange and get your children to agree to have your brain preserved and analysed when you are done with it." "The brain of no great woman, nor even of a remarkable one, has ever yet been preserved," Gardener ("Heathen Helen," she signed her note) wrote. Brain weight was a matter of some interest to late-nineteenth-century Americans, and the readers of the woman's rights press knew that men's average brain weight (forty-nine ounces) was greater than women's (forty-four ounces); the assumption was widely shared that "the size and weight of the brain are in direct relation to the mental capacity." On the back of Gardener's missive, in Stanton's hand, appears the cheerful directive, "You must save my brain for Heathen Helen's statistics." This was neither a secret nor a joke; in 1900, Gardener published a poem to Stanton about their brains being bequeathed to Cornell "for the benefit of science," and in February 1900, Stanton approved a "Bequest of Brain to Cornell University" that sits in its archives still.[92]

The funeral was small, especially for someone who so loved being the center of a party. Stanton's children were there, as were old friends and a few younger suffragists; Antoinette Brown Blackwell and the abolitionist Moncure Conway helped lead the service, and close relatives, such as Elizabeth Smith Miller, came great distances to attend. The casket was covered with flowers, with Susan B. Anthony's picture displayed above it. Anthony believed, plausibly, that Stanton wished to be cremated, but her children had her buried rather conventionally, with her brain still inside her head, in the Bronx.[93] A prominent headstone reads, "Mother Author Orator Woman Suffrage Leader" and lists some of her accomplishments.

The public and the private were as inseparable in Elizabeth Cady Stanton's death as they had been in her life. Headlines proclaimed the news, and obituaries overflowed with praise. Newspapers throughout the world celebrated Stanton's contributions to a movement nearly all had once scorned. Though few went so far as the *Free Thought Magazine* in calling her "the greatest woman that the world has ever produced," there was much editorial self-congratulation that Stanton's demand for woman suffrage, once deemed so radical, was now so widely shared. Even the *New York Tribune*, which had long continued Horace Greeley's revenge of referring to Stanton as "Mrs. Henry Stanton," honored her in its obituary by giving her, at last, "the name by which the world knew her."[94]

Friends wrote Susan B. Anthony that they could "hardly imagine" her personal loss, and indeed, she was stunned by grief.[95] None of the deaths of parents, siblings, colleagues, and friends had prepared Anthony for this, and none of the accolades or condolences helped. Struggling desperately to remember that it was the cause that mattered, she spoke to a local reporter the day after Stanton's death about her friend's life and work. "I cannot express myself at all as I feel," she admitted, unable for once to maintain the facade of commitment and detachment that she had worked to perfect. "I am too crushed to say much, but if she had outlived me she would have found fine words with which to express our friendship. I can't say it in words. She always said she wished to outlive me, that she might pay her tribute to me to the world, for she knew I couldn't pay my tribute to her." Letters kept arriving, expressing sympathy and loss, but Anthony could not quite absorb it: "it is an awful hush," she wrote Ida Husted

Harper, "it seems impossible—that the voice is hushed—that I have longed to hear for 50 years." Months later, still staggering, she cried to Theodore Stanton, "Dear me! how lonesome I do feel, not to have any Mrs. Stanton to write to, to think of going to see, and talking to! It was a great going out of my life when she went, but she is gone not to return and we only can follow, where? and answers, where?"[96]

Stanton took some time to quiet down even after her death. She had been so busy dictating articles in her final days that newspapers were still printing them for weeks to come. Indeed, a small competition arose over which published statement—the one about marriage and divorce laws, or about the church's hold over women, or about the prospects for a suffrage victory—was Stanton's actual "last word." Eerily, the words tumbled out for days and weeks after she had been buried. A year later, on what would have been Stanton's eighty-eighth birthday, Anthony did what she did best: she organized a meeting. The Rochester press accorded it prominent space: "Honors Paid to a Dead Leader. Interesting Gathering at the Anthony Home. Elizabeth Cady Stanton. Anniversary of her Birthday Observed by Suffrage Sympathizers Under Roof of the Last of the Great Leaders, Susan B. Anthony."[97]

CONCLUSION

I f I could live my life over again," Elizabeth Cady Stanton wrote to her daughter Harriot Stanton Blatch at the age of eighty-four, "it seems to me I would more conscientiously guard every word and thought." Perhaps so, though Hattie may have thought it unlikely. The pleasure of speaking out, of provoking opposition, and of being so clearly—in her mind at least—*right* about everything was too great to resist. But Stanton did feel some disquiet about what she would leave behind. Sometime in the mid-1890s, she "look[ed] over my papers, destroying many and putting the rest in order." "Well," she noted cheerfully, "I have thinned mine out and may try it again should I remain on this planet half a dozen years longer." She would die six years later almost to the day, without recording any further bursts of thinning. Her children would take up that chore where she left off; Harriot in particular devoted herself to polishing up her mother's historical memory in what she viewed as the best interests of her mother and the cause.[1]

Elizabeth Cady Stanton was happy to risk public censure for an idea, but she was careful to nurture the seeds of her legacy as a radical thinker long before she had completed her work. In 1869, biographer James Parton and others compiled *Eminent Women of the Age*, a collective biography in which Elizabeth Cady Stanton appears, uniquely, as both a subject and a major contributor. Stanton's section on "The Woman's Rights Movement and Its Champions in the United States," with laudatory biographies of fourteen of her friends and associates, was her first foray into history writing. In another chapter, Theodore Tilton takes on the task of writing Stanton's own biography; he apologized that his sketch was but a "poor, opaque copy" of an extraordinary woman, and he quoted her words at length. Here readers learned that Elizabeth Cady Stanton was the originator of the very notion of woman's rights: by calling the convention at Seneca Falls she had "jarred . . . into sudden wakefulness" women's "slumbering" political rights. She was also, in Tilton's gushing account, the kindest woman alive, with "a perpetual good-humor, and an irresistible flow of spirits." "Pity is her chief vice," he noted, "charity, her besetting sin." In truth she was a saint: "She would willingly give her body to be burned, for the sake of seeing her sex enfranchised."[2]

Hardly anyone was as over the top as Tilton, but Stanton was mindful of how even her friends influenced her historical reputation, and she rectified their alleged errors when she could. In 1899, William Lloyd Garrison, Jr., published a list of living abolitionists in *The Nation* that, purposely or not, omitted her name. Stanton was furious: "As I am proud of my record as an abolitionist and as I am still living, I would like to be mentioned as one of the soldiers in that grand battle against slavery," she informed him. ". . . In your next public pronunciamento, please accord me the honor of being an abolitionist, and being still alive to declare the faith that is in me."[3] Stanton was acutely aware of her place in history, and was eager to be remembered for representing the cutting edge of every radical thought and act of her generation.

Oppositional skeptics such as Elizabeth Cady Stanton are tough to nail down, and evaluating Stanton's legacy has never been easy. If she had stayed still, rather than leaping from one outrageous idea to another, it would be simpler to label her contributions. If she had lived to see the fulfillment of major legislation on behalf of women—the Nineteenth Amendment, most obviously, but also an equal rights amendment not formulated in her lifetime—assessing her impact would be more straightforward. But Stanton's genius lay in her very momentum: in her impatience with limiting herself even to the radical demand for suffrage, in her efforts to loosen the laws of marriage and divorce, and in her opposition to the pervasive power that organized religion had over women's lives. Given her tendency to utter the most radical conclusion she could imagine at any given time, it is not surprising that her legacy has remained slippery, or that the next generation of activists saw in Susan B. Anthony a more appropriate icon for the march to woman suffrage.

By the early twentieth century, Anthony was widely celebrated as the sole founder and leader of the cause of woman's rights. On some level the confusion between Stanton and Anthony had long been a joke: Theodore Tilton playfully noted, "It has been sometimes suspected that Mrs. Stanton and Miss Anthony are two distinct persons, united by a cartilage like the Siamese twins, but in the absence of any medical or other scientific proof of this hypothesis, I remain of the opinion that, like Liberty and Union, they are 'one and inseparable.'" But seventy years after Elizabeth Cady Stanton declared suffrage a central component of woman's rights, her name was largely absent from the reports of its achievement. "Senators to Vote on Suffrage Today," read the headline in the *New York Times* in 1918. "Fate of Susan B. Anthony Amendment Hangs in Balance on Eve of Final Test."[4]

This labeling of the Nineteenth Amendment irritated Harriot Stanton Blatch to no end. Perhaps her campaign to resurrect her mother's memory might therefore be seen merely as a personal grievance. But there were more serious consequences to activists' and historians' acceptance of Susan B. Anthony's sole leadership, and in Anthony's tight focus on mobilizing for the right to vote, in shaping how we think about woman's rights itself. Within a few years of her death, Stanton had been largely superseded by her friend in movement legend, her reputation damaged by the *Woman's Bible* controversy and by her insistence on being remembered as an intellectual radical. Several controversial and unsavory biographies and movement histories further hardened this view. After the achievement of woman suffrage, activists sought to find their place in American history and politics, now clouded, as were all progressive causes, by the conservative post–World War I atmosphere. As part of that postwar movement, Harriot Stanton Blatch sought urgently to "rehabilitate her mother's historical reputation" and to grant her the prominence she deserved. She collaborated with Alma Lutz on a 1940 biography, providing personal stories, family lore, and a mid-twentieth-century assessment of

Stanton's once-radical views on marriage, divorce, and sex.[5] By then, of course, few were seeking feminist icons in the American past.

With the rise of a new feminist movement in the late 1960s and 1970s and the emergence of academic women's history, Elizabeth Cady Stanton gained new celebrity. The very things that signaled the decline of her reputation earlier on, especially her views on marriage and motherhood, gained new favor. Nearly all high school and college U.S. history textbooks now include the obligatory inset about Stanton and Seneca Falls, though they are inevitably both overblown and overly narrow. Biographies by Elisabeth Griffith and Lois Banner were valuable celebrations of Stanton's intellectual and political legacy, establishing her, in some sense, as the founding mother of a century of rights-bearing women. A movie by Ken Burns, *Not for Ourselves Alone*, further publicized Stanton and Anthony as a pair without whom, as one historian put it with some exaggeration, "there is no women's history." Serious histories of the radicalism of the woman suffrage movement, notably by Ellen Carol DuBois, placed Elizabeth Cady Stanton squarely in a national political narrative, and thus refused to isolate women intellectually from the larger world of which Stanton herself was very much a part. Conferences and collections of articles—including a forum honoring Stanton on the occasion of the one hundredth anniversary of her death—have offered more nuanced explorations of Stanton's political legacy.[6] The last thirty years of scholarship have greatly complicated our understanding of nineteenth-century reform movements, of elite women's cultural and political authority, of the pervasiveness of racism and economic inequalities, and of American women's identities based on their race, class, religion, and region. All this work has reshaped how we think about each and every leading political thinker in this nation's history, Stanton among them.

This book offers a view of Elizabeth Cady Stanton that is more critical and, I think, more complicated than any of these. By setting Stanton firmly in her time and place, it refuses to dismiss either her relationship to a community of reformers or her elitism and racism. Stanton's fiery words on behalf of woman's rights offer stunning moments of moral absolutism in the American liberal tradition. She had a thrilling ability to hone in on one facet of the world's complexity: the fact that, by virtue of being born female, women were considered lesser than men, which in turn explained denying them the rights necessary to independence itself. She was brilliant at pulling together strands of thought that floated past and turning them into a coherent set of arguments about one of the most pervasive categories of American life: gender itself. Once she had digested and polished a thought, she had a way with words that few could match. Intellectually impatient, she thought and wrote at a pace that left most people breathless. She welcomed applause and censure in about equal measure—and hardly ever suffered any doubts about the utter correctness of her views.

Elizabeth Cady Stanton left a huge legacy, and it gets no smaller by complicating it; for all her limitations, few nineteenth-century women loom quite as large. But Stanton was as flawed and complex as other human beings, and the limitations in her thinking have shaped some of the limitations in more contemporary movements for social change, feminism included. They influence how we conceive of rights, and how we go about expanding them; they shape whom we embrace as worthy of equality and independence, and whom we consider lesser or marginal or alien. Stanton insisted that the rights and responsibilities of individual citizenship be granted to women on the same terms that they were granted to men, and she demanded that state, church, and family adapt to that truth; it is hard, now, to argue with her logic, even harder to imagine how frightening it all was to her opposition. But if Stanton's power lay in her absolutism, so did her weakness. Like most people who are utterly sure that theirs is the only way to view the world, Stanton did not, or not really, allow her political imagination to include the myriad people who were largely outside the borders of her particular American experience. She simply could not see that other priorities, other ways of viewing political authority, or other communal or collective identities might reflect equally radical understandings of social transformation. Nor did Stanton consider that her own privileged position, including her identification with the nation's founding elite, constituted as narrow a perch as anyone else's from which to declaim universal truths. Her legacy to us is complicated by the fact that she could not evaluate her own prejudices, her racism, or her astonishing positive self-regard, and that she failed to acknowledge the moral complexity of those who disagreed with her.

How do we measure the success of an idea? Traditionally, scholars have argued that the very length of time that it took to gain passage of the federal woman suffrage amendment—some seventy years after the demand was formally made—meant that the idea was anathema to most Americans. Indeed, politicians were relatively slow to notice that the idea of woman suffrage had seeped into the woodwork, that it had, little by little, crept out of conventions of radical reformers and into the schools where their daughters learned, and the magazines they read. If we are to judge from the crowds that gathered to hear Stanton and her colleagues speak, the press reports, and the serious consideration of the subject by politicians, the idea of women voting was, by the post–Civil War decades, a matter of common discussion. It was by then harder to take seriously the Pennsylvania legislator who in 1872 referred to woman suffrage as "this startling innovation, this pernicious heresy." Decades before its final passage, woman suffrage had come to seem in many circles both inevitable and unremarkable, a plank of respectable liberals, not outrageous or marginal radicals. That this demand could be seen, as Theodore Tilton reflected on the occasion of Stanton's eightieth birthday, as "your mere typical claim for the ballot," underscores this achievement. By then, Stanton had gathered up her intellect, her courage, her outrage, and her flaws, and had moved on.[7]

It is impossible not to wonder who Elizabeth Cady Stanton would have been had she been born a century and a half later—an exercise that tells us a great deal about both her and ourselves. Stanton was an ambitious daughter of wealthy parents whose own daughters attended Vassar; she would no doubt have attended, and excelled at, an elite college. After graduation, given her firm belief that the law both created injustice and could resolve it, she would have become a lawyer. Neither meticulous nor patient, and known for her intellectual acumen and witty writing (one scholar believes she had "the most astute legal mind of her generation of reformers"), she might have become a professor and a scholar.[8] Students would have found her a demanding teacher; colleagues would have thought her better at declaring great innovations than at carrying them out; administrators would have pulled their hair out at her dismissiveness of institutional constraints. Perhaps she would have met a modern version of Henry Stanton who would support her ambitions, defend her cause, and be her shadow; probably not. Certainly she would have had fewer than seven children. Brilliant, passionate about legal and social change, and happy to charm politicians, Elizabeth Cady might have become a judge. If one needs any evidence of the change from her time to ours, consider how little the imagination must stretch to picture her sitting on the Supreme Court, or to reflect on the searing briefs she would have composed. She would have loved writing dissents.

It is ironic and, to generations of professional women, humbling, however, to note that almost any career a contemporary Elizabeth Cady Stanton followed would have offered her a narrower scope than the one she actually inhabited. The nineteenth century grievously restricted economic, political, and intellectual opportunities for women such as Stanton, and we ought to feel no sentimental longing to go back. But in that time and place, with a plethora of reform movements and an eager audience for new ideas, Stanton became a public intellectual with a stature and impact that is now inconceivable. The opportunity to form and join social movements offered expansive opportunities to her and to other women of her generation to think and act independently, to share in what Oliver Wendell Holmes, Jr. (an actual "Great Dissenter" on the Supreme Court), once called "the passion and action" of their times.[9] She could elaborate theories and positions and strategies without restraint; propose her ideas to attentive crowds of activists; and command the respectful attention of the nation's leading politicians. Through the podium and the press, she challenged the commonplace assumptions of her time, and counted on her opponents to scatter her ideas so widely that they hardly noticed that they had helped make them acceptable. Her own career offered material support, which she needed; travel, which she sometimes hated; and public adulation, which she always loved; it guaranteed that she would never lack for argument or controversy. At a time when women's intellects were said to be inferior to men's, Elizabeth Cady Stanton used hers to become internationally famous, to be loved by admiring strangers, and to change the world.

And change it she did. Indeed, Stanton's confidence in the rightness of her views was matched only by her conviction that they would ultimately triumph. "This sounds like a very radical proposition now," she predicted more than once, "but be sure that some day in the future Americans will ask how these things could ever have been done otherwise."[10] For all her flaws and limitations, Stanton prodded an entire nation into envisioning women as full citizens, and with such success that it is indeed difficult to imagine that it was only recently any other way. Yet even as we measure it an achievement that many of her once-radical demands are so widely accepted, Stanton herself barely paused before excavating yet more evidence of women's oppression and shattering the assumptions on which it rested. It is perhaps in her intellectual momentum, her unwillingness to rest satisfied with the pace and nature of change, that we find the lesson and the legacy of Elizabeth Cady Stanton's life.

NOTES

A word about citations. If a quote appears in Ann D. Gordon, ed., *The Selected Papers of Elizabeth Cady Stanton and Susan B. Anthony* (New Brunswick, N.J.: Rutgers University Press, 1997–2006), volumes 1–4, I have cited it there, as the most accessible and reliable source. A date in square brackets reflects Gordon's best guess; her overall discussion of editorial practice can be found in *Selected Papers* 1:xxxiii–xxxviii. When a document was not included in *Selected Papers*, I relied on Patricia Holland and Ann D. Gordon's microfilm collection, *The Papers of Elizabeth Cady Stanton and Susan B. Anthony* (Wilmington, Del.: Scholarly Resources, 1991), which contains nearly all speeches, letters, newspaper clippings, and diaries. The microfilm sources are scattered throughout many archives and private collections; I have cited them as "Film," with the microfilm reel number. A date in square brackets is Holland and Gordon's estimate, although I have cited printed sources with their date of publication so that readers can find them elsewhere. In those cases when the microfilm copied documents directly from Theodore Weld Stanton and Harriot Stanton Blatch, eds., *Elizabeth Cady Stanton*, or Ida Husted Harper's *Life and Work of Susan B. Anthony*, I have cited those sources as the most accessible, recognizing that each is, in its own way, problematic. Here, too, brackets indicate Holland and Gordon's dating.

I have struggled mightily to resist the scholar's habit of offering additional citations in support of particular points. In those instances when I have succumbed, I have tried to cite examples that appear in *Selected Papers*, since they are both the most available to readers and offer excellent explanations and annotations.

INTRODUCTION

1. Article by ECS, March 15, [1883], in Gordon, ed., *Selected Papers*, 4:224.
2. ECS, "My Grace," inscription to Elizabeth Boynton Harbert, n.d., Film, Reel 45. She would frequently inscribe this on the backs of her photos and in books as well. See also *New Era* 1, Nov. 1885, 327, Film, Reel 24, for slightly different wording.
3. Elizabeth Cady Stanton, *Eighty Years and More: Reminiscences 1815–1897* (New

York: Schocken Books, 1971; reprinted from T. Fisher Unwin edition, 1898), 300–301.

4. ECS to Susan B. Anthony, [Sept. 10], 1855, in Theodore Weld Stanton and Harriot Stanton Blatch, eds., *Elizabeth Cady Stanton* (hereafter *ECS*) (New York: Harper & Bros., 1922), 2:59–60.

5. Rogers M. Smith, *Civic Ideals: Conflicting Visions of Citizenship in U.S. History* (New Haven, Conn.: Yale University Press, 1997), 3.

6. Ellen Carol DuBois, *Harriot Stanton Blatch and the Winning of Woman Suffrage* (New Haven, Conn.: Yale University Press, 1997), 37.

7. Harriot Stanton Blatch and Alma Lutz, *Challenging Years: The Memoirs of Harriot Stanton Blatch* (New York: G.P. Putnam's Sons, 1940), 34. Four-year-old Helen Blatch died in 1896 in England. Elizabeth Cady Stanton remained stoic, at least publicly; Harriot Blatch, as determinedly composed as her mother, never mentioned her second child in her memoir. Theodore Stanton rushed to England to attend the "sad affair" of the child's funeral and cremation; he reported that his sister "broke down for a moment on meeting me but she does not look so worn out as I feared would be the case. She has worked like a Trojan since Thursday" (Theodore Stanton to ECS, June 14, 1896, Film, Reel 35). That Theodore's letter ended up in Clara Colby's papers suggests that Stanton, rather than rewrite the news, simply forwarded her son's letter to her friends. On Anthony's distress, see SBA to Harriot Stanton Blatch, July 3, 1896, Film, Reel 35.

8. ECS to Martha Coffin Wright, March 8, [1873], in Gordon, ed., *Selected Papers*, 2:597.

9. Theodore Tilton, "Mrs. Elizabeth Cady Stanton," in James Parton, et al., *Eminent Women of the Age* (Hartford, Conn: S. M. Betts & Co., 1869), 358; Elizabeth Cady Stanton, Diary, in Stanton and Blatch, eds., *ECS*, 2:192; ECS, "Reminiscences of Angelina Grimké," in Elizabeth Cady Stanton, Susan B. Anthony, and Matilda Joslyn Gage, *History of Woman Suffrage* (hereafter referred to as *HWS*) (New York: Fowler and Wells, 1881), 1:392; ECS to Elizabeth Cady McMartin Baldwin, May 29, [1883], Film, Reel 23.

10. ECS to Mary B. Hall, March 12, [1869], Film, Reel 13.

11. ECS to Paulina Wright Davis, [April 1, 1871], Film, Reel 15.

12. ECS to Sara Jane Lippincott, May 30, 1873, Stanton and Blatch, eds., *ECS*, 2:141.

13. ECS to SBA, Matilda Joslyn Gage, [before July 10], 1873, Film, Reel 17; ECS to Theodore Stanton, March 2, [1896], Film, Reel 35.

14. ECS to Harriot Stanton Blatch, *Woman's Journal*, Jan. 5, 1895, Film, Reel 33; ECS to Clara Colby, [Dec. 1885], Film, Reel 24 ("In your chapter please avoid the following words, to wit. 'Suffragists' 'old workers' 'pioneers in the field' 'in the harness' 'women dentists' 'lady lawyers' 'gentlemen friends' 'women teachers.' "); ECS to SBA, (Jan. 8, 1887), in Gordon, ed., *Selected Papers*, 4:539. Like many letters written by Stanton while she was in Europe, this one was quoted in Clara Colby's *Woman's Tribune*, March 1887, and was also quoted with slightly different wording as a letter to the 1887 National Woman Suffrage Association convention, *HWS*, 4:113. Also see "Mrs. Stanton on Literary Style," *Woman's Tribune*, May 16, 1903, Film, Reel 24; ECS to Editor, *Woman's Journal*, March 13, 1886, Film, Reel 24.

15. Tilton, "Mrs. Elizabeth Cady Stanton," 360; ECS to SBA, [Aug. 1883], Film, Reel 23.
16. There are many reports of this event on Film, Reel 34. See, for example, "Event of the Century," *New York Recorder*, Nov. 13, 1895; "Honors for Mrs. Stanton," *New York Tribune*, Nov. 13, 1895; *Woman's Tribune* (Washington, D.C.), Dec. 28, 1895; "More Adoration for Mrs. Stanton," *New York Herald*, Nov. 24, 1895; *San Francisco Chronicle*, Nov. 13, 1895.
17. SBA to Mary Anthony, Jan. 26, 1883, in Ida Husted Harper, *The Life and Work of Susan B. Anthony* (hereafter *SBA*), 3 vols. (Indianapolis, Ind.: The Hollenbeck Press, 1898; 1908), 2:565; Marietta Holley, *My Opinions and Betsey Bobbet's* (Hartford, Conn.: American Publishing Co., 1875), 313–14.
18. ECS to Olympia Brown, May 8, [1889], Film, Reel 27.
19. ECS, "The Solitude of Self" (1892), in Ellen Carol DuBois, ed., *Elizabeth Cady Stanton/Susan B. Anthony: Correspondence, Writings, Speeches* (New York: Schocken Books, 1981), 251.
20. ECS to Theodore W. Stanton, Nov. 2, 1880, in Gordon, ed., *Selected Papers*, 4:14; Edward P. Furlong, Account of ECS Attempt to Vote, Nov. 3, 1880, Film, Reel 21. In 1868, women in Vineland, New Jersey, had voted, casting 157 Republican votes and 4 Democratic ones; 7 of the women were African American (*Revolution* 2:19, Nov. 12, 1868, 289).
21. ECS to Elizabeth Boynton Harbert, July 25, 1901, Film, Reel 42; DuBois, *Harriot Stanton Blatch*, 243.
22. Amy Dykeman, "To Look a Gift Horse in the Mouth: The History of the Theodore Stanton Collection," *Journal of Library History* 17 (1982): 471. Fittingly, he was "Stricken While Preparing to Open Library as Memorial to His Mother" in 1925 (*New York Times*, March 3, 1925). Harriot completed the trans action, without restrictions.
23. Smaller collections of writings and speeches have been published over the years as well, notably DuBois, ed., *Elizabeth Cady Stanton/Susan B. Anthony: Correspondence, Writings, Speeches*, and Mari Jo Buhle and Paul Buhle, eds., *The Concise History of Woman Suffrage* (Urbana, Ill.: University of Illinois Press, 2005).
24. Tilton, "Mrs. Elizabeth Cady Stanton," 359; ECS to Catherine Fish Stebbins, "Suffragists' Golden Wedding," *Woman's Journal*, Aug. 29, 1896, Film, Reel 35.

1. THE TWO WORLDS OF ELIZABETH CADY (1815–1840)

1. Stanton, *Eighty Years and More*, 10–12.
2. Horatio Gates Spafford, *Gazetteer of the State of New York* (Albany, N.Y.: B. D. Packard, 1824).
3. See Judith Klinghoffer and Lois Elkis, " 'The Petticoat Electors': Women's Suffrage in New Jersey, 1776–1807," *Journal of the Early Republic* 12 (1992); Jeanne Boydston, "Making Gender in the Early Republic," in James Horn, Jan Ellen Lewis, and Peter S. Onuf, eds., *The Revolution of 1800* (Charlottesville: University of Virginia Press, 2002), 240–66.
4. Stanton, *Eighty Years and More*, 20; Ellen Carol DuBois, *Feminism and Suffrage: The Emergence of an Independent Women's Movement in America, 1848–1869* (Ithaca, N.Y.: Cornell University Press, 1978), 25.

5. Stanton, *Eighty Years and More*, 3–4, 12.

6. Blatch and Lutz, *Challenging Years*, 16.

7. Stanton, *Eighty Years and More*, 12; Blatch and Lutz, *Challenging Years*, 16, 19. By 1868, Margaret Cady was a supporter of woman suffrage (*Revolution* 1:8, Feb. 26, 1868: 121). Elizabeth Cady Stanton noted that her mother, while pregnant with Elizabeth, "took the deepest interest" in her husband's 1815 election to Congress, but the remark serves only to suggest that her own passion for political rights may have been prenatal (Stanton, *Eighty Years and More*, 2).

8. Stanton, *Eighty Years and More*, 5, 16–17; Stanton referred to him by his last name in Editorial Correspondence, *Revolution* 2:10, Sept. 10, 1868. See also Christine Stansell, "Missed Connections: Abolitionist Feminism in the Nineteenth Century," in Ellen Carol DuBois and Richard Cándida Smith, eds., *Elizabeth Cady Stanton: Feminist as Thinker: A Reader in Documents and Essays* (New York: New York University Press, 2007), 36; and Kathi Kern, *Mrs. Stanton's Bible* (Ithaca: Cornell University Press, 2001), 22–30.

9. Peter Eisenstadt and Laura-Eve Moss, eds., "Slavery," *The Encyclopedia of New York State* (Syracuse, N.Y.: Syracuse University Press, 2005), 1418–22. New York City, which had had nearly 3,000 slaves in 1800, had seen that population decline to 518 by 1820, with well over 10,000 free African Americans in the city. The Cadys were not alone among the parents of future abolitionists in holding slaves; the fathers of both Henry Stanton and Gerrit Smith were slaveowners in earlier days.

10. Stanton, *Eighty Years and More*, 31. She had become angry when she heard "the tears and complaints of the women who came to my father for legal advice," and frustrated when the judge could only "take down his books and show me the inexorable statutes." Once, she determined to rip the offending laws from her father's books, until he convinced her that it would do no good, all of which, she later wrote, indicated that "the future object of my life was foreshadowed" (Stanton, *Eighty Years and More*, 31–32).

11. Stanton, *Eighty Years and More*, 14, 17.

12. Ibid., 21–23. Interestingly, she seems not to have recognized that her mother was a great horsewoman.

13. Ibid., 22, 33.

14. Ibid., 35.

15. See Mary Kelley, *Learning to Stand and Speak: Women, Education, and Public Life in America's Republic* (Chapel Hill: University of North Carolina Press, 2006).

16. *Emma Willard and Her Pupils, or Fifty Years of Troy Female Seminary, 1822–1872* (New York: Mrs. Russell Sage, 1898); on Millers, see 82–83; on Cadys, see 147–49.

17. All quotes about school here are in Stanton, *Eighty Years and More*, 32–40; quote on "young masculinity" in ECS to Elizabeth Smith Miller, May 10, 1863, in Gordon, ed., *Selected Papers*, 1:487.

18. All quotes here are from Stanton, *Eighty Years and More*, 41–45.

19. Kern, *Mrs. Stanton's Bible*, 42; Stanton, *Eighty Years and More*, 26.

20. Stanton, *Eighty Years and More*, 47, 5, 9, 45.

21. Lawrence J. Friedman, *Gregarious Saints: Self and Community in American Abo-*

litionism, 1830–1870 (Cambridge: Cambridge University Press, 1982), 100; Beverly Wilson Palmer, ed., *Selected Letters of Lucretia Coffin Mott* (Urbana: University of Illinois Press, 2002), 33. The explanation for these nicknames is in Gordon, ed., *Selected Papers*, 1:383, note 1.

22. Stanton, *Eighty Years and More*, 62; Alma Lutz, *Created Equal: A Biography of Elizabeth Cady Stanton* (New York: John Day Company, 1940), 13; Stansell, "Missed Connections," 36; ECS to Peter Smith, Jan. 27, [1836], Film, Reel 6. There is more information on Harriet Powell in Judith Wellman, *The Road to Seneca Falls: Elizabeth Cady Stanton and the First Woman's Rights Convention* (Urbana: University of Illinois Press, 2004), 39–40, and Laurel Thatcher Ulrich, *Well-Behaved Women Seldom Make History* (New York: Alfred A. Knopf, 2007), 106–11. In Stanton's later recollection (*HWS*, 1:471), she "told [Harriet Powell] of the laws for women such as we then lived under, and remarked on the parallel condition of slaves and women." This seems extremely unlikely.

23. Stanton, *Eighty Years and More*, 48, 44, 45.

24. Ibid., 45–46; Lutz, *Created Equal*, 16–17, 23. Harriot Stanton Blatch wrote about her mother's romantic past to Alma Lutz on May 16, 1930, and June 27, 1937. Alma Lutz Papers, Special Collections, Vassar College Library. See also "Elizabeth Cady Stanton's Fight for Freedom," *The American Weekly*, Jan. 11, 1948.

25. Stanton, *Eighty Years and More*, 45; ECS to Isabella Beecher Hooker, Jan. 21, [1873], Film, Reel 16; Barbara Goldsmith, *Other Powers: The Age of Suffrage, Spiritualism, and the Scandalous Victoria Woodhull* (New York: Alfred A. Knopf, 1998), 45. Several weeks later, Stanton renewed their confidences and begged Hooker to "tell no one else all I said that moonlight, even Susan never had such a complete view of my soul" (ECS to Isabella Beecher Hooker, Feb. 20, [1873], Film, Reel 16); ECS to Harriot Stanton Blatch, Oct. 1, 1889, Film, Reel 27.

26. Blatch and Lutz, *Challenging Years*, 16, 20; DuBois, *Harriot Stanton Blatch*, 18, 256.

27. Stanton's quotes are all in *Eighty Years and More*, 58–60; Lutz, *Created Equal*, 19.

28. The major sources about Henry Stanton are his own aptly named *Random Recollections*, 3rd ed. (New York: Harper and Brothers, 1887), and Arthur Harry Rice, "Henry B. Stanton as a Political Abolitionist," Ed.D. thesis, Columbia University, 1968.

29. Quote is in Robert Brewster Stanton, "Reminiscences," manuscript in New York Public Library. Henry did help support his mother, apparently "with cheerfulness" (Henry Stanton to James Birney, Aug. 11, 1845, in Dwight L. Dumond, *Letters of James Gillespie Birney, 1831–1857* [Gloucester, Mass.: Peter Smith, 1966], 2:959).

30. Stanton, *Random Recollections*, 27. See also Paul E. Johnson, *Sam Patch, the Famous Jumper* (New York: Hill and Wang, 2003).

31. Rice, "Henry B. Stanton," 18, 21–22, 24.

32. Ibid., 57.

33. Theodore Weld to James Birney, May 23, 1837, in Dumond, *Letters of James Gillespie Birney*, 1:382; Quotes are from Rice, "Henry B. Stanton," 77; Lydia Maria Child to ECS, May 24, 1863, Film, Reel 10; Debora Weston quoted in Rice, "Henry B. Stanton," 71; Charles Finney to Theodore Dwight Weld, July 21,

1836, in Gilbert H. Barnes and Dwight L. Dumond, eds., *Letters of Theodore Dwight Weld, Angelina Grimké Weld, and Sarah Grimké, 1822–1844* (Gloucester, Mass.: Peter Smith, 1965), 1:319–20.

34. Rice, "Henry B. Stanton," 78, 74, 93.

35. Ibid., 164–65.

36. Stanton, *Eighty Years and More*, 58–59. On pro-slavery mobs, see Henry Stanton, *Random Recollections*, 48–55.

37. She recalled with both irony and fondness an evening when Henry was asked to reflect on music: "Now, said I to myself, for once he will be at a loss for something to say," and she was amazed when he produced a coherent speech on the subject (ECS to Theodore Stanton, [after Jan. 14, 1887], in Gordon, ed., *Selected Papers*, 4:541).

38. Stanton, *Eighty Years and More*, 60–61.

39. Letter quoted in Gordon, ed., *Selected Papers*, 1:4, note 6.

40. Henry B. Stanton to Elizabeth Cady, Jan. 4, [1840], Film, Reel 6; Stanton, *Eighty Years and More*, 71; Gordon, ed., *Selected Papers*, 1:7, note 7; Lutz, *Created Equal*, 21; Stanton, *Eighty Years and More*, 62; ECS to Ann Fitzhugh Smith, March 4, [1840], in Gordon, ed., *Selected Papers*, 1:5; Stanton, *Eighty Years and More*, 71.

41. Gordon, ed., *Selected Papers*, introd., 1, xxix; Richard Webb to Elizabeth Pease, Nov. 4, 1840, in Clare Taylor, *British and American Abolitionists: An Episode in Transatlantic Understanding* (Edinburgh: Edinburgh University Press, 1974), 119–20; Angelina Grimké Weld to Gerrit and Ann Smith, June 18, 1840, in Barnes and Dumond, *Letters of Theodore Dwight Weld, Angelina Grimké Weld, and Sarah Grimké*, 2:842.

42. Henry B. Stanton to Gerrit Smith, Feb. 27, 1840, quoted in Rice, "Henry B. Stanton," 203; Stanton, *Eighty Years and More*, 74. Stanton, ibid., 71, says, incorrectly, that the wedding was held on Friday, May 10.

43. William Lloyd Garrison to Harriot Minot, March 19, 1833, in Taylor, *British and American Abolitionists*, 22.

44. Theodore Dwight Weld to Lewis Tappan, April 10, 1840, in Barnes and Dumond, eds., *Letters of Theodore Dwight Weld, Angelina Grimké Weld, and Sarah Grimké*, 2:828. Charles P. Bossom estimated the total cost at $330 per person for a three-month stay (Bossom to William Lloyd Garrison, "Expense of a Trip to England," *Liberator*, March 20, 1840, 46).

45. Stanton, *Eighty Years and More*, 73–75.

46. ECS to Gerrit Smith, Aug. 3, 1840, in Gordon, ed., *Selected Papers*, 1:16; Stanton, *Eighty Years and More*, 74.

47. Mary Grew, Diary, June 6, 1840, Alma Lutz Collection, Women's Studies Manuscript Collections from the Schlesinger Library, Radcliffe College, Series 1, Woman's Suffrage (Bethesda, Md.: University Publications of America, 1990), M-59, Reel 973, No. M 13; Stanton, *Eighty Years and More*, 85; ECS to Angelina Grimké Weld and Sarah Grimké, June 25, 1840, in Gordon, ed., *Selected Papers*, 1:11.

48. *HWS*, 1:420.

49. Ann Greene Phillips is frequently quoted: e.g., James Brewer Stewart, *Wendell Phillips: Liberty's Hero* (Baton Rouge: Louisiana State University Press, 1986),

81. *Proceedings of the General Anti-Slavery Convention, Called by the Committee of the British and Foreign Anti-Slavery Society, and Held in London, from Friday, June 12th, to Tuesday, June 23rd, 1840* (London: British and Foreign Anti-Slavery Society, 1841), 24, 31, 25.

50. Stanton, *Eighty Years and More*, 79; Garrison to Helen Garrison, June 29, 1840, in Taylor, *British and American Abolitionists*, 93; *HWS*, 1:61; Rice, "Henry B. Stanton," 207. While Lucretia Mott found that Elizabeth Stanton was "gaining daily in our affections," Henry was "not so strong in confidence in moral power as desirable." Lucretia Mott, Diary, June 20, 1840, in Frederick Tolles, ed., "Slavery and the 'Woman Question': Lucretia Mott's Diary of Her Visit to Great Britain to Attend the World's Anti-Slavery Convention of 1840," Supplement #23 to the *Journal of the Friends' Historical Society* (Haverford, Pa.: Friends' Historical Association, 1952), 41. Henry did, Mott noted, "plead for the right" in trying to get the women's protest on the record, Diary, June 23, 1840, ibid., 44.

51. Rice, "Henry B. Stanton," 163–64, 143–44. Henry had never been reliable on this issue. Two years earlier he had considered it an unnecessary distraction to resolve to include women on equal terms with men, and so he had voted against it (Palmer, ed., *Selected Letters of Lucretia Coffin Mott*, 48, note 2: Convention of May 29–31, 1838).

52. Quoted in Andrea Constantine Hawkes, "The Life of Elizabeth McClintock Phillips, 1821–1896: A Story of Family, Friends, Community, and a Self-Made Woman," Ph.D. dissertation, University of Maine, 2005, 84; Stanton, *Eighty Years and More*, 79. Garrison's was "a great act of self-sacrifice that should never be forgotten by women," Elizabeth Cady Stanton would recall (ibid., 82). See William Lloyd Garrison to Helen Garrison, June 29, 1840, in Taylor, *British and American Abolitionists*, 91–93.

53. Stanton, *Eighty Years and More*, 83; ECS to Sarah Grimké and Angelina Grimké Weld, June 25, 1840, in Gordon, ed., *Selected Papers*, 1:10; Theodore Dwight Weld to Angelina Grimké, August 26, 1837, in Barnes and Dumond, eds., *Letters of Theodore Dwight Weld, Angelina Grimké Weld, and Sarah Grimké*, 1:436; Mary Grew, Diary, May 19 and 26, 1840.

54. Stanton, *Eighty Years and More*, 83; Lucretia Coffin Mott to Richard and Hannah Webb, April 2, 1841, in Palmer, ed., *Selected Letters of Lucretia Coffin Mott*, 93; Mott to ECS, March 23, 1841, in ibid., 90.

55. Mott to Richard and Hannah Webb, April 2, 1841, in ibid., 93; Mott to Maria Weston Chapman, July 29, 1840, in ibid., 79; ECS to Edward M. Davis, Dec. 5, [1880], in Gordon, ed., *Selected Letters*, 4:27.

56. William Lloyd Garrison to Helen Garrison, June 29, 1840, in Taylor, *British and American Abolitionists*, 93; ECS to SBA, April 2, 1852, in Stanton and Blatch, eds., *ECS*, 2:40; Dorothy Sterling, *Ahead of Her Time: Abby Kelley and the Politics of Antislavery* (New York: W. W. Norton, 1991), 166.

57. Mott to ECS, March 16, 1855, in Palmer, ed., *Selected Letters of Lucretia Coffin Mott*, 233; Mott to Abigail Kelley, March 18, 1839, in ibid., 47.

58. Stanton, *Eighty Years and More*, 82–83; Mott to ECS, March 16, 1855, in Palmer, ed., *Selected Letters of Lucretia Coffin Mott*, 236. For an important challenge to this narrative, see Nancy Isenberg, *Sex and Citizenship in Antebellum America* (Chapel Hill: University of North Carolina Press, 1998), 2–6.

2. "LONG-ACCUMULATING DISCONTENT" (1840–1851)

1. ECS to Elizabeth J. Neall, Jan. 25, [1841], in Gordon, ed., *Selected Papers*, 1:18; Stanton, *Eighty Years and More*, 111, 143.
2. Ever happy to draw on his political connections, Henry counted on New York lawyers to change the law so that he could practice there as well (HBS to ECS, June 23, 1842, in Gordon, ed., *Selected Papers*, 1:35–36).
3. Stephen Thernstrom, *The Other Bostonians: Poverty and Progress in the American Metropolis, 1880–1970* (Cambridge, Mass.: Harvard University Press, 1973), 5; quoted in Madelon Bedell, *The Alcotts: Biography of a Family* (New York: Clarkson N. Potter, 1980), 34.
4. Lucretia Mott to James Miller McKim, Dec. 29, 1839, in Palmer, ed., *Selected Letters of Lucretia Coffin Mott*, 68; Mott to ECS, March 23, 1841, in ibid., 90; Sarah M. Grimké to ECS, Dec. 31, 1842, in Gordon, ed., *Selected Papers*, 1:39.
5. Phyllis Cole, "Stanton, Fuller, and the Grammar of Romanticism," *The New England Quarterly* 73, no. 4 (Dec. 2000): 540; ECS to Elizabeth J. Neall, Feb. 3, [1843], in Gordon, ed., *Selected Papers*, 1:41.
6. See, e.g., Richard Webb to Edmund Quincy, Aug. 17, 1844, in Taylor, *British and American Abolitionists*, 225. As late as 1851 Abby Kelley Foster would write that "altho' personally, almost a stranger to you I feel that I know you and I regard you with feelings of high esteem" (Foster to ECS, Jan. 11, 1851, in Gordon, ed., *Selected Papers*, 1:176).
7. ECS to Neall, Nov. 26, [1841], in Gordon, ed., *Selected Papers*, 1:24–25; ECS to Neall, Feb. 3, [1843], in ibid., 1:41.
8. Stanton, *Eighty Years and More*, 133.
9. Sarah Grimké to ECS, Dec. 31, 1842, in Gordon, ed., *Selected Papers*, 1:39; Henry B. Stanton to ECS, [Oct. 4, 1842], Film, Reel 6; Henry B. Stanton to ECS, [June 23, 1841], in Gordon, ed., *Selected Papers*, 1:35; Henry B. Stanton to ECS, [Oct. 4, 1842], Film, Reel 6.
10. Stanton, *Eighty Years and More*, 142; ECS to Elizabeth Smith Miller, [April 15, 1847], in Gordon, ed., *Selected Papers*, 1:63; Stanton, *Eighty Years and More*, 144.
11. For a beautifully imagined description of what Stanton's surroundings were like, see Wellman, *Road to Seneca Falls*, 1–14.
12. *Seneca County Courier*, Aug. 4, 1848. Reference to *Albany Patriot* being Liberty League paper and supported by Gerrit Smith: *Liberator* 18, Feb. 18, 1848.
13. ECS to Elizabeth J. Neall, Nov. 26, [1841], in Gordon, ed., *Selected Papers*, 1:25.
14. *Seneca County Courier*, July 21, 1848; ECS to Marguerite Berry Stanton, Oct. 7, 1881, in Gordon, ed., *Selected Papers*, 4:114; Robert Brewster Stanton, "Reminiscences." There are many examples of Stanton's freely offered advice. See ECS, Editorial Correspondence, *Revolution* 4:23, Dec. 9, 1869; *Revolution*, Dec. 30, 1869.
15. Stanton, *Eighty Years and More*, 163. Angelina Grimké Weld reassured his mother that she would try to write, but "no news will be good news." Grimké Weld to ECS, [April 1, 1851], in Gordon, ed., *Selected Papers*, 1:181.
16. ECS to Daniel C. Stanton, Dec. 10, [1851], in Gordon, ed., *Selected Papers*, 1:188–89.
17. ECS to Elizabeth Smith Miller, [Feb. 10, 1851], in ibid., 1:178; ECS to Lucretia

Mott, Oct. 22, 1852, in ibid., 1:212; DuBois, *Harriot Stanton Blatch*, 9. Wellman, *Road to Seneca Falls*, 169, suggests she may have had a miscarriage in 1849. In a diary entry at age sixty-five, Stanton reflected on her younger self who "knew no better than to have seven children in quick succession" (Stanton and Blatch, eds., *ECS*, 2:177). But it is plausible that Thomas McClintock's drugstore in Waterloo offered some preventive contraceptive options; certainly other married nineteenth-century women used abstinence, extended breastfeeding, and abortion to limit births.

18. Stanton, *Eighty Years and More*, 145–47; on housewives' mental limitations: *HWS*, 1:21.

19. ECS to Daniel Cady Eaton, Aug. 18, 1840, Film, Reel 6; *Liberator* 18:11, March 17, 1848; Palmer, ed., *Selected Letters of Lucretia Coffin Mott*, 166; *Liberator* 18:21, May 26, 1848, 82. On Rose: *HWS*, 1:100.

20. Quoted in Andrea Moore Kerr, *Lucy Stone: Speaking Out for Equality* (New Brunswick, N.J.: Rutgers University Press, 1995), 46; "The Rights of Woman," *Liberator* 18:22, June 2, 1848, 86; ECS to Elizabeth J. Neall, Nov. 26, [1841], in Gordon, ed., *Selected Papers*, 1:25. This phrase pleased reformers enough for them to quote it widely. See Lucretia Mott to Richard and Hannah Webb, Feb. 25, 1842, in Palmer, ed., *Selected Letters of Lucretia Coffin Mott*, 111. "Reminiscences. Emily Collins," in *HWS*, 1:88–89.

21. Michael D. Pierson, *Free Hearts and Free Homes: Gender and American Antislavery Politics* (Chapel Hill: University of North Carolina Press, 2003), 44; *Albany Patriot* 5:5, Dec. 10, 1845; Lori D. Ginzberg, *Untidy Origins: A Story of Woman's Rights in Antebellum New York* (Chapel Hill: University of North Carolina Press, 2005); Isenberg, *Sex and Citizenship in Antebellum America*, xiii. Lucretia Mott noted in 1842 that Elizabeth Cady Stanton had requested many copies of Sarah Grimké's *Letters on the Equality of the Sexes* (Mott to Richard and Hannah Webb, Feb. 25, 1842, in Palmer, ed., *Selected Letters of Lucretia Coffin Mott*, 111).

22. ECS to Elizabeth J. Neall, Nov. 26, [1841], in Gordon, ed., *Selected Papers*, 1:26.

23. Wellman, *Road to Seneca Falls*, 188.

24. On Richard Hunt, see ibid., 189; Stanton, *Eighty Years and More*, 148–49.

25. Wellman, *Road to Seneca Falls*, 189–90; ECS to Elizabeth McClintock, [July 14, 1848], in Gordon, ed., *Selected Papers*, 1:69. In *HWS*, 1:67–68, Stanton doesn't mention Lizzie McClintock among the organizers, which she says were a group of four ladies, and suggests that a larger group came up with the model for the Declaration of Sentiments.

26. For information on the Hunt and McClintock families, see Hawkes, "Life of Elizabeth McClintock." Quotes are from 155, 6; on Bayard, see 138–39.

27. Ibid., 74.

28. *HWS*, 1:68; ECS to Elizabeth McClintock, [July 14, 1848], in Gordon, ed., *Selected Papers*, 1:69.

29. "Woman's Rights Convention, Held at Seneca Falls," in Gordon, ed., *Selected Papers*, 1:82.

30. ECS to SBA, April 2, 1852, in Stanton and Blatch, eds., *ECS*, 2:39.

31. The text of the Declaration of Sentiments can be found in "Woman's Rights Convention, Held at Seneca Falls," in Gordon, ed., *Selected Papers*, 1:75–88 and

HWS, 1:70–73. It has also been reprinted as a small fascimile pamphlet of *Report of the Woman's Rights Convention, Held at Seneca Falls, N.Y., July 19th and 20th, 1848* (Rochester: John Dick, 1848) for the Women's Rights National Historical Park (Eastern National, 2003).

32. The Anti-Slavery Convention of American Women, *Proceedings* (New York: William S. Dorr, 1837), 9; Sarah Grimké to Mary Parker, Sept. 6, 1837, in Elizabeth Ann Bartlett, ed., *Sarah Grimké: Letters on the Equality of the Sexes and Other Essays* (New Haven, Conn.: Yale University Press, 1988), 72.

33. Wellman, *Road to Seneca Falls*, 193.

34. ECS to Elizabeth Pease, Feb. 12, [1842], in Gordon, ed., *Selected Papers*, 1:29–30.

35. Wellman, *Road to Seneca Falls*, 121–22, 128. Mary Bascom Bull said, incorrectly, that everyone present had signed the Declaration; neither she nor her father did (ibid., 201). On Free Soilers at the convention, see ibid., 207–208.

36. Hawkes, "Life of Elizabeth McClintock," 165; *HWS*, 1:372. As late as 1852, Mott wrote George Combe, "As to the turmoil of political life, *as it is*, or any preparation for the exercise of a government by physical force, I ever distinctly avow a decided & conscientious opposition to it—indeed for men as well as for women—still I can but feel the force of the claim of the *right* of suffrage for our sex equally with that of men" (May 21, 1852, in Palmer, ed., *Selected Letters of Lucretia Coffin Mott*, 215).

37. Among historians, Ellen DuBois has offered the most compelling analysis of suffrage as the demand "around which women's boldest aspirations coalesced" over the next century (DuBois, "The Last Suffragist: An Intellectual and Political Autobiography," in Ellen Carol DuBois, *Woman Suffrage and Women's Rights*, [New York: New York University Press, 1998], 3). See also "The Radicalism of the Woman Suffrage Movement: Notes Toward the Reconstruction of Nineteenth-Century Feminism," originally *Feminist Studies* 3 (1975), republished in DuBois, *Woman Suffrage and Women's Rights*, 30–42.

38. DuBois, "Outgrowing the Compact of the Fathers," in *Woman Suffrage and Women's Rights*, 86.

39. ECS to Mary Ann White Johnson and Salem convention, April 7, [1850], in Gordon, ed., *Selected Papers*, 1:166; *HWS*, 1:16.

40. Hawkes, "Life of Elizabeth McClintock," 184.

41. *New York Tribune*, Oct. 25, 1850, in John F. McClymer, *This High and Holy Moment: The First National Woman's Rights Convention, Worcester, 1850* (Orlando, Fl.: Harcourt Brace and Company, 1999), 114.

42. Sylvia D. Hoffert, *When Hens Crow: The Woman's Rights Movement in Antebellum America* (Bloomington: Indiana University Press, 1995), 34.

43. Stanton, *Eighty Years and More*, 149. Once the *Liberator* did take notice, in late August, they printed the *Courier's* report and the "Declaration of Sentiments" in their entirety. *Liberator* 18:34, Aug. 25, 1848, 136.

44. Quoted in Wellman, *Road to Seneca Falls*, 210. "This convention was novel in its character, and the doctrines broached in it are startling to those who are wedded to the present usages and laws of society," the paper noted blandly. "The resolutions are of the kind called radical . . . Some will be regarded with respect—others with disapprobation and contempt" (*Seneca County Courier*, July 21, 1848).

45. ECS and Elizabeth McClintock to Editors, *Seneca County Courier*, [after July 23, 1848], in Gordon, ed., *Selected Papers*, 1:88; *Seneca County Courier*, Aug. 4, 1848. *HWS*, 1:802–806, contains some of the press attacks and Stanton's response.

46. Stanton, *Eighty Years and More*, 149; Hoffert, *When Hens Crow*, 114.

47. Stanton, *Eighty Years and More*, 149. The list of those who signed the Declaration of Sentiments is in *HWS*, 1:809–10 and reprinted in Wellman, *Road to Seneca Falls*, 87, and in Gordon, ed., *Selected Papers*, 1:81–82, with no indication of who might have withdrawn.

48. Wellman, *Road to Seneca Falls*, 211, 209; Hawkes, "Life of Elizabeth McClintock," 170.

49. Stanton, *Eighty Years and More*, 151; ECS to Amy Post, Sept. 24, [1848], in Gordon, ed., *Selected Papers*, 1:124; *Liberator* 18:37, Sept. 15, 1848, 148.

50. Henry B. Stanton to ECS, [Sept. 8, 1848], Film, Reel 6.

51. Quote is Lucretia Mott's, in Gordon, ed., *Selected Papers*, 1:94–95. Quotes that follow are from ECS, "Address on Woman's Rights," [Sept. 1848], in ibid., 1:95–116. Apparently Stanton did not give an extended speech at Seneca Falls. Although she often gave the impression that her ideas were entirely original, she did an enormous amount of research for her speeches and articles. This Waterloo speech, for instance, depended heavily on Lydia Maria Child's *History of the Condition of Women* for historical information. Ibid., 1:117, note 3.

52. In this, Stanton followed such writers as Mary Wollstonecraft, whose *Vindication of the Rights of Women* (1792) argues that women exist not simply to please men, but to use their rational faculties, and that education should aim to lessen sexual differences rather than exacerbate them.

53. Stanton, *Eighty Years and More*, 153; quoted in Ida Husted Harper, *SBA*, 3:1263.

54. Hawkes, "Life of Elizabeth McClintock," 178; ECS to Martha Coffin Wright, [April 1856], Film, Reel 8; Lucretia Mott to Elizabeth Neall Gay, May 27, 1856, in Palmer, ed., *Selected Letters of Lucretia Coffin Mott*, 250; Lucretia Mott to ECS, Oct. 3, 1848, in Gordon, ed., *Selected Papers*, 1:127.

55. ECS to Amy Kirby Post, Sept. 24, [1848], in ibid., 1:123; ECS to SBA, [after May 25, 1852], in ibid., 1:197; ECS to SBA, Jan. 16, 1854, in ibid., 1:237. See also ECS, "Appeal to the Women of the State of New York," [July 1, 1852], in ibid., 1:201–205.

56. Proceedings of the Ohio Women's Convention, in ibid., 1:168, note 1; Paulina Wright Davis, *A History of the National Woman's Rights Movement for Twenty Years; with the Proceedings of the Decade Meeting Held at Apollo Hall, October 20, 1870, from 1850 to 1870* (New York: Journeymen Printers' Co-operative Association, 1871), 8. On the Salem convention, see Isenberg, *Sex and Citizenship*.

57. Anthony, "Woman's Half-Century of Evolution," *North American Review* 175 (Dec. 1902): 806. Greeley and Stanton would later fall out, but in the early days his *New York Tribune* contained "No ridicule of our cause, no sneers at its advocates" (*HWS*, 1:126).

58. ECS to Mott, Oct. 22, 1852, in Gordon, ed., *Selected Papers*, 1:212.

59. ECS, "Our Costume," *Lily* 3:4, April 1851, 31; Stanton, *Eighty Years and More*, 204; see Gordon, ed., *Selected Papers*, 4:14, note 5, on Willard's age. See also Gerrit Smith Stanton, "How Aged Housekeeper Gave Her All to Cause of

Woman Suffrage," unidentified clipping, n.d., E. C. Stanton Papers, Archives Collection 37, box 38, folder 5, Seneca Falls Historical Society.
60. Stanton, *Eighty Years and More*, 204.
61. "Divorce," *Lily* 2:4, April 1850, 31; "Legislative Doings," *Lily* 2:5, May 1850, 38; "Housekeeping," *Lily* 2:9, Sept. 1850, 68.
62. ECS to Abigail Kelley Foster, [Jan. 12, 1851], in Gordon, ed., *Selected Papers*, 1:178.

3. "AT THE BOILING POINT" (1851–1861)

1. Susan B. Anthony to Nora Blatch, Nov. 24, 1902, Film, Reel 42. The story of their meeting, as Ann Gordon suggests, is a "slippery" one, including a probably incorrect version in Ida Husted Harper's biography of Susan B. Anthony. See "Editorial Note," in Gordon, ed., *Selected Papers*, 1:182–84; Harper, *SBA*, 1:64.
2. Stanton, *Eighty Years and More*, 162–63. As in many cases, Stanton repeated the story elsewhere, with slight variations. See *HWS*, 1:456–68.
3. Stanton, *Eighty Years and More*, 159, 161.
4. Elisabeth Griffith, *In Her Own Right: The Life of Elizabeth Cady Stanton* (New York: Oxford University Press, 1984), 34.
5. Anthony, "Woman's Half-Century of Evolution," *North American Review* 175 (Dec. 1902): 806.
6. Stanton was notoriously sloppy about dates, and she misreported the timing of the bloomer experiment, *Eighty Years and More*, 201. Amelia Willard, Stanton's housekeeper, also wore the outfit from the first. See Gerrit Smith Stanton, "How Aged Housekeeper Gave Her All to Cause of Woman's Suffrage."
7. Catharine E. Beecher, *A Treatise on Domestic Economy, for the Use of Young Ladies at Home, and at School* (Boston: Marsh, Capen, Lyon, and Webb, 1841), 97.
8. Hoffert, *When Hens Crow*, 26; Stanton, *Eighty Years and More*, 202, has a different version.
9. ECS to Henry B. Stanton, [April 11], 1851, in Stanton and Blatch, eds., *ECS*, 2:27; Robert Brewster Stanton, "Reminiscences"; ECS to Elizabeth Smith Miller, Oct. 18, 1851, in Stanton and Blatch, eds., *ECS*, 2:36–37; ECS to Elizabeth Smith Miller, [March 10, 1889], in ibid., 2:257.
10. ECS to Daniel Cady, Jan. 12, 1853, in ibid., 2:46.
11. Henry B. Stanton to ECS, [Feb. 15, 1851], Film, Reel 7; ECS to Elizabeth Smith Miller, June 4, 1851, in Stanton and Blatch, eds., *ECS*, 2:29.
12. Stanton, *Eighty Years and More*, 202; George Thompson to Anne Weston Warren, Feb. 28, 1851, in Taylor, *British and American Abolitionists*, 367; Gerrit Smith to ECS, Dec. 1, 1855, (Broadside), Film, Reel 8; Gerrit Smith to SBA, quoted in Harper, *SBA*, 1:147.
13. ECS to Daniel Cady Stanton, Oct. 14, 1851, in Stanton and Blatch, eds., *ECS*, 2:35–36; ECS, "Eulogy at Memorial Service" of Lucretia Mott, *HWS*, 1:431.
14. Stanton, *Eighty Years and More*, 201; ECS, "The New Dress," *Lily* 4:4, April 1852, 27; ECS to Elizabeth Smith Miller, June 4, 1851, in Stanton and Blatch, eds., *ECS*, 2:30.
15. On Amelia Bloomer, see Harper, *SBA*, 1:114; Sarah Grimké to ECS, March 29, [1854], Film, Reel 7; "Bloomerism in the Mills," *Lily* 3:7, July 1851, 53.

16. From Elizabeth Smith Miller Collection at New York Public Library, quoted on www.NYhistory.com/GerritSmith/esm.htm.

17. Lucy Stone to Susan B. Anthony, Feb. 13, 1854, Film, Reel 7.

18. Susan B. Anthony and ECS to Lucy Stone, Feb. 16, 1854, in Gordon, ed., *Selected Papers*, 1:260–61.

19. Harper, *SBA*, 1:115, 117; Susan B. Anthony to Lucy Stone, Feb. 9, 1854, in Gordon, ed., *Selected Papers* 1:239.

20. In a letter from Antoinette Brown Blackwell to Lucy Stone, Jan. 1, 1853, Alice Stone Blackwell added this reminiscence by her aunt, in Carol Lasser and Marlene Deahl Merrill, *Friends and Sisters: Letters Between Lucy Stone and Antoinette Brown Blackwell, 1846–1893* (Urbana: University of Illinois Press, 1987), 131n; ECS to Elizabeth Smith Miller, June 13, 1853, in Stanton and Blatch, eds., *ECS*, 2:50n; Susan B. Anthony to Lucy Stone, March 7, 1854, in Gordon, ed., *Selected Papers*, 1:262. Mary Bascom Bull claimed that Stanton looked terrible in the outfit: "I have seen scarecrows that did credit to farmers' boys' ingenuity, but never one better calculated to scare all birds, beasts and human beings than was Mrs. Stanton in the Bloomer dress" (Mary S. Bull, "Woman's Rights and Other 'Reforms' in Seneca Falls," *Good Company* 5, 1880: 335). Stanton, although she enjoyed Bull's article, was "vexed" by the added suggestion that she was "beyond the becoming point of plumpness" (ECS to Amelia Jenks Bloomer, July 25, [1880], in Gordon, ed., *Selected Papers*, 3:550).

21. *Address to the Legislature of New-York, Adopted by the State Woman's Rights Convention, Held at Albany*, [Feb. 14, 1854], in ibid., 1:240–55. Quotes are on 240, 243, 253, 241. Here, as in so many instances, Ann Gordon and her colleagues have sorted out the chronological confusions that frequently occur in Stanton's accounts. The story Stanton told—that she practiced her speech before her skeptical father before presenting it to the legislature—was apparently a dramatic creation of her own. "Editorial Note," Gordon, ed., *Selected Papers* 1:240.

22. There are several versions of this letter. The quote is in Ida Harper, "Early Letters of Elizabeth Cady Stanton," *Independent* 55, May 21, 1903, 1190, Film, Reel 9. Another appears as ECS to Susan B. Anthony, July 4, 1858, Film, Reel 9.

23. Rice, "Henry B. Stanton," 339.

24. ECS to SBA, Feb. 15, 1855, in Stanton and Blatch, eds., *ECS*, 2:59.

25. Kerr, *Lucy Stone*, 86; SBA to Antoinette Brown Blackwell, Sept. 4, 1858, in Gordon, ed., *Selected Papers*, 1:378.

26. ECS to Daniel Cady, Jan. 12, 1853, in Stanton and Blatch, eds., *ECS*, 2:46; Henry B. Stanton to Margaret Stanton, Jan. 16, 1857, in *Life Sketch of Elizabeth Cady Stanton by Her Granddaughter, Nora Stanton Barney* (1948), E. C. Stanton Papers, Archives Collection 37, box 38, folder 2, Seneca Falls Historical Society; Henry B. Stanton to ECS, Feb. 14, 1858, Film, Reel 8.

27. Henry B. Stanton to ECS, [Feb. 15, 1851], Film, Reel 7.

28. Lucretia Mott to ECS, Oct. 3, 1848, in Palmer, ed., *Selected Letters of Lucretia Coffin Mott*, 172; ECS to Isabella Beecher Hooker, Sept. 8, 1859, in Gordon, ed., *Selected Papers*, 2:264; Henry B. Stanton to ECS, [Feb. 17, 1859], Film, Reel 9; Edward P. Mitchell, *Memoirs of an Editor: Fifty Years of American Journalism* (New York: Charles Scribner's Sons, 1924), 216.

29. Rice, "Henry B. Stanton," 297; Lucretia Mott to Richard and Hannah Webb, Feb. 25, 1842, in Palmer, ed., *Selected Letters of Lucretia Coffin Mott*, 111; Rice, "Henry B. Stanton," 345. In reflecting on the 1850s, Rice considered Henry's "serious character flaw" to be "his vanity and desire for personal gain through political preferment" (Rice, ibid., 351).

30. Henry B. Stanton to ECS, Oct. 26, 1848, Film, Reel 6; Henry B. Stanton to ECS, March 6, 1851, Film, Reel 7; Henry B. Stanton to ECS, Feb. 20, 1851, Film, Reel 7; Stanton, *Eighty Years and More*, 71; ECS to SBA, [Jan. 16, 1854], in Gordon, ed., *Selected Papers*, 1:238.

31. Mitchell, *Memoirs*, 216; Rice, "Henry B. Stanton," 3; SBA to Antoinette Brown Blackwell, Sept. 4, 1858, in Gordon, ed., *Selected Papers*, 1:379; "Mr. Stanton's Death," *New York Times*, Jan. 15, 1887; Rice, "Henry B. Stanton," 351.

32. Blatch and Lutz, *Challenging Years*, 35.

33. ECS to Elizabeth Smith Miller, June 4, 1851, in Stanton and Blatch, eds., *ECS*, 2:28–31.

34. "I am rejoiced to say that Henry is heart and soul in the Republican movement and is faithfully stumping the state once more," Stanton wrote Anthony several years later. "I have attended all the Republican meetings and have had Senator John P. Hale staying with us" (ECS to SBA, Nov. 4, 1856, in Stanton and Blatch, eds., *ECS*, 2:62–63).

35. ECS to SBA, [after May 25, 1851], in Gordon, ed., *Selected Papers*, 1:197; ECS to SBA, April 2, 1852, in Stanton and Blatch, eds., *ECS*, 2:41–42. Stanton's children apparently edited this letter to incorporate several under this date. See DuBois, ed., *Elizabeth Cady Stanton/Susan B. Anthony: Correspondence, Writings, Speeches*, 54–55.

36. ECS to SBA, [Jan. 16, 1854], in Gordon, ed., *Selected Papers*, 1:238; Stanton, *Eighty Years and More*, 165. Several years later, after assisting one of her sisters with her new baby, Anthony wrote to Stanton, somewhat tongue in cheek, "O this babydom, what a constant never-ending, all-consuming strain! We should never ask anything else of the woman who has to endure it." She continued: "I realize more and more that rearing children should be looked upon as a profession which, like any other, must be made the primary work of those engaged in it" (quoted in Harper, *SBA*, 1:213).

37. SBA to ECS, June 5, [1856], in Gordon, ed., *Selected Papers*, 1:321.

38. ECS to SBA, June 10, 1856, in ibid., 1:325; SBA to Lucy Stone, Dec. 13, 1852, in ibid., 1:232; SBA to ECS, June 5, [1856], in ibid., 1:322; SBA to Antoinette Brown Blackwell, Apr. 22, 1858, in ibid., 1:360; ECS to SBA, June 10, 1856, in ibid., 1:325; ECS to SBA, [1853], in Harper, "Early Letters," 1191; SBA to Antoinette Brown Blackwell, Sept. 4, 1858, in Gordon, ed., *Selected Papers*, 1:379; ECS to Antoinette Brown Blackwell, March 13, [1861], in ibid., 1:462.

39. ECS to SBA, June 10, 1856, in ibid., 1:325; SBA [to Antoinette Brown Blackwell], [before Sept. 29, 1858], in Harper, *SBA*, 1:168; ECS to SBA, [Aug. 20, 1857], in Gordon, ed., *Selected Papers*, 1:351.

40. ECS to SBA, [Nov. 2], 1857, Film, Reel 8; SBA to sister, [Fall 1857], in Harper, *SBA*, 1:158.

41. "I am regarded as a perfect wonder," she bragged to Henry soon after Theodore's birth (ECS to HBS, Feb. 13, 1851, in Stanton and Blatch, eds., *ECS*, 2:26).

42. ECS to SBA, Aug. [20], 1857, in Gordon, ed., *Selected Papers*, 1:351–52; Caroline Severance to ECS, Oct. 24, 1858; Charles W. Slack to ECS, Nov. 9, 1858; Caroline Thayer to ECS, Nov. 11, 1858. All on Film, Reel 9.

43. ECS to Elizabeth Smith Miller, Dec. 1, 1858, in Gordon, ed., *Selected Papers*, 1:383.

44. ECS to SBA, April 2, [1859], Film, Reel 9; ECS to SBA, April 10, [1859], in Gordon, ed., *Selected Papers*, 1:387.

45. ECS to SBA, [Dec. 13, 1859], in Gordon, ed., *Selected Papers*, 1:400.

46. All quotes in *HWS*, 1:679–84. Lydia Mott lived in Albany, and kept others in the movement aware of the happenings in the state capital. *HWS*, 1:686n, 744–75.

47. William Lloyd Garrison to ECS, March 23, 1860, Film, Reel 9; Garrison to J. Miller McKim, Oct. 21, 1860, in Louis Ruchames, ed., *Letters of William Lloyd Garrison: Volume IV: From Disunion to the Brink of War, 1850–1860* (Cambridge, Mass.: Harvard University Press, 1975), 4:697.

48. Henry Mayer, *All on Fire: William Lloyd Garrison and the Abolition of Slavery* (New York: St. Martin's Griffin, 1998), 511–12.

49. "Mrs. Stanton and the Wide-Awakes," *National Anti-Slavery Standard*, Oct. 13, 1860; Henry B. Stanton to ECS, Oct. 1, 1860, Film, Reel 9. A long account of the speech is in a letter from SBA to Henry B. Stanton, Jr., and Gerrit Smith Stanton, Sept. 27, 1860, in Gordon, ed., *Selected Letters*, 1:441–43.

50. "Tenth Annual Woman's Rights Convention," May 10 and 11, 1860, in *HWS*, 1.688–737. (Quotes are in *HWS*—Wright, 1:689; SBA, 1:689; Rose, 1:693; ECS, 1:716n); Kathleen Barry, *Susan B. Anthony: A Biography of a Singular Feminist* (New York: New York University Press, 1988), 137. An excerpt from the convention, including ECS speech, is in Gordon, ed., *Selected Papers*, 1:418–30. As early as 1850, Rev. Henry Bellows, editor of the *New York Christian Inquirer*, had noted his own gradually changing view, from one who had been "among those who have regarded this movement with decided distrust and distaste" to, a year later, an understanding that "the Woman's Rights question has now made good its title to be heard in the superior court" of public opinion (*HWS*, 1:243–44). The Cooper Union for the Advancement of Science and Art was founded in a building commonly known as the Cooper Institute and the names were used interchangeably.

51. Quotes are in *HWS*—Blackwell, 1:729; Phillips, 1:732; Stanton, 1:718.

52. *HWS*, 1:482, 598. See Ellen DuBois, " 'The Pivot of the Marriage Relation': Stanton's Analysis of Women's Subordination in Marriage," in DuBois and Smith, eds., *ECS: Feminist as Thinker*, 82–92.

53. SBA to Lucy Stone, May 1, 1853, in Gordon, ed., *Selected Papers*, 1:220; Lucy Stone to ECS, April 14, 1853, in ibid., 1:224; Lucy Stone to ECS, March 16, [1860], Film, Reel 9; quoted in Kerr, *Lucy Stone*, 72. See also Lucy Stone to ECS, Aug. 14, 1853, in Gordon, ed., *Selected Papers*, 1:224; ECS to SBA, April 24, 1860, in Stanton and Blatch, eds., *ECS*, 2:77; *HWS*, 1:723n.

54. *HWS*, 1:732; Wendell Phillips to ECS, Aug. 21, [1860], in Gordon, ed., *Selected Papers*, 1:439.

55. ECS to Martha Coffin Wright, [May 28], 1860, in Stanton and Blatch, eds., *ECS*, 2:80–81.

56. ECS to SBA, June 14, 1860, in Stanton and Blatch, eds., *ECS*, 2:82–83.
57. Ibid., 2:82.
58. ECS to SBA, in Harper, *SBA*, 1:244.

4. WAR AND RECONSTRUCTION (1861–1868)

1. ECS to Frances Seward, Sept. 21, [1861], Film, Reel 10; Henry B. Stanton to ECS, Jan. 12, 1861, in Gordon, ed., *Selected Papers*, 1:454–55.
2. Mayer, *All on Fire*, 551; Gordon, ed., *Selected Papers*, 1:530, note 8; Blatch and Lutz, *Challenging Years*, 15.
3. ECS to Frances Seward, Sept. 21, [1861], Film, Reel 10; Henry B. Stanton to ECS, Jan. 12, 1861, in Gordon, ed., *Selected Papers*, 1:455.
4. The main evidence for this story is in a county history, which claims that when James Ashcroft organized a company after Lincoln's first call for troops, the Nineteenth Infantry included "two sons of Hon. H. B. Stanton" and that "Mrs. Stanton expressed her regret that her two younger sons were not old enough to enlist also" (*History of Seneca Co., New York* [Philadelphia: Everts, Ensign & Everts, 1876], 58). Antoinette Brown Blackwell wrote Susan B. Anthony, April 30, 1861: "So Mrs. Stantons [*sic*] two boys have 'gone to the wars,'" and Ann Gordon includes the information from the county history (both in Gordon, ed., *Selected Papers*, 1:466–67). Ellen Carol DuBois, in contrast, suggests that Neil had "refused to enlist" (*Harriot Stanton Blatch and the Winning of Woman Suffrage*, 21). I have found no confirming evidence that Daniel Cady Stanton (Neil) enlisted, though Henry Jr.'s name is listed briefly in the New York Civil War Rosters, Adjutant Generals Report, Third New York Artillery (http://sunsite.utk.edu /civil-war/warweb.html). I thank Carol Reardon for her assistance in tracking down this source.
5. ECS to Ellen Dwight Eaton, July 2, [1861], Film, Reel 10; ECS to William H. Seward, Sept. 19, 1861, ibid.; Lutz, *Created Equal*, 122; ECS to Gerrit Smith, Jan. 14, [1862], Film, Reel 10. Gerrit Smith Stanton later wrote that he had been a "drummer boy in the Army of the Potomac" (G. Smith Stanton, *Renting a Furnished Apartment: A Narrative Setting Forth the Experiences of an Out-of-Town Family in the Metropolis* [New York: J. S. Ogilvie Publishing Co., 1916], 117) and his *New York Times* obituary (Apr. 25, 1927) says that he was a "volunteer soldier." It is possible that Harriot Blatch, who was Lutz's source, confused the stories of two of her older brothers in reporting that Henry, or Kit, ran away to the army.
6. Henry B. Stanton to ECS, Jan. 7, 1862, Film, Reel 10; Blatch and Lutz, *Challenging Years*, 13–14. Ellen DuBois suggests astutely, "It was almost as if Susan Anthony, not the absent Henry Stanton, played the role for Harriot of bad parent, a perfect contrast for her portrait of her all-loving mother" (DuBois, *Harriot Stanton Blatch*, 20).
7. Margaret Stanton Lawrence, "As a Mother," Appendix, in Gordon, ed., *Selected Papers*, 4:558; Blatch and Lutz, *Challenging Years*, 5; ECS to Gerrit Smith, Jan. 14, [1862], Film, Reel 10; SBA to ECS, Nov. 11, 1861, Film, Reel 10.
8. Stanton sold the house and land in Seneca Falls in April 1862 for $2,500, for which she received final payment two years later. Mortgage agreement by John Edwards to ECS, April 21, 1862, Archives Collection, Seneca Falls Historical Society, and on Film, Reel 10.

9. On Civil War–era New York, see Edwin G. Burrows and Mike Wallace, *Gotham: A History of New York City to 1898* (New York: Oxford University Press, 1999), chaps. 48–50. Dodge quote is on 877.

10. Gordon, ed., *Selected Papers*, 1:487, note 1; SBA Diary, Oct. 16, 1865, in ibid., 1:557.

11. Henry B. Stanton to ECS, Jan. 12, 1861, in ibid., 1:455; SBA to Beriah Green, [after May 22, 1861], in Harper, *SBA*, 1:215; ECS, *Eighty Years and More*, 254. In fact, women had suffered some losses, as the New York Legislature took back some of the custody rights it had recently granted them, to Anthony's horror (*HWS*, 1:747–48*n*).

12. Theodore Tilton to SBA, Jan. 11, 1863, in Harper, *SBA*, 1:225–26.

13. Henry B. Stanton to SBA, Jan. 18, 1863, in ibid., 1:226.

14. Call and appeal are in *HWS*, 2:51–53, note.

15. Ibid., 2:2–3. The League was called by three different names in ibid., 2:50, 66, 80. By whatever name, it boasted some five thousand members (ibid., 2:81). Lengthy accounts of the several days' meeting are in the *New York Daily Tribune*, May 15, 1863; May 17, 1863.

16. This version of the quote is in Lutz, *Created Equal*, 126. See also "Meeting of the Loyal Women of the Republic," in Gordon, ed., *Selected Papers* 1:488, which refers to "every subject of the Government."

17. All quotes from this meeting are in *HWS*, 2:58–61.

18. Ibid., 2:62–66. On Abby Kelley Foster's and Maria Weston Chapman's ambivalence, see Dorothy Sterling, *Ahead of Her Time: Abby Kelley and the Politics of Antislavery* (New York: W. W. Norton, 1991), 337–38. "I regard this work of moving Congress . . . as the last great act of our anti-slavery enterprise," Mary Grew wrote. "Verily, the end is nigh" (Mary Grew to SBA, [before Nov. 28, 1863], in Gordon, ed., *Selected Papers*, 1:504).

19. *HWS*, 2:893, 79, 81; Lutz, *Created Equal*, 128, says four hundred thousand names had been gathered by August 1864.

20. Iver Bernstein, "Securing Freedom: The Challenges of Black Life in Civil War New York," in Ira Berlin and Leslie M. Harris, *Slavery in New York* (New York: New Press, 2005), 297; Burrows and Wallace, *Gotham*, 884–85; Bernstein, "Securing Freedom," 291. See Iver Bernstein, *The New York City Draft Riots: Their Significance for American Society and Politics in the Age of the Civil War* (New York: Oxford University Press, 1990).

21. George Templeton Strong, July 13, 1863, *Diary of the Civil War, 1860–1865* (New York: Macmillan, 1962), 336; Burrows and Wallace, *Gotham*, 890. The Gibbonses' correspondence about the riots is in Sarah Hopper Emerson, ed., *Life of Abby Hopper Gibbons, Told Chiefly Through Her Correspondence* (New York: G. P. Putnam's Sons, 1896), 2:43–69. Quotes are from: Julia Gibbons to Abby Hopper Gibbons, July 15, 1863, 2:43; James Gibbons to Edward Hopper, July 16, 1863, 2:45–47; James Gibbons to George E. Baker, July 15, 1863, 2:43. Interestingly, the Quaker Gibbons was prepared to defend his home "with my pistol in hand."

22. Bernstein, *New York City Draft Riots*, 27; Burrows and Wallace, *Gotham*, 896–97.

23. The orphan asylum was on Fifth Avenue and Forty-third Street, and draft headquarters was on Third Avenue and Forty-sixth Street.

24. ECS to Ann Fitzhugh Smith, July 20, 1863, Film, Reel 10; Rice, "Henry B. Stanton," 401.

25. James S. Gibbons to Edward Hopper, July 16, 1863, in Emerson, *Life of Abby Hopper Gibbons*, 2:47; Frances Seward to Henry Seward, July 18, 1863, Microfilm of The Papers of William H. Seward, Department of Rare Books, Rush Rhees Library, University of Rochester, Reel 114; Frances Seward to Henry Seward, July 24, 1863, ibid., Reel 114; Frances Seward to Augustus Seward, July 20, 1863, ibid., Reel 115; Frances Seward to Frederick Seward, July 23, [1863], ibid., Reel 115. George Templeton Strong noted in his diary that there were outbreaks of "Irish anti-conscription Nigger-murdering mob[s]" in Albany, Troy, Yonkers, Hartford, Boston, and elsewhere. Strong, July 16, 1863, *Diary of the Civil War*, 341.

26. ECS to Ann Fitzhugh Smith, July 20, 1863, Film, Reel 10.

27. ECS to Gerrit Smith, July 3, [1864], in Gordon, ed., *Selected Papers*, 1:528.

28. Rice, "Henry B. Stanton," 446.

29. *New York Times*, Nov. 1, 1863; *New York Times*, Stanton letter, Nov. 6, 1863; ECS to Gerrit Smith, July 3, [1864], in Gordon, ed., *Selected Papers*, 1:528. See also ECS to Horace Greeley, Jan. 18, [1864], in ibid., 1:509. The most thorough discussion of the scandal is in Rice, "Henry R. Stanton," 422–62.

30. ECS to Gerrit Smith, July 3, [1864], in ibid., 1:528.

31. Robert Brewster Stanton, "Reminiscences"; quote on Warmoth is in Richard N. Current, "Carpetbaggers Reconsidered," in Kenneth M. Stampp and Leon F. Litwack, *Reconstruction: An Anthology of Revisionist Writings* (Baton Rouge: Louisiana State University Press, 1969), 245. See also Eric Foner, *Reconstruction: America's Unfinished Revolution, 1863–1877* (New York: Harper and Row, 1988), various pages, and Current, "Carpetbaggers Reconsidered," 223–40. Robert Brewster Stanton, "Reminiscences," claimed that Neil served a term as a state senator. Gordon, ed., *Selected Papers*, 2:xxvi, note 19, was unable to confirm this. In her Alumnae Questionnaire for the Emma Willard Association, Elizabeth Stanton noted that Daniel Cady Stanton had been a member of the Louisiana Legislature. Since the form is in Margaret Stanton Lawrence's handwriting, it seems that Maggie at least considered the claim plausible. ECS, Alumnae Questionaire [1898], Emma Willard Association, Film, Reel 39.

32. Margaret Stanton Lawrence, "As a Mother," in Gordon, ed., *Selected Papers*, Appendix, 4:559; ECS to SBA, summer 1877, Film, Reel 19. One historian believes that Neil "remained her favorite and could do no wrong in her eyes," but there is nothing explicit to suggest this, nor have I found much information about his marriage, divorce, and daughter. Griffith, *In Her Own Right*, 121, 172–73.

33. Wendell Phillips to ECS, Sept. 27, [1864], in Gordon, ed., *Selected Papers*, 1:531.

34. Mayer, *All on Fire*, 577–80.

35. The phrase is Leon F. Litwack's, *Been in the Storm So Long: The Aftermath of Slavery* (New York: Alfred A. Knopf, 1979), 292.

36. Foner, *Reconstruction*, 67; William S. McFeely, *Frederick Douglass* (New York: W. W. Norton, 1991), 246.

37. Foner, *Reconstruction*, 282; Eleventh National Woman's Rights Convention, *HWS*, 2:172; ECS, "Universal Suffrage," [July 29, 1865], in Gordon, ed., *Selected Papers*, 1:551.

38. American Anti-Slavery Society convention, May 9, 1866, in Gordon, ed., *Selected Papers*, 1:581; American Equal Rights Association convention, 1867, in ibid., 2:66.
39. "Thanksgiving Sermons," *New York Times*, Dec. 8, 1865; *New York World*, May 6, 1869, quoted in DuBois, *Feminism and Suffrage*, 152; "Mr. Blackwell's Seventieth Birthday," *Woman's Journal*, May 11, 1895, Film, Reel 33.
40. Quoted in Carol Faulkner, *Women's Radical Reconstruction: The Freedmen's Aid Movement* (Philadelphia: University of Pennsylvania Press, 2004), 40; DuBois, *Feminism and Suffrage*, 75.
41. McFeely, *Frederick Douglass*, 251; HWS, 2:331. On Northern states, see Alexander Keyssar, *The Right to Vote: The Contested History of Democracy in the United States* (New York: Basic Books, 2000), 89.
42. Quote in Keyssar, *Right to Vote*, 177; "The Anniversaries," *New York Times*, May 10, 1865; *National Anti-Slavery Standard*, Nov. 25, 1865, 3; Kerr, *Lucy Stone*, 121–22; HWS, 2:833–34. On black women's support for universal voting rights, see Rosalyn Terborg-Penn, *African American Women in the Struggle for the Vote, 1850–1920* (Bloomington: Indiana University Press, 1998), 24–35, and Martha S. Jones, *All Bound Up Together: The Woman Question in African American Political Culture, 1830–1900* (Chapel Hill: University of North Carolina Press, 2007), 140–49.
43. HWS, 2:174, 152–56.
44. Harper, *SBA*, 1:262.
45. ECS to Wendell Phillips, Oct. 12, [1866], Film, Reel 11; ECS to Frederick Douglass, Oct. 20, [1885], Film, Reel 24; HWS, 2:180–81. See "Elizabeth Cady Stanton for Congress," *National Anti-Slavery Standard*, Oct. 13, 1866, Film, Reel 11.
46. *The New-Orleans Weekly Times*, 3:155, Nov. 17, 1866, 7 (retrieved from NewsBank database); HWS, 2:181.
47. ECS, "Reconstruction," [Feb. 19, 1867], in Gordon, ed., *Selected Papers*, 2:28; HWS, 2:320; ECS, "Female Suffrage Committee," [June 19, 1867], in Gordon, ed., *Selected Papers*, 2:72. She used that phrase elsewhere, e.g., ECS to Sojourner Truth, March 24, [1867], in Gordon, ed., *Selected Papers*, 2:47; it also appears in the Constitution of the American Equal Rights Association, 1866, in HWS, 2:173. Even Lucretia Mott, though loyal to Stanton, thought this "emphatically the negro's hour," and told Stanton so. (See Mott to Wendell Phillips, April 17, 1866, in Palmer, ed., *Selected Letters of Lucretia Coffin Mott*, 371.)
48. HWS, 2:181. There are numerous similar references. See, for example, ECS, "Female Suffrage Committee," [June 14, 1867], in Gordon, ed., *Selected Papers*, 2:72.
49. ECS to Editor, *National Anti-Slavery Standard*, in Gordon, ed., *Selected Papers*, 1:564–65; HWS, 2:214.
50. *Revolution* 1:1, Jan. 8, 1868, 1.
51. Kerr, *Lucy Stone*, 124; Lucy Stone to ECS, April 10, 1867, in Gordon, ed., *Selected Papers*, 2:48.
52. Stanton, *Eighty Years and More*, 250; DuBois, *Feminism and Suffrage*, 94. "Of all the twisted intellects in *The Sun*'s crankdom George Francis Train was easily monarch" (Mitchell, *Memoirs of an Editor*, 237).

53. *HWS*, 2:254, reminiscence of Helen Ekin Starrett; Harper, *SBA*, 1:295; Stanton, *Eighty Years and More*, 256. In George Francis Train's memoir, *My Life in Many States and Foreign Lands* (New York: D. Appleton and Company, 1902), he mentions woman suffrage only once (136), in referring to his daughter, "Sue, who could never be President, unless the Woman's Suffrage movement moves along very much faster than it has up to this time." Decades later, Stanton would admit that "Susan & I were so desperate we said to each other when considering Train's proposition Yes we would work with the Devil if he would advocate our cause" (ECS to Clara Colby, June 16, [1890], Film, Reel 28).
54. *HWS*, 2:248. "[I]t was not the woman suffrage question that killed the negro question," she declared to an audience in St. Louis, Missouri, "it was Republican leaders . . . they killed it themselves" (Nov. 25, 1867, in Gordon, ed., *Selected Papers*, 2:108).
55. Quoted in McFeely, *Frederick Douglass*, 268; quoted in James A. Colaiaco, *Frederick Douglass and the Fourth of July* (New York: Palgrave Macmillan, 2006), 92.
56. *HWS*, 2:382–83.
57. Ibid., 2:382–84.
58. Vivian Gornick, "Elizabeth Cady Stanton: The Long View," in DuBois and Smith, eds., *Elizabeth Cady Stanton: Feminist as Thinker*, 25.
59. Foner, *Reconstruction*, 261–63. On African American political organizing during Reconstruction, see Steven Hahn, *A Nation Under Our Feet: Black Political Struggles in the Rural South from Slavery to the Great Migration* (Cambridge: Harvard University Press, 2003).
60. *HWS*, 2:382.
61. Ibid., 2:23–26; Clara Barton to Mary Norton, Oct. 15, 1869, Alma Lutz Collection, Women's Studies Manuscript Collections from the Schlesinger Library, Radcliffe College, Series 1, Woman's Suffrage (Bethesda, Md.: University Publications of America, 1990), A-110, Reel M-105.
62. *Revolution* 1:4, Jan. 29, 1868, 50; Stansell, "Missed Connections," in DuBois and Smith, eds., *Elizabeth Cady Stanton: Feminist as Thinker*, 44; DuBois, "Outgrowing the Compact of the Fathers," *Woman Suffrage and Women's Rights*, 92; Editorial, *Revolution*, March 18, 1869, in Gordon, ed., *Selected Papers*, 2:229. "To the end of her days," as Stansell bluntly puts it, "Stanton was oblivious to the costs of her towering disregard for black women" ("Missed Connections," 46).
63. *HWS*, 2:320.
64. ECS, "Manhood Suffrage," [Dec. 24, 1868], in Gordon, ed., *Selected Papers*, 2:194; ECS to Martha Coffin Wright, March 21, [1871], in ibid., 2:426; ECS, "Woman Suffrage" speech, 1874, in ibid., 3:82.
65. ECS, "Manhood Suffrage"; ECS, "The Sixteenth Amendment," April 29, 1869, in ibid., 2:237. See, too, Meeting of the Illinois Woman Suffrage Association, Feb. 12, 1869, in ibid., 2:217.
66. ECS to Editor, *National Anti-Slavery Standard* 26, July 22, 1865; Elsa Barkley Brown, "Negotiating and Transforming the Public Sphere: African American Political Life in the Transition from Slavery to Freedom," *Public Culture* 7 (1994): 123.
67. Hahn, *A Nation Under Our Feet*, 227–28; Barkley Brown, "Negotiating and Transforming," 119; Jones, *All Bound Up Together*, 146–48; Hahn, ibid., 213.

68. *HWS*, 4:41. Old friends became either enemies, like Lucy Stone, or wary associates, as in the case of Douglass, who "seldom," as one biographer puts it, "lost a
friend for long" (McFeely, *Frederick Douglass*, 315). The conflict, Stanton and
Anthony later recalled, "cost us the friendship of Horace Greeley and the support of the *New York Tribune*, heretofore our most powerful and faithful allies"
(*HWS*, 2:269). It did not help that Stanton and Anthony headed a petition for
woman suffrage with the name of "Mrs. Horace Greeley," intending to embarrass
her husband; out of pique and irritation, Greeley vowed to use a similar tactic
against her, from then on referring to her in the *Tribune* as "Mrs. Henry B. Stanton." Though the *History of Woman Suffrage* called this "An Amusing Encounter,"
it rankled (ibid., 2:287).
69. Sally G. McMillen, *Seneca Falls and the Origins of the Women's Rights Movement*
(New York: Oxford University Press, 2008), 161; Gornick, "Elizabeth Cady Stanton," DuBois and Smith, eds., *Elizabeth Cady Stanton: Feminist as Thinker*, 25.
Ellen DuBois has called this era "one of those turning points in history that
requires . . . continually revised interpretation" (DuBois, "The Last Suffragist," in
DuBois, *Woman Suffrage and Women's Rights*, 10). For a range of historians'
analyses, see DuBois and Smith, eds., *Elizabeth Cady Stanton: Feminist as
Thinker*; DuBois, *Feminism and Suffrage*; Angela Davis, *Women, Race, and Class*
(New York: Vintage Press, 1983); Eleanor Flexner, *Century of Struggle: The
Woman's Rights Movement in the United States* (Cambridge: Harvard University
Press, 1959); Ann D. Gordon, ed., *African American Women and the Vote,
1837–1965* (Amherst: University of Massachusetts Press, 1997); Nell Irvin
Painter, *Sojourner Truth: A Life, a Symbol* (New York: W. W. Norton, 1996);
Terborg-Penn, *African American Women in the Struggle for the Vote*; and Lisa
Marguerite Tetrault, "The Memory of a Movement: Woman Suffrage and Reconstruction America, 1865–1890," Ph.D. dissertation (University of Wisconsin,
2004).
70. *Revolution* 1:22, June 4, 1868, 337; ECS, "Women and Black Men," in ibid., 3:6,
Feb. 11, 1869, 88.
71. "A," in ibid., 3:10, March 11, 1869, 148.
72. ECS, Editorial, in ibid., March 7, [1869], in Gordon, ed., *Selected Papers*,
2:228–29.

5. *REVOLUTION* AND THE ROAD (1868–1880)

1. *Revolution* 1:4, Jan. 29, 1868, 50.
2. ECS to SBA, [June ca. 13], 1870, Film, Reel 14; ECS to Isabella Beecher
Hooker, [Aug. 1872], Film, Reel 16; *HWS*, 2:322.
3. ECS to Ellen D. Eaton, Dec. 17, [1867], in Gordon, ed., *Selected Papers*, 2:117.
4. *Cincinnati Commercial*, quoted in Lutz, *Created Equal*, 160. No one else,
thought Susan B. Anthony, could "make the pages burn & freeze—laugh & cry"
as Stanton and Pillsbury did (SBA to Laura De Force Gordon, [Feb. 9, 1871], in
Gordon, ed., *Selected Papers*, 2:417).
5. "The Jews and the Chinese—A Warning," *Revolution* 3:11, March 18, 1869,
166; "Let the Jews Alone," in ibid., 3:14, April 8, 1869, 220. There were one
hundred subscribers in California as of 1868 (Gordon, ed., *Selected Papers*,
2:295, note 1).

6. *Revolution* 1:3, Jan. 22, 1868, 34; *Cincinnati Enquirer*, quoted in Lutz, *Created Equal*, 159.

7. *Revolution* 2:20, Nov. 19, 1868; ibid., 2:23, Dec. 10, 1868. And yet neither *The Revolution* nor the women activists it represented were helpless; petitions and a mass demonstration sponsored by the Working Women's Association, followed by a meeting between Elizabeth Cady Stanton and the governor of Pennsylvania, likely influenced him to commute the death sentence, and exile Vaughn to her native England instead (Stanton, Editorial Correspondence, *Revolution* 2:23, Dec. 10, 1868, 353–54.)

8. ECS, Editorial Correspondence, *Revolution* 4:4, July 29, 1869, 49–50.

9. George Cooper, *Lost Love: A True Story of Passion, Murder, and Justice in Old New York* (New York: Random House, 1994), 138: *Revolution* 4:25, Dec. 23, 1869; ECS speech, "Mass Meeting of Women," [May 17, 1870], in Gordon, ed., *Selected Papers*, 2:338; *Revolution* 4:25, Dec. 23, 1869.

10. Kerr, *Lucy Stone*, 148. For an excellent analysis of *The Revolution*'s stance on matters of political economy, and their implications for the women's movement, see Tetrault, "Memory of a Movement," chap. 3.

11. *Revolution* 1:15, April 16, 1868, 227; ibid., 1:17, April 30, 1868, 264; Meeting of the Working Women's Association, [Sept. 17, 1868], in Gordon, ed., *Selected Papers*, 2:164–65. For Stanton's views, see "On Labor," ed. Ellen DuBois, *Signs* 1 (Autumn 1975): 260–63. The best assessment of *The Revolution*'s alliance with labor leaders remains DuBois, *Feminism and Suffrage*, 110–25. Gordon, ed., *Selected Papers*, 2:168, note 5, says Lewis worked in the print shop of Robert J. Johnson, where *The Revolution* was printed, until 1869—and may have been fired for her union activities.

12. SBA to ECS, March 20, 1870, in Gordon, ed., *Selected Papers*, 2:311. Anthony spent three weeks each winter at Mr. and Mrs. C. W. Spofford's Riggs House, an elegant hotel one block from the White House, which she considered her head-quarters in Washington. By 1892 the hotel had been sold and the delegation had to move on (*HWS*, 4:188).

13. ECS to SBA, [Dec. 28, 1869], in Stanton and Blatch, eds., *ECS*, 2:125.

14. SBA to ECS, Jan. 2, 1871, in Gordon, ed., *Selected Papers*, 2:401; ECS, after Oct. 29, 1869, in Lutz, *Created Equal*, 182–83; ECS to Thomas Wentworth Higginson, Nov. 3, 1868, Film, Reel 13.

15. ECS to SBA, [Dec. 28], 1869, in Stanton and Blatch, eds., *ECS*, 2:124–25.

16. ECS to Isabella Beecher Hooker, Dec. 1, [1870], Film, Reel 14; Isabella Beecher Hooker to ECS, Dec. 21, 1870, ibid.; ECS to Isabella Beecher Hooker, Dec. 28, [1870], ibid.

17. ECS to SBA, [before July 10], 1873, Film, Reel 17.

18. Martha Coffin Wright to ECS, March 16, 1873, Film, Reel 17.

19. ECS to Martha Coffin Wright, Dec. 27, 1870, Film, Reel 14; ECS to Theodore Tilton, July 14, [1870], ibid.

20. Historians have suggested that Anthony's situation resulted because, as an unmarried woman, only she could be responsible for debts (McMillen, *Seneca Falls*, 172), but by 1870 that was no longer the case. The question of why Stanton burdened her friend with the debt is a distasteful one, an act that even an admiring biographer calls "unconscionable" (Griffith, *In Her Own Right*, 145).

21. ECS to SBA, [June ca. 13], 1870, Film, Reel 14.

22. See Vassar Encyclopedia, "Preparatory School," vcencyclopedia.vassar.edu. The 1872–1873 *Cornell University Register* states total costs were about $265 a term, with books costing about $20–$30 per year. Thanks to Elaine Engst, at the Cornell University Library, for this information. Theodore Stanton got his AB degree in 1876 and his MA in 1877; Robert Livingston Stanton got his BS in 1880 (*Cornell University: A History*, compiled by Frank R. Homes and Lewis A. Williams, Jr. [New York: University Publishing Society, 1905], 517).

23. Blatch and Lutz, *Challenging Years*, 36. Daniel Cady's will was so complicated that it took eighteen years for his sons-in-law to settle it. Holland and Gordon, eds., *The Papers of Elizabeth Cady Stanton and Susan B. Anthony: Guide and Index to the Microfilm Edition*, p. 18, Film, Reel 45.

24. ECS to Henry B. Stanton, Oct. 9, 1867, in Gordon, ed., *Selected Papers*, 2:96.

25. Anthony's brother D.R. had moved to Kansas in 1854 as part of the antislavery migration, founded and edited the *Leavenworth Times*, and, in 1863, became Leavenworth's mayor. Her youngest brother, Jacob Merritt, had moved to Kansas in 1856 and immediately become caught up in John Brown's raid.

26. ECS to Thomas Wentworth Higginson, Nov. 3, 1868, Film, Reel 13; *Revolution* 1:18, May 7, 1868, 281. When she sold the house, she received $11,000, a tidy sum (warranty deed, May 26, 1887, Film, Reel 25).

27. ECS, "Notes and Comments," *Golden Age* (New York), April 8, 1871, Film, Reel 15; ECS to Ezra Cornell, Feb. 13, [1872], Film, Reel 16.

28. Margaret Stanton Lawrence, "As a Mother," in Gordon, ed., *Selected Papers*, Appendix, 4:559; interview with Elizabeth Boynton Harbert, "Woman's Kingdom," *Inter-Ocean* (Chicago), Oct. 23, 1880, Film, Reel 21; ECS to Martha Coffin Wright, [Oct. 10, 1874], in Gordon, ed., *Selected Papers*, 3:117–18; ECS to Elizabeth Smith Miller, Aug. 16, 1877, Film, Reel 19.

29. Tetrault, "Memory of a Movement," 214; SBA to Lepha Johnson Canfield, Jan. 2, 1871, in Gordon, ed., *Selected Papers*, 2:399; Martha Coffin Wright to ECS, May 9, 1870, Film, Reel 14.

30. Stanton, *Eighty Years and More*, 290.

31. SBA to Lucy Read Anthony, [July 31, 1871], in Harper, *SBA*, 1:393.

32. SBA Diary, [Jan. 1–9, 1872], in Gordon, ed., *Selected Papers*, 2:463; "I shall say this winter $85 to $100" (ECS to Charles Mumford, July 18, 1870, Film, Reel 14); Tetrault, "Memory of a Movement," 226, 234; ECS to Gerrit Smith, Jan. 25, [1870], in Gordon, ed., *Selected Papers*, 2:299.

33. ECS, Editorial Correspondence, *Revolution*, April 21, 1870, in Gordon, ed., *Selected Papers*, 2:319. She added, "my usually placid soul has been so terribly tempest-tossed" (ibid., 2:320).

34. ECS to Margaret Stanton, Dec. 1, 1872, Film, Reel 16.

35. ECS, "The Greatest of Bugaboos," in Gordon, ed., *Selected Papers*, 2:442.

36. Woodhull quoted in Goldsmith, *Other Powers*, 274; SBA to Woodhull, Feb. 4, 1871, in Gordon, ed., *Selected Papers*, 2:415; Victoria Woodhull, Address, Jan. 11, 1871, in *HWS*, 2:444–48; ECS to Lucretia Mott, April 1, [1871], in Gordon, ed., *Selected Papers*, 2:427–28.

37. ECS to SBA, May 27, [1871], in ibid., 2:431.

38. Applegate, *The Most Famous Man in America*, 421–22; Bull, "Woman's Rights and Other 'Reforms' in Seneca Falls," 330.

39. SBA to ECS and Isabella Beecher Hooker, March 13, 1872, in Gordon, ed., *Selected Papers*, 2:485; announcement of a People's Convention, [March 1872], in ibid., 2:489–90; SBA Diary, May 8, 1872, in ibid., 2:493.

40. The fourteenth plank of the Republican Party platform is quoted in ibid., 2:505, note 2; ECS to Isabella Beecher Hooker, [June 14, 1872], in ibid., 2:511.

41. Martha Coffin Wright to ECS, Sept. 4, 1872, Film, Reel 16; interview with SBA by Anne E. McDowell in Philadelphia, [June 11, 1872], in Gordon, ed., *Selected Papers*, 2:508; ECS to Lucy Stone and Henry Blackwell, July 13, 1872, in ibid., 2:517.

42. Martha Coffin Wright to ECS, Sept. 4, 1872, Film, Reel 16; *HWS*, 2:407–10.

43. SBA to ECS, Nov. 5, 1872, in Gordon, ed., *Selected Papers*, 2:524. For the names of those women who voted in that election in Rochester, see Editorial Note, in ibid., 2:527–29. See also Allison L. Sneider, *Suffragists in an Imperial Age: U.S. Expansion and the Woman Question, 1870–1929* (New York: Oxford University Press, 2008), 53–54; *HWS*, 2:587, 3:813.

44. *An Account of the Proceedings of the Trial of Susan B. Anthony on the Charge of Illegal Voting* (Rochester, N.Y., 1874), 2.

45. ECS to SBA and Matilda Joslyn Gage, [before July 10], 1873, Film, Reel 17; SBA to Isabella Beecher Hooker, July 14, 1873, in Gordon, ed., *Selected Papers*, 2:618.

46. SBA, "Work, Wages and the Ballot," [April 15, 1870], in ibid., 2:321; SBA "Women Already Voters," [Oct. 19, 1871], in ibid., 2:456–61.

47. ECS to SBA, [June 27, 1870], in Stanton and Blatch, eds., *ECS*, 2:127; SBA Diary, Aug. 18, 1871, in Gordon, ed., *Selected Papers*, 2:439; ECS, "Woman Suffrage" speech, Grand Rapids, [1874], in ibid., 3:81.

48. ECS to SBA, [Sept. 15], 1872, Film, Reel 16; ECS to SBA, [Dec. 28, 1869], in Harper, *SBA*, 1:357, and Stanton and Blatch, eds., *ECS*, 2:124.

49. *HWS*, 2:254n; "Mrs. E. C. Stanton on Marriage and Divorce," *Wisconsin Daily Journal* (Madison), Nov. 28, 1870, Film, Reel 14; "The Suffrage Question," *Chicago Tribune*, Nov. 23, 1876, Film, Reel 12; "The Champions of Woman Suffrage," *San Francisco Chronicle*, July 11, 1871, Film, Reel 15; Illinois Woman Suffrage Association, Founding Convention, Feb. 12, 1869, in Gordon, ed., *Selected Papers*, 2:213. Tetrault, "Memory of a Movement," offers information and analysis of Stanton and Anthony's celebrity in the West.

50. "Mrs. Cady Stanton to the Women of Illinois," *Agitator*, March 13, 1869, Film, Reel 13.

51. Wendy Hamand Venet, *A Strong-Minded Woman: The Life of Mary Livermore* (Amherst: University of Massachusetts Press, 2005), 202.

52. Keyssar, *Right to Vote*, 187.

53. Declaration of the Rights of the Women of the United States, [July 4, 1876], in Gordon, ed., *Selected Papers*, 3:234; newspaper quotes in *HWS*, 3:42–44; Keyssar, *Right to Vote*, 190. The text of the Declaration is in Gordon, ed., *Selected Papers*, 3:234–41. Stanton said it was written jointly and then "put together in my language" (ECS to Isabella Beecher Hooker, July 5, 1876, in Gordon, ed., *Selected Papers*, 3:241).

54. ECS to Isabella Beecher Hooker, April 1, [1871], Film, Reel 15.

55. *HWS*, 464–65. In spite of Stanton's implication that she was the lone radical in

her family, her sister Catherine Wilkeson's name appeared on the Call to the Worcester Convention (Gordon, ed., *Selected Papers*, 1:172, note 5).

56. Quoted in Goldsmith, *Other Powers*, 218.

57. SBA to Lucy Read Anthony, [Sept. 1, 1871], in Harper, *SBA*, 1:396.

58. ECS to SBA, Nov. 5, 1872, Film, Reel 16; ECS to SBA, Dec. 28, 1869, Stanton and Blatch, eds., *ECS*, 2:125; ECS to SBA, Feb. 6, 1871, in ibid., 2:130; ECS to SBA, Nov. 20, 1872, Film, Reel 16; ECS to Elizabeth Boynton Harbert, Sept. 29, [1880], Film, Reel 21.

59. ECS to Theodore Stanton, March 30, 1880, Film, Reel 21.

6. MAKING A PLACE IN HISTORY (1880–1902)

1. Robert Browning, "Rabbi Ben Ezra," in ECS Diary, Stanton and Blatch, eds., *ECS*, 2:175; Diary, Nov. 14, 1880, ibid., 2:178; Diary, Nov. 12, 1880, ibid., 2:177.

2. ECS to SBA, Feb. 1, 1877, Film, Reel 19; ECS, SBA, Matilda Joslyn Gage, Partnership Agreement, Nov. 15, 1876, Film, Reel 18; "Woman Suffrage," unidentified clipping, Oct. 27, 1880, Film, Reel 21; *HWS*, 3:iv. The fourth volume was coedited by Anthony and Ida Husted Harper, and the rest by Harper. For historical assessments of the *History of Woman Suffrage*, and how it has shaped the narrative of women's history itself, see Ellen Carol DuBois, "Making Women's History: Historian-Activists of Women's Rights, 1880–1940," in DuBois, *Woman Suffrage and Women's Rights*, and Tetrault, "Memory of a Movement."

3. *HWS*, 1:13; Tetrault, "Memory of a Movement," 25–26, 4; *HWS*, 3:v.

4. ECS to Elizabeth Smith Miller, Aug. 16, 1877, Film, Reel 19; quoted in Sally Roesch Wagner, introduction to Matilda Joslyn Gage, *Woman, Church, and State* (Watertown, Mass.: Persephone Press, 1980), xxvi. Anthony's father had long before suggested that it might "be wise to preserve the many and amusing observations by the different papers, that years hence . . . you and maybe your children can look over the views of both the friends and opponents of the cause" (Daniel Anthony to SBA, [winter 1855], in Harper, *SBA*, 1:125).

5. Tetrault, "Memory of a Movement," 34.

6. Stanton, *Eighty Years and More*, 326. It was, Anthony's biographer notes, "torture for her to give up her active life and sit poring over the musty records of the past" (Harper, *SBA*, 2:525).

7. SBA to Clara Colby, May 3, 1897, Film, Reel 36.

8. SBA to Amelia Bloomer, Oct. 25, 1880, in Gordon, ed., *Selected Papers*, 4:12: "all her men are quartered in the city for the winter," Anthony wrote happily. The quoted description of the project comes from Margaret Stanton Lawrence, "As a Mother," in Gordon, ed., *Selected Papers*, Appendix, 4:559–60. Stanton herself "laughed heartily over the way Maggie sewed Susan & me up & it is all quite true" (ECS to Elizabeth Boynton Harbert, [Oct. 19, 1885], Film, Reel 24). The disagreements took various forms: on occasion Anthony pleaded with Gage to "scan the *law* & the *logic*" of some position of Stanton's that she considered absurd, agreeing that "if you & she see the matter alike—of course I shall surrender" (SBA to Matilda Joslyn Gage, April 27, 1886, in Gordon, ed., *Selected Papers*, 4:503).

9. ECS to Elizabeth Boynton Harbert, Sept. 29, [1876], in Gordon, ed., *Selected Papers*, 3:264; SBA to Clara Barton, Sept. 19, 1876, in ibid., 3:263; ECS to Frederic Allen Hinckley, Jan. 30, [1882], in ibid., 4:148; ECS to SBA, July 26, [1877], Film, Reel 19.

10. Lucy Stone to ECS, Aug. 3, 1876, in Gordon, ed., *Selected Papers*, 3:249; ECS to Harriet Hanson Robinson, Nov. 1, [1881], Film, Reel 22.

11. ECS to Harriet Hanson Robinson, Oct. 26, [1881], in Gordon, ed., *Selected Papers*, 4:118; Blatch and Lutz, *Challenging Years*, 61; DuBois, *Harriot Stanton Blatch*, 50–51; Stanton, *Eighty Years and More*, 337.

12. Stanton, *Eighty Years and More*, 342.

13. ECS, "Eulogy at Memorial Service" of Lucretia Coffin Mott, Jan. 19, 1881, *HWS*, 1:407–31. Quotes on p. 431.

14. ECS to SBA, May 4, 1879, in Gordon, ed., *Selected Papers*, 3:443; Gerrit Smith Stanton, "How Aged Housekeeper Gave Her All to Cause of Woman's Suffrage," Seneca Falls Historical Society. Back in New York years later, when asked his opinion of woman suffrage, he made no mention of his famous parent, offering only the view that "an educational and property qualification, especially the former, should determine the question of the elective franchise" (G. Smith Stanton, *Renting a Furnished Apartment*, 117). For his life story, see also Gerrit Smith Stanton, *When the Wildwood Was in Flower: A Narrative Covering the Fifteen Years' Experiences of a Stockman on the Western Plains and His Vacation Days in the Open* (New York: J. S. Ogilvie Publishing Co., 1909).

15. ECS to SBA, [before June 11], 1870, Film, Reel 14; ECS to Marguerite Berry Stanton, March 8, [1885], in Gordon, ed., *Selected Papers*, 4:406; ECS to Harriot Stanton Blatch, Sept. 21, 1884, Film, Reel 23. It was for Bob that sister Hattie reserved her highest compliment—that he "displayed no sex superiority" (Blatch and Lutz, *Challenging Years*, 34).

16. Blatch and Lutz, *Challenging Years*, 17; "What Women May Wear," *New York Times*, May 22, 1895.

17. ECS to Benjamin F. Underwood, Oct. 19, [1885], in Gordon, ed., *Selected Papers*, 4:443. "I am rather ambitious for the success of this young man," she wrote Joseph Pulitzer, "as I am his mother & I should esteem it a great favor if you would make him your Paris correspondent" (ECS to Joseph Pulitzer, Dec. 29, 1885, Film, Reel 24).

18. See, for example, ECS speech to the Scottish demonstration of women at Glasgow in November 1882, in Gordon, ed., *Selected Papers*, 4:194–96; interview with SBA, in ibid., 4:222; ECS to Mary Post Hallowell, July 16, [1882], in ibid., 4:171; ECS to Robert L. Stanton, June 17, [1887], Film, Reel 25. On her feelings about "Old World" intransigence, see Priscilla Bright McLaren to ECS, July 17, 1883, in ibid., 4:282.

19. Article by ECS, March 5, [1883], in Gordon, ed., *Selected Papers*, 4:226; SBA Diary, in Harper, *SBA*, 2:636; SBA to Elizabeth Smith Miller, Jan. 26, 1888, Film, Reel 25. As the story goes, Stanton arrived at the 1888 convention with no speech prepared; Anthony apparently locked her in a room in the Riggs House for three days until she had written one (Harper, *SBA*, 2:636).

20. Frenchwomen Jeanne Deroin and Pauline Roland had long ago written from their prison cells that news of the American women's struggle "has filled our

souls with inexpressible joy" (Bonnie S. Anderson, *Joyous Greetings: The First International Women's Movement, 1830–1860* [New York: Oxford University Press, 2000], 8–9, 24).

21. SBA to Frederick Douglass, Feb. 6, 1888, Film, Reel 26.

22. Quotes are in *HWS*, 4:133–35; National Woman Suffrage Association, *Report, International Council of Women* (Washington, D.C., 1888), 436, Film, Reel 26.

23. ECS Address, [Sept. 1848], in Gordon, ed., *Selected Papers*, 1:104.

24. *Revolution* 1:1, Jan. 8, 1868, 1; "Meeting of the American Equal Rights Association," May 9, 1867, in Gordon, ed., *Selected Papers*, 2:65; *Revolution* 1:14, April 9, 1868, 212–13; ECS to Editor, *Ballot Box*, in Gordon, ed., *Selected Papers*, 3:284. See also ECS on "Manhood Suffrage," in Gordon, ed., *Selected Papers*, 2:195; Train's "National Party" plank in ibid., 2:146, note 3.

25. ECS to Matilda Joslyn Gage and National Woman Suffrage Association [before May 24, 1877], in Gordon, ed., *Selected Papers*, 3:310; SBA to Robert Stanton, April 15, 1904, Film, Reel 44; ECS, "Immigration and Suffrage," *Wisconsin Citizen* (Racine), Feb. 1893.

26. ECS to Clara Colby, Jan. 17, [1898], Film, Reel 37.

27. Harriot Stanton Blatch to ECS, *Woman's Journal*, Dec. 22, 1894. Evidently the two women continued to argue the point. (See Blatch, "Universal Suffrage Symposium," *Woman's Journal*, Oct. 9, 1897.)

28. ECS to Harriot Stanton Blatch, Jan. 4, [1895], Film, Reel 33; ECS to editors, *Woman's Journal*, Dec. 22, 1894, Film, Reel 33; ibid., Nov. 13, 1897, Film, Reel 37; National Council of Women, U.S. triennial meeting held in Washington, D.C., *American Woman's Journal* 9 (March–April 1895): 90–92, Film, Reel 33; ECS to Harriot Stanton Blatch, *Woman's Journal*, Jan. 5, 1895. Three years later Stanton remained unmoved. Although she knew that "Susan does not see eye to eye with me this time neither does my daughter Hattie," she remained certain that "I am right" (ECS to Clara Colby, Jan. 24, [1898], Film, Reel 38).

29. Sneider, *Suffragists in an Imperial Age*, 6; ECS to William Lloyd Garrison, Jr., July 21, [1899], Film, Reel 40; William Lloyd Garrison, Jr., to ECS, July 26, 1899, Film, Reel 40.

30. ECS, "The Solution of the Race Question," *Woman's Tribune*, May 17, 1902, Film, Reel 42; ECS, "The Woman Suffrage Association," *Boston Investigator*, July 22, 1899, Film, Reel 40; ECS Diary, Feb. 11, 1893, in Stanton and Blatch, eds., *ECS*, 292.

31. ECS to Clara Colby, Dec. 8, [1892], Film, Reel 30; ECS to Clara Colby, March 6, [1890], Film, Reel 28; ECS to Clara Colby, June 16, [1890], Film, Reel 28. Stanton had already concluded, "A personal quarrel between Susan & Lucy was the corner stone of the division" (ECS to Clara Colby, April 10, [1890], Film, Reel 28).

32. "Mrs. Stanton's Remarks," National Woman Suffrage Association, Final Executive Session, *Woman's Tribune*, March 8, 1890; ECS to Olympia Brown, May 8, [1889], Film, Reel 27; ECS to Clara Colby, June 16, [1890], Film, Reel 28.

33. The exchange (and all quotes) are in SBA to ECS, Jan. 27, 1884, in Gordon, ed., *Selected Papers*, 4:323–26; ECS to Frederick Douglass, Jan. 27, [1884], enclosed in letter from ECS to Douglass dated May 27, [1884], in ibid., 4:353–55; Frederick Douglass to ECS, May 30, 1884, in ibid., 4:356.

34. ECS to Elizabeth Smith Miller, June 30, [1880], Film, Reel 24; ECS Diary, Sept. 6, 1883, in Stanton and Blatch, eds., *ECS*, 2:210.
35. Griffith, *In Her Own Right*, 170.
36. ECS to Isabella Beecher Hooker, Sept. 8, 1869, in Gordon, ed., *Selected Papers*, 2:263–64.
37. On Henry's presence in the household see, for example, ECS to Marguerite Berry Stanton, March 8, [1885], in Gordon, ed., *Selected Papers*, 4:406 or in a domestic tale, ECS to Harriot Stanton, June 8, 1880, in ibid., 3:544.
38. Interview with Elizabeth Boynton Harbert, "Woman's Kingdom," *Inter-Ocean* (Chicago), Oct. 23, 1880, Film, Reel 21.
39. ECS, "Reminiscences: Washington, Troy, Albany," *Woman's Tribune*, July 18, 1891, Film, Reel 29; "Mr. Stanton's Recollections," *New York Times*, July 5, 1887.
40. Henry B. Stanton, *Random Recollections* (3rd edition), 68; ECS to Theodore Stanton, [after Jan. 14, 1887], in Gordon, ed., *Selected Papers*, 4:541; ECS, "Reminiscences: Washington, Troy, Albany." According to his obituary, when Henry did "assert his personality," people found him "instantly attractive" ("Henry B. Stanton's Death," *New York Times*, Jan. 15, 1887).
41. ECS to Elizabeth Smith Miller, [Summer 1885], Film, Reel 24; "Henry B. Stanton's Death," *New York Times*, Jan. 15, 1887. The attendance was thin at Henry's funeral, including Elizabeth Cady Stanton's sisters and brothers-in-law and two Stanton sons, Henry, Jr., and Bob.
42. ECS Diary, Jan. 12, 1887, in Stanton and Blatch, eds., *ECS*, 2:236; ECS to George Burt Lincoln, Aug. 24, [1889], Film, Reel 27; Surrogate Court document, County of New York, filed Jan. 19, 1887; Lutz, *Created Equal*, 265.
43. Interview with New York paper, *Woman's Tribune*, May 13, 1893, Film, Reel 31; Kerr, *Lucy Stone*, 2; Livermore quoted in Goldsmith, *Other Powers*, 185; *Revolution* 1:14, April 9, 1868, 212–13; ECS to Paulina Wright Davis, Dec. 6, [1852], in Gordon, ed., *Selected Papers*, 1:215.
44. Quoted in McFeely, *Frederick Douglass*, 333; John Swinton to ECS, Dec. 29, 1897, Film, Reel 37. On Swinton, see obituary, *New York Times*, Dec. 16, 1901. Even Lucy Stone, while refusing to meet with Stanton, admitted she was "as bright and witty as ever" (Stone to Antoinette Brown Blackwell, Jan. 10, 1886, Lasser and Merrill, *Friends and Sisters*, 250).
45. ECS to Frederick Douglass, May 27, [1884], in Gordon, ed., *Selected Papers*, 4:353; ECS to Laura Curtis Bullard, Dec. 18, [1884], in ibid., 4:385.
46. All quotes in Ellen DuBois, ed., *Elizabeth Cady Stanton/Susan B. Anthony: Correspondence, Writings, Speeches*, doc. 20, "The Solitude of Self," 247–54. Also excerpted in *HWS*, 4:189–91.
47. Lutz, *Created Equal*, 290; Kerr, *Lucy Stone*, 236; ECS to Clara Colby, Dec. 30, [1893], Film, Reel 31; ECS to Clara Colby, [March 9], 1894, Film, Reel 32.
48. ECS to SBA, [before April 27, 1886], in Gordon, ed., *Selected Papers*, 4:502; "Woman Suffrage Gaining," *Sun* (New York), April 19, 1894, Film, Reel 32; DuBois, *Feminism and Suffrage*, 17.
49. ECS to Theodore Stanton, May 1, 1894, Film, Reel 32; "Women Ruled the Meeting," *New York Times*, May 8, 1894. New York's electoral defeat that year made her feel "Depressed, indignant, humiliated, anxious and apprehensive for

the future," she told a reporter (ECS to editor, *Sun*, Aug. 24, 1894, Film, Reel 32).

50. Kathi Kern, " 'Free Woman Is a Divine Being, the Savior of Mankind': Stanton's Exploration of Religion and Gender," in DuBois and Smith, eds., *Elizabeth Cady Stanton: Feminist as Thinker*, 102; ECS to Sara Underwood, Nov. 1, [1887], Film, Reel 25; SBA to ECS, Sept. 8, 1896, Film, Reel 35; ECS to Elizabeth Smith Miller, March 5, [1887], Film, Reel 25. On at least two occasions, Stanton had her head examined for significant bumps, and was pleased by the evidence that "Approbativeness and Self-Esteem, was quite noticeable" (Jessie Allen Fowler, "The Late Elizabeth Cady Stanton," *Phrenological Journal* 115, [March 1903], 82–86, Film, Reel 42).

51. Indeed, Matilda Joslyn Gage would soon publish *Woman, Church and State*, which openly challenged the common view that Christianity and its teachings were responsible for raising women's status.

52. *HWS*, 2:891; ECS to William Lloyd Garrison, Jr., Jan. 6, [1896], Film, Reel 35.

53. "Fear of Woman Rule," *Washington Post*, March 1, 1896, Film Reel 35; ECS to Sara Underwood, Dec. 13, [1887], Film, Reel 25; ECS to Clara Colby, March 25, [1896], Film, Reel 35.

54. ECS, "The Woman's Bible," [Aug. 19, 1886], in Gordon, ed., *Selected Papers*, 4:510. One typical plea is that of ECS to May Wright Sewall, Oct. 10, [1886], Film, Reel 25.

55. See Kern, *Mrs. Stanton's Bible*, 100–103. "I have not the scholarship demanded by the work," wrote Mary Livermore to ECS, Sept. 1, 1886, Film, Reel 14. Antoinette Brown Blackwell no longer remembered Hebrew and Greek. "Most women college graduates understand Greek fairly," she wrote. "All the early Oberlin women collegiates studied Hebrew; but I can recall only one who might possibly help you by a living knowledge of Hebrew, and she is extremely doubtful, as her chief attention for many years has been given to modern languages" (Antoinette Brown Blackwell to ECS, Aug. 10, 1886, Film, Reel 24).

56. Ibid.; Elizabeth Smith Miller to ECS, Aug. 29, 1886, Film, Reel 24; Elizabeth Smith Miller to ECS, Sept. 2, 1886, in Gordon, ed., *Selected Papers*, 4:513; SBA to ECS, [1895], in Harper, *SBA*, 2:856–57; SBA to ECS, Dec. 2, 1898, Film, Reel 38; Florence Wallace Legge Pomeroy to ECS, Dec. 24, 1886, Film, Reel 25; Caroline Coulomb de Barrau to ECS, Nov. 15, [1886], in Gordon, ed., *Selected Papers*, 4:530.

57. SBA to ECS, [April 1896], in Harper, *SBA*, 2:857; SBA to ECS, July 24, 1895, Film, Reel 34.

58. ECS, "The Woman's Bible," *Index*, Oct. 21, 1886, Film, Reel 25; SBA to ECS, July 24, 1895, Film, Reel 34.

59. Kern, *Mrs. Stanton's Bible*, 168.

60. ECS, "The Antagonism of Sex: World's Columbian Exposition," *National Bulletin* 2, June 1893, Film, Reel 31; National American Woman Suffrage Association, Meeting, Jan. 21, 1885, in Gordon, ed., *Selected Papers*, 4:392; ECS to Mary Clemmer Ames, June 20, [1880], Film, Reel 21. Stanton dismissed the criticism as unimportant, noting only that the resolution "raised a row among some Jews in the convention" (Diary, Jan. 22, 1885, in Stanton and Blatch, eds., *ECS*, 2:223).

61. Kern, *Mrs. Stanton's Bible*, 172; ECS birthday celebration, *New York Recorder*, Dec. 13, 1895, Film, Reel 34.
62. Kern, *Mrs. Stanton's Bible*, 182.
63. ECS to Clara Colby, Jan. 28, [1896], Film, Reel 35; Kern, *Mrs. Stanton's Bible*, 182–84.
64. SBA to ECS, [Feb. 10], 1896, in Harper, *SBA*, 2:855.
65. "Go on, O sacred scribe & commentator!" he wrote, promising to read "in pious satisfaction" "everything that comes from your biblical pen!" Tilton to ECS, March 28, 1897, Film, Reel 36.
66. ECS to Theodore Stanton, Sept. 4, 1898, Film, Reel 38.
67. SBA to ECS, Sept. 7, 1897, Film, Reel 37; SBA to ECS, [July 1891], in Harper, *SBA*, 2:712; SBA to Adelaide Johnson, March 20, 1904, Film, Reel 44. Few reminiscences of Neil Stanton survive. But "This is Neal's birthday," Stanton had written in March. "Had he lived, he would have been forty-nine, nearly half a century. And yet it seems so short a time since he was a baby—my first one—in my arms. I dreamed of him last night" (ECS Diary, March 2, 1891, in Stanton and Blatch, eds., *ECS*, 272). ECS, with Maggie and Bob, moved to the apartment at 250 West 61st Street in April 1892; the building is now named "The Stanton" ("You Say Stanton," *New Yorker*, April 21, 2008).
68. ECS to Theodore Stanton, March 2, [1896], Film, Reel 35; ECS to Harriot Stanton Blatch, July 28, 1892, Film, Reel 30; ECS to SBA, [Dec. 1887], in Harper, *SBA*, 2:635.
69. SBA to Ellen Wright Garrison, [Jan. 1899], Film, Reel 39; Tilton, "Mrs. Elizabeth Cady Stanton," 343. In 1868, she told Theodore Tilton, who would be writing this sketch, that she weighed "176 solid pounds" (ECS to Tilton, [Aug. 16, 1868], in Gordon, ed., *Selected Papers*, 2:160).
70. ECS to Elizabeth Smith Miller, Sept. 11, [1888], Film, Reel 26.
71. "Elizabeth Cady Stanton: How She Has Preserved Her Health," reprinted from the *Journal of Hygiene* in *Free Thought Magazine*, March 1896, 171, Film, Reel 35; ECS to Elizabeth Smith Miller, [Sept. 11, 1888], Film, Reel 26.
72. Tilton, "Mrs. Elizabeth Cady Stanton," 357; "Elizabeth Cady Stanton: How She Has Preserved Her Health," 170; ECS to Harriot Stanton, [Nov. 4], 1882, in Gordon, ed., *Selected Papers*, 4:196.
73. Nearing her seventy-fifth birthday, she wrote Margaret that she had been observing herself in the mirror "with intense satisfaction," hoping to see a resemblance to Hattie. "Now I perceive another feature that must be concealed. *My ears*: they are very large, quite unnecessarily so" (ECS to Margaret Stanton Lawrence, Oct. 27, [1890], Film, Reel 28). Anthony was not without vanity, pleading with an editor to destroy some particularly unattractive woodcuts of Stanton and herself; "it can not be said that I am a beauty," she admitted, "therefore am I more sensitive at being made to look more ugly than truth absolutely demands" (SBA to Editor, *Cincinnati Commercial Gazette*, Dec. 29, 1883, in Gordon, ed., *Selected Papers*, 4:321).
74. ECS, "Interview with Haryot [sic] Holt Cahoon on Success," *Success* 1 (June 1898), Film, Reel 38; ECS to Harriot Stanton Blatch, July 11, 1899, Film, Reel 40. The *North American Review* "gave me twenty-five dollars for my article and the Cosmopolitan gave me one hundred. I am busy all the time" (ECS to Theodore Stanton, Dec. 3, 1900, Film, Reel 41).

75. ECS to Harriot Stanton Blatch, July 11, 1899, Film, Reel 40; ECS et al., "Old Age the Happiest Part of a Well-Spent Life," *World*, Feb. 26, 1899, Film, Reel 39; ECS to Theodore Stanton, July 24, 1896, Film, Reel 35.

76. SBA to ECS, Dec. 1, 1897, Film, Reel 37; SBA to Rachel Avery, Dec. 29, 1897, Film, Reel 37.

77. For Whittier and Rose eulogies, see National American Woman Suffrage Association, *Proceedings of the Twenty-fifth Annual Convention of the NAWSA* (Washington, D.C., 1893), 21. On Stone, see *Proceedings of the Twenty-sixth Annual Convention of the NAWSA*, ed., Harriet Taylor Upton (Warren, Ohio, 1894), 72. "Lucy Stone did a brave thing in keeping her name," Stanton admitted in her comments, "and it is strange that so few women follow her example."

78. After Douglass had spoken, Anthony, perhaps to dull the implied criticism of her friend and her convention, reacted tartly: "I was sorry that Frederick violated her last and strongest wish by giving her the name of Blackwell," an error he rarely made (*Proceedings of the Twenty-sixth Annual Convention of the NAWSA*, 85).

79. *Free Thought Magazine* 13, April 1895, 214, Film, Reel 33.

80. ECS to SBA, [before Dec. 7, 1896], in Stanton and Blatch, eds., *ECS*, 2:321–22.

81. Lucretia Mott to ECS, March 16, 1855, in Palmer, ed., *Selected Letters of Lucretia Coffin Mott*, 233–34; Griffith, *In Her Own Right*, 207.

82. ECS to Clara Colby, Feb. 15, [1898], Film, Reel 38; ECS to Maria Palmer Thomas [1898], Film, Reel 38; ECS to Emily Howland, Feb. 18, [1898], Film, Reel 38; www.abebooks.com (viewed Dec. 14, 2006); ECS to Marietta Holley, May 9, [1898], Film, Reel 38.

83. ECS to William Lloyd Garrison, Jr., Feb. 15, [1898], Film, Reel 38; ECS review of *Eighty Years and More*, in *Journalist* (New York), [1898], Film, Reel 38.

84. Quote on "jackasses" in Griffith, *In Her Own Right*, 208; Diary, July 4, 1894, in Stanton and Blatch, eds., *ECS*, 2:306; ECS, "Our Boys on Sunday," *Forum* 1, April 1886, Film, Reel 24. Stanton consistently opposed Blue Laws; for example, at the 1892 National American Woman Suffrage Association convention she offered a resolution in favor of "keeping the World's Fair open on Sunday, which was advocated and opposed with great earnestness" (*HWS*, 4:185).

85. *San Francisco Examiner*, Jan. 20, 1896, Film, Reel 35 (the Vassar College archive has a fascinating website about the claims and ads for this product: projects .vassar.edu/1896/medicine.html); ECS Endorsement of Fairy Soap, *Ladies' Home Journal* 16, Sept. 1899, 31; "Mrs. Stanton's Views on Fire," to *New York Recorder*, reprinted in *Woman's Journal* (Boston), May 18, 1895, Film, Reel 34; ECS to Harriet Hanson Robinson, *True Republic* 4, March 1895, 4, Film, Reel 33.

86. ECS to SBA, [Feb.] 1884, Film, Reel 23.

87. ECS to Lillie D. Blake, June 14, 1899, Film, Reel 39. "You have not been treated by our young co-adjutors with less consideration than I have been," she assured a colleague who had been slighted. "They refused to read my letters and resolutions to the conventions. They have denounced the Woman's Bible unsparingly; not one of them has ever reviewed or expressed the least appreciation of 'Eighty Years and More.' Not one of my suffrage friends has ever thought it worth a complimentary notice in any of the metropolitan journals, or even in the Woman's papers . . . For all this I make no public protest, I propose no revenge."

88. SBA to Ednah Dow Cheney, April 16, 1895, Film, Reel 33; ECS to Elizabeth Boynton Harbert, July 25, 1901, Film, Reel 42.

89. Harriot Stanton Blatch to SBA, Sept. 25, 1902, Film, Reel 42; ECS to Ida Husted Harper, Sept. 30, 1902, Film, Reel 42.

90. ECS to editor, *Woman's Journal*, Sept. 27, 1902, Film, Reel 42; ECS to Theodore Roosevelt, Oct. 22, 1902, in *Independent* 54, Nov. 6, 1902, 2621, Film, Reel 42.

91. Harriot Stanton Blatch to SBA, Oct. 26, 1902 (telegram, notation in SBA's hand), Film, Reel 42; Theodore Stanton, Harriot Stanton Blatch to SBA, (after Oct. 29), 1902, Film, Reel 42; Harriot Stanton Blatch to SBA, Oct. 26, 1902 (second telegram), Film, Reel 42. Officially, Stanton died of heart failure. Only the day before, experiencing trouble breathing, she had apparently instructed the doctor that if she were "not to feel brighter and more like work again," she be "give[n] . . . something to send me pack-horse speed to heaven" (quoted in Griffith, *In Her Own Right*, 217).

92. DuBois, *Harriot Stanton Blatch*, 86; Helen Hamilton Gardener to ECS, July 25, 1887, Film, Reel 25; "Brain Weight," *The Woman's Tribune*, August 1883; Helen Hamilton Gardener, "Brains at Cornell," *Free Thought Magazine* 18, Feb. 1900, 94–95; ECS, "Bequest of Brain to Cornell University," Feb. 2, 1900, Film, Reel 40. The *New York Times* of Nov. 20, 1902, in reporting on "Tributes to Mrs. Stanton," referred to the absence of Helen Gardener, "who figured prominently in the controversy with the Stanton family which followed the circulation of reports that Mrs. Cady Stanton had willed her brain to Cornell University."

93. SBA to Clara Colby, Oct. 31, 1902, published in *Woman's Tribune*, Nov. 8, 1902, Film, Reel 42; Anthony, "Were Friends for Fifty Years," *Democrat and Chronicle* (Rochester, N.Y.), Oct. 26, 1902, Film, Reel 42.

94. *Free Thought Magazine* 21, Jan. 1903, Film, Reel 42. ECS's obituary was in the *Tribune*, Oct. 27, 1902. Harriot's remark about the paper's use of her mother's name is on the back of a manuscript, ECS, "Battling for the Ballot," [1894], Film, Reel 33.

95. Clara Colby to SBA, Oct. 29, 1902, Film, Reel 42. In the same letter, Clara Colby suggested that "because you are spare, take exercise, & eat frugally [you] have a much better chance for longevity than did she," an astonishing comment about the death of someone who was nearly eighty-seven. Anna Howard Shaw recalled that "Mrs. Stanton could always make Miss Anthony smile" (*Buffalo Daily Courier*, Oct. 30, 1902, Film, Reel 42).

96. Anthony, "Were Friends for Fifty Years"; SBA to Ida Husted Harper, Oct. 28, 1902, Film, Reel 42; SBA to Theodore Stanton, May 18, 1903, Film, Reel 43.

97. "Honors Paid to a Dead Leader," *Democrat and Chronicle* (Rochester, N.Y.), Nov. 13, 1903, Film, Reel 43.

CONCLUSION

1. ECS to Harriot Stanton Blatch, Oct. 1, 1889, Film, Reel 27; ECS Diary, Oct. 1, 1896, in Stanton and Blatch, eds., *ECS*, 321; DuBois, *Harriot Stanton Blatch*, chap. 9. Maggie, too, helped to define her mother's role in the cause, writing letters to newspapers to correct their historical accounts. Undated clippings in E.C. Stanton Archives Collection, Box 38, folder 6, Seneca Falls Historical Society.

2. Tilton, "Mrs. Elizabeth Cady Stanton," 332, 346, 361, 359.

3. ECS to William Lloyd Garrison, Jr., Dec. 5, 1899, Film, Reel 40.

4. Theodore Tilton, *Golden Age*, July 1, 1871, reprinted in *Revolution*, July 6, 1871, quoted in Holland and Gordon, *Papers of Stanton and Anthony: Guide and Index*, 2, Film, Reel 45; *New York Times*, Sept. 26, 1918. Alice Paul's faction of the woman suffrage movement designated it the Susan B. Anthony amendment in 1914. See DuBois, *Harriot Stanton Blatch*, 250.

5. DuBois, *Harriot Stanton Blatch*, 257. "Many years later, [Alice] Paul told an interviewer that the problem with Harriot was that she was 'just like her mother, that she was just involved in too many things and could not commit herself steadily to one goal' " (DuBois, *Harriot Stanton Blatch*, 248–49).

6. Ken Burns, *Not For Ourselves Alone*, PBS, 1999; DuBois, *Feminism and Suffrage*; DuBois and Smith, eds., *Elizabeth Cady Stanton: Feminist as Thinker*.

7. *Debates of the Convention to Amend the Constitution of Pennsylvania* (Harrisburg, Pa.: Benjamin Singerly, 1873), 540; Theodore Tilton to ECS, Nov. 1, 1895, Film, Reel 34.

8. Mayer, *All On Fire*, 607.

9. Oliver Wendell Holmes, Jr., "An Address Delivered for Memorial Day, May 30, 1884," in Richard A. Posner, ed., *The Essential Holmes: Selections from the Letters, Speeches, Judicial Opinions, and Other Writings of Oliver Wendell Holmes, Jr.* (Chicago: University of Chicago Press, 1992), 80–87.

10. ECS to Martha Coffin Wright, Feb. 10, 1861, in Stanton and Blatch, eds., *ECS*, 2:87.

BIBLIOGRAPHY

Anderson, Bonnie S. *Joyous Greetings: The First International Women's Movement, 1830–1860* (New York: Oxford University Press, 2000).

An Account of the Proceedings of the Trial of Susan B. Anthony on the Charge of Illegal Voting (Rochester, N.Y., 1874).

Anti-Slavery Convention of American Women. *Proceedings* (New York: William S. Dorr, 1837).

Applegate, Debby. *The Most Famous Man in America. The Biography of Henry Ward Beecher* (New York: Doubleday, 2006).

Banner, Lois. *Elizabeth Cady Stanton: A Radical for Women's Rights* (Boston: Little, Brown, 1980).

Barkley Brown, Elsa. "Negotiating and Tranforming the Public Sphere: African American Political Life in the Transition from Slavery to Freedom." *Public Culture* 7 (1994): 107–46.

Barnes, Gilbert H., and Dwight L. Dumond, eds. *Letters of Theodore Dwight Weld, Angelina Grimké Weld, and Sarah Grimké, 1822–1844* (Gloucester, Mass.: Peter Smith, 1965).

Barry, Kathleen. *Susan B. Anthony: A Biography of a Singular Feminist* (New York: New York University Press, 1988).

Bartlett, Elizabeth Ann, ed. *Sarah Grimké: Letters on the Equality of the Sexes and Other Essays* (New Haven, Conn.: Yale University Press, 1988).

Barton, Clara. Letters. Alma Lutz Collection. Women's Studies Manuscript Collections from the Schlesinger Library, Radcliffe College. Series 1, Woman's Suffrage (Bethesda, Md.: University Publications of America, 1990).

Bedell, Madelon. *The Alcotts: Biography of a Family* (New York: Clarkson N. Potter, 1980).

Beecher, Catharine E. *A Treatise on Domestic Economy, for the Use of Young Ladies at Home, and at School* (Boston: Marsh, Capen, Lyon, and Webb, 1841).

Berlin, Ira, and Leslie M. Harris. *Slavery in New York* (New York: The New Press, 2005).

Bernstein, Iver. *The New York City Draft Riots: Their Significance for American Society and Politics in the Age of the Civil War* (New York: Oxford University Press, 1990).

Blatch, Harriot Stanton, and Alma Lutz. *Challenging Years: The Memoirs of Harriot Stanton Blatch* (New York: G. P. Putnam's Sons, 1940).

Boydston, Jeanne, Mary Kelley, and Anne Margolis. *The Limits of Sisterhood: The Beecher Sisters on Women's Rights and Woman's Sphere* (Chapel Hill: University of North Carolina Press, 1988).

———. "Making Gender in the Early Republic." In James Horn, Jan Ellen Lewis, and Peter S. Onuf, eds. *The Revolution of 1800* (Charlottesville: University of Virginia Press, 2002): 240–66.

Brown, Ira V. *Mary Grew: Abolitionist and Feminist (1813–1896)* (Selinsgrove, Pa.: Susquehanna University Press, 1991).

Buhle, Mari Jo, and Paul Buhle, eds. *The Concise History of Woman Suffrage* (Urbana, Ill.: University of Illinois Press, 2005).

Bull, Mary S. "Woman's Rights and Other 'Reforms' in Seneca Falls." *Good Company* 5 (1880): 328–36.

Cole, Phyllis. "Stanton, Fuller, and the Grammar of Romanticism." *The New England Quarterly* 73:4 (Dec. 2000): 533–59.

Cooper, George. *Lost Love: A True Story of Passion, Murder, and Justice in Old New York* (New York: Random House, 1994).

Davis, Angela. *Women, Race, and Class* (New York: Vintage Press, 1983).

Davis, Paulina Wright. *A History of the National Woman's Rights Movement for Twenty Years; with the Proceedings of the Decade Meeting Held at Apollo Hall, October 20, 1870, from 1850 to 1870* (New York: Journeymen Printers' Co-operative Association, 1871).

DuBois, Ellen Carol. *Feminism and Suffrage: The Emergence of an Independent Women's Movement in America, 1848–1869* (Ithaca, N.Y.: Cornell University Press, 1978).

———. *Harriot Stanton Blatch and the Winning of Woman Suffrage* (New Haven, Conn.: Yale University Press, 1997).

———. *Woman Suffrage and Women's Rights* (New York: New York University Press, 1998).

DuBois, Ellen Carol, ed. *Elizabeth Cady Stanton/Susan B. Anthony: Correspondence, Writings, Speeches* (New York: Schocken Books, 1981).

DuBois, Ellen Carol, and Richard Cándida Smith, eds. *Elizabeth Cady Stanton: Feminist as Thinker: A Reader in Documents and Essays* (New York: New York University Press, 2007).

Dykeman, Amy. " 'To Pour Forth from My Own Experience': Two Versions of Elizabeth Cady Stanton." *The Journal of the Rutgers University Libraries* 44:1 (June 1982): 1–16.

———. "To Look a Gift Horse in the Mouth: The History of the Theodore Stanton Collection." *Journal of Library History* 17:4 (Fall 1982): 468–73.

Eisenstadt, Peter, and Laura-Eve Moss, eds. *The Encyclopedia of New York State* (Syracuse, N.Y.: Syracuse University Press, 2005).

Emerson, Sarah Hopper, ed. *Life of Abby Hopper Gibbons Told Chiefly Through Her Correspondence*, 2 vols. (New York: G. P. Putnam's Sons, 1896).

Emma Willard and Her Pupils, or Fifty Years of Troy Female Seminary, 1822–1872 (New York: Mrs. Russell Sage, 1898).

Faulkner, Carol. *Women's Radical Reconstruction: The Freedmen's Aid Movement* (Philadelphia: University of Pennsylvania Press, 2004).

BIBLIOGRAPHY

Flexner, Eleanor. *Century of Struggle: The Woman's Rights Movement in the United States* (Cambridge: Harvard University Press, 1959).

Foner, Eric. *Reconstruction: America's Unfinished Revolution, 1863–1877* (New York: Harper and Row, 1988).

Friedman, Lawrence J. *Gregarious Saints: Self and Community in American Abolitionism, 1830–1870* (Cambridge: Cambridge University Press, 1982).

Gage, Matilda Joslyn. *Woman, Church and State.* Introduction by Sally Roesch Wagner (Watertown, Mass.: Persephone Press, 1980; orig. 1893).

Ginzberg, Lori D. *Women and the Work of Benevolence: Morality, Politics, and Class in the Nineteenth-Century United States* (New Haven, Conn.: Yale University Press, 1990).

———. *Untidy Origins: A Story of Woman's Rights in Antebellum New York* (Chapel Hill: University of North Carolina Press, 2005).

———. *Women in Antebellum Reform* (Wheeling, Ill.: Harlan Davidson, 2000).

Goldsmith, Barbara. *Other Powers: The Age of Suffrage, Spiritualism, and the Scandalous Victoria Woodhull* (New York: Alfred A. Knopf, 1998).

Gordon, Ann D., ed. *The Selected Papers of Elizabeth Cady Stanton and Susan B. Anthony,* vols. 1–4 (New Brunswick, N.J.: Rutgers University Press, 1997–2006).

———. *African American Women and the Vote, 1837–1965* (Amherst: University of Massachusetts Press, 1997).

Gornick, Vivian. *The Solitude of Self: Thinking About Elizabeth Cady Stanton* (New York: Farrar, Straus and Giroux, 2005).

Grew, Mary. Diary. Alma Lutz Collection. Women's Studies Manuscript Collections from the Schlesinger Library, Radcliffe College. Series 1, Woman's Suffrage (Bethesda, Md.: University Publications of America, 1990).

Griffith, Elisabeth. *In Her Own Right: The Life of Elizabeth Cady Stanton* (New York: Oxford University Press, 1984).

Gustafson, Melanie Susan. *Women and the Republican Party, 1854–1924* (Urbana: University of Illinois Press, 2001).

Harper, Ida Husted. *The Life and Work of Susan B. Anthony: Including Public Addresses, Her Own Letters and Many from Her Contemporaries During Fifty Years.* 3 vols. (Indianapolis, Ind.: The Hollenbeck Press, vols. 1 and 2, 1898; vol. 3, 1908).

Hawkes, Andrea Constantine. "The Life of Elizabeth McClintock Phillips, 1821–1896: A Story of Family, Friends, Community, and a Self-Made Woman." Ph.D. dissertation, University of Maine, 2005.

Hersh, Blanche Glassman. *The Slavery of Sex: Feminist-Abolitionists in America* (Urbana: University of Illinois Press, 1978).

Hoffert, Sylvia D. *When Hens Crow: The Woman's Rights Movement in Antebellum America* (Bloomington: Indiana University Press, 1995).

Holland, Patricia G., and Ann D. Gordon, eds. *The Papers of Elizabeth Cady Stanton and Susan B. Anthony.* 45 microfilm reels (Wilmington, Del.: Scholarly Resources, 1991).

Holley, Marietta. *My Opinions and Betsey Bobbet's* (Hartford, Conn.: American Publishing Co., 1875).

Isenberg, Nancy. *Sex and Citizenship in Antebellum America* (Chapel Hill: University of North Carolina Press, 1998).

Jeffrey, Julie Roy. *The Great Silent Army of Abolitionism: Ordinary Women in the Antislavery Movement* (Chapel Hill: University of North Carolina Press, 1998).

———. *Abolitionists Remember: Antislavery Autobiographies and the Unfinished Work of Emancipation* (Chapel Hill: University of North Carolina Press, 2008).

Johnson, Paul E. *Sam Patch, the Famous Jumper* (New York: Hill and Wang, 2003).

Jones, Martha S. *All Bound Up Together: The Woman Question in African American Political Culture, 1830–1900* (Chapel Hill: University of North Carolina Press, 2007).

Kelley, Mary. *Learning to Stand and Speak: Women, Education, and Public Life in America's Republic* (Chapel Hill: University of North Carolina Press, 2006).

Kern, Kathi, *Mrs. Stanton's Bible* (Ithaca, N.Y.: Cornell University Press, 2001).

Kerr, Andrea Moore. *Lucy Stone: Speaking Out for Equality* (New Brunswick, N.J.: Rutgers University Press, 1995).

Keyssar, Alexander. *The Right to Vote: The Contested History of Democracy in the United States* (New York: Basic Books, 2000).

Klinghoffer, Judith, and Lois Elkis. "'The Petticoat Electors': Women's Suffrage in New Jersey, 1776–1807." *Journal of the Early Republic* 12 (1992): 159–93.

Lasser, Carol, and Marlene Deahl Merrill, eds. *Friends and Sisters: Letters Between Lucy Stone and Antoinette Brown Blackwell, 1846–1893* (Urbana: University of Illinois Press, 1987).

Litwack, Leon F. *Been in the Storm So Long: The Aftermath of Slavery* (New York: Alfred A. Knopf, 1979).

Lutz, Alma. *Created Equal: A Biography of Elizabeth Cady Stanton* (New York: John Day Company, 1940).

Mayer, Henry. *All on Fire: William Lloyd Garrison and the Abolition of Slavery* (New York: St. Martin's Griffin, 1998).

Maynard, Douglas H. "The World's Anti-Slavery Convention of 1840." *The Mississippi Valley Historical Review* 47:3 (Dec. 1960): 452–71.

McClymer, John F. *This High and Holy Moment: The First National Woman's Rights Convention, Worcester, 1850* (Orlando, Fl.: Harcourt Brace and Company, 1999).

McFadden, Margaret H. *Golden Cables of Sympathy: The Transatlantic Sources of Nineteenth-Century Feminism* (Lexington: University Press of Kentucky, 1999).

McFeely, William S. *Frederick Douglass* (New York: W. W. Norton, 1991).

McMillen, Sally G. *Seneca Falls and the Origins of the Women's Rights Movement* (New York: Oxford University Press, 2008).

Merrill, Marlene Deahl, ed. *Growing Up in Boston's Gilded Age: The Journal of Alice Stone Blackwell, 1872–1874* (New Haven, Conn.: Yale University Press, 1990).

Merrill, Walter M. *The Letters of William Lloyd Garrison. Volume II: A House Dividing Against Itself* (Cambridge, Mass.: Harvard University Press, 1971).

———. *The Letters of William Lloyd Garrison. Volume III: No Union with Slaveholders, 1841–1849* (Cambridge, Mass.: Harvard University Press, 1973).

Mitchell, Edward P. *Memoirs of an Editor: Fifty Years of American Journalism* (New York: Charles Scribner's Sons, 1924).

Oates, Stephen B. *A Woman of Valor: Clara Barton and the Civil War* (New York: The Free Press, 1994).

O'Brien, Frank M. *The Story of the Sun, New York, 1833–1928* (New York: George H. Doran Company, 1918).

Painter, Nell Irvin. *Sojourner Truth: A Life, a Symbol* (New York: W. W. Norton, 1996).

Palmer, Beverly Wilson, ed. *Selected Letters of Lucretia Coffin Mott* (Urbana: University of Illinois Press, 2002).

Parton, James, et al. *Eminent Women of the Age* (Hartford, Conn.: S. M. Betts & Co., 1869).

Penney, Sherry H., and James D. Livingston. *A Very Dangerous Woman: Martha Wright and Women's Rights* (Amherst: University of Massachusetts Press, 2004).

Perry, Mark. *Live Up Thy Voice: The Grimké Family's Journey from Slaveholders to Civil Rights Leaders* (New York: Penguin Books, 2001).

Pierson, Michael. *Free Hearts and Free Homes: Gender and American Antislavery Politics* (Chapel Hill, N.C.: University of North Carolina Press, 2003).

Proceedings of the General Anti-Slavery Convention, Called by the Committee of the British and Foreign Anti-Slavery Society, and Held in London, from Friday, June 12th, to Tuesday, June 23rd, 1840 (London: British and Foreign Anti-Slavery Society, 1841).

Pugh, Sarah. *Memorial of Sarah Pugh: A Tribute of Respect from Her Cousins* (Philadelphia, Pa.: J. B. Lippincott & Co., 1888).

Rice, Arthur Harry. "Henry B. Stanton as a Political Abolitionist." Ed.D. thesis. Columbia University, 1968.

Ruchames, Louis, ed. *Letters of William Lloyd Garrison: Volume IV: From Disunion to the Brink of War, 1850–1860* (Cambridge, Mass.: Harvard University Press, 1975).

Seward, William H. Microfilm of The Papers of William H. Seward, Department of Rare Books, Rush Rhees Library, University of Rochester.

Smith, Rogers M. *Civic Ideals: Conflicting Visions of Citizenship in U.S. History* (New Haven, Conn.: Yale University Press, 1997).

Sneider, Allison L. *Suffragists in an Imperial Age: U.S. Expansion and the Woman Question, 1870–1929* (New York: Oxford University Press, 2008).

Spafford, Horatio Gates. *Gazetteer of the State of New York* (Albany: B. D. Packard, 1824).

Stampp, Kenneth, and Leon F. Litwack. *Reconstruction: An Anthology of Revisionist Writings* (Baton Rouge: Louisiana State University Press, 1969).

Stanton, Elizabeth Cady. *Eighty Years and More: Reminiscences (1815–1897)* (New York: Schocken Books, 1971; reprinted from T. Fisher Urwin edition, 1898).

———. *The Woman's Bible* (New York: European Publishing Company, 1895, 1898).

Stanton, Elizabeth Cady, Susan B. Anthony, and Matilda Joslyn Gage. *History of Woman Suffrage*, 3 vols. (New York: Fowler and Wells, 1881, 1882; Rochester, N.Y.: Susan B. Anthony, 1886).

Stanton, Gerrit Smith. *Renting a Furnished Apartment: A Narrative Setting Forth the Experiences of an Out-of-Town Family in the Metropolis* (New York: J. S. Ogilvie Publishing Co., 1916).

————. *When the Wildwood Was in Flower: A Narrative Covering the Fifteen Years' Experiences of a Stockman on the Western Plains and His Vacation Days in the Open* (New York: J. S. Ogilvie Publishing Co., 1909).

————. "How Aged Housekeeper . . . Woman's Suffrage." Unidentified clipping, n.d. (E. C. Stanton Papers, Archives Collection 37, box 38, folder 5, Seneca Falls Historical Society).

Stanton, Henry B. *Random Recollections*, 3rd ed. (New York: Harper and Brothers, 1887).

Stanton, Theodore Weld, and Harriot Stanton Blatch, eds. *Elizabeth Cady Stanton*, 2 vols. (New York: Harper & Bros., 1922).

Stanton, William A. *A Record, Genealogical, Biographical, Statistical, of Thomas Stanton* (Albany, N.Y.: 1891).

Sterling, Dorothy. *Ahead of Her Time: Abby Kelley and the Politics of Antislavery* (New York: W. W. Norton, 1991).

Stewart, James Brewer. *Wendell Phillips: Liberty's Hero* (Baton Rouge: Louisiana State University Press, 1986).

Strong, George Templeton. *Diary of the Civil War, 1860–1865* (New York: Macmillan, 1962).

Taylor, Clare. *British and American Abolitionists: An Episode in Transatlantic Understanding* (Edinburgh: Edinburgh University Press, 1974).

Terborg-Penn, Rosalyn. *African American Women in the Struggle for the Vote, 1850–1920* (Blommington: Indiana University Press, 1998).

Tetrault, Lisa Marguerite. "The Memory of a Movement: Woman Suffrage and Reconstruction America, 1865–1890." Ph.D. dissertation, University of Wisconsin, 2004.

Thernstrom, Stephen. *The Other Bostonians: Poverty and Progress in the American Metropolis, 1880–1970* (Cambridge, Mass.: Harvard University Press, 1973).

Tolles, Frederick, ed. "Slavery and the 'Woman Question': Lucretia Mott's Diary of Her Visit to Great Britain to Attend the World's Anti-Slavery Convention of 1840." Supplement #23 to the *Journal of the Friends' Historical Society* (Haverford, Pa.: Friends Historical Association, 1952).

Train, George Francis. *My Life in Many States and in Foreign Lands* (New York: D. Appleton and Company, 1902).

Ulrich, Laurel Thatcher. *Well-Behaved Women Seldom Make History* (New York: Alfred A. Knopf, 2007).

Venet, Wendy Hamand. *A Strong-Minded Woman: The Life of Mary Livermore* (Amherst: University of Massachusetts Press, 2005).

Ward, Geoffrey C., and Ken Burns. *Not for Ourselves Alone: The Story of Elizabeth Cady Stanton and Susan B. Anthony: An Illustrated History* (New York: Alfred A. Knopf, 1999).

Wellman, Judith. *The Road to Seneca Falls: Elizabeth Cady Stanton and the First Woman's Rights Convention* (Urbana: University of Illinois Press, 2004).

Yellin, Jean Fagan, and John C. Van Horne, eds. *The Abolitionist Sisterhood: Women's Political Culture in Antebellum America* (Ithaca, N.Y.: Cornell University Press, 1994).

ACKNOWLEDGMENTS

As challenging as it has been to tell Elizabeth Cady Stanton's story succinctly, it is harder to thank in a few words the people who helped. The idea for this book originated with Louis Masur, and I am deeply grateful for his, and Thomas Slaughter's, ongoing enthusiasm. Thomas LeBien has been an exemplary and astute editor who, with Elizabeth Maples and others at Hill and Wang, made every stage of this project a pleasure.

Librarians and archivists were uniformly gracious. I want especially to thank those at the Schlesinger Library on the History of Women in America at Radcliffe College, the New York Public Library, the Library of Congress, the Rush Rhees Library at the University of Rochester, Syracuse University, the Seneca Falls Historical Society, the Library Company of Philadelphia, the Cornell University Library, and the Vassar College Library. I owe special thanks to Debora Cheney and her colleagues at Penn State's Pattee and Paterno libraries, whose generosity and flexibility made the research for this book far less daunting. I am also grateful for the extensive historical resources available on the Web through such databases as ProQuest, the Women and Social Movements Project, the Making of America digital library at the University of Michigan, and Accessible Archives. For permission to publish illustrations from their collections, I thank the Seneca Falls Historical Society, Bryn Mawr College, the Library of Congress, the Harriet Beecher Stowe Center, the New York Public Library, and, especially, Khyber Oser.

I was extremely fortunate to receive a National Endowment for the Humanities Fellowship to work on this book. I am also pleased to thank Penn State University's College of Liberal Arts for a sabbatical leave and the Research and Graduate Studies Office for a research grant. Department heads Sally McMurry, Lorraine Dowler, and Carolyn Sachs, as well as Dean Susan Welch, offered intellectual and financial support.

Scholars and colleagues aided this project in ways large and small: I thank Iver Bernstein, Anne Boylan, Nancy Cott, Anne Derousie, Ellen DuBois, Carol Faulkner, Tamara Gaskell, Terry Godlove, Andrea Constantine Hawkes, Nancy Hewitt, Mary Kelley, Kathi Kern, Peter Kolchin, Susan McCormick, Stephanie McCurry, Hélène Quanquin, Carol Reardon, Mrinalini Sinha, Lisa Tetrault, Judith Wellman, Nan Woodruff, and Susan Zaeske. It is a pleasure once again to express my appreciation for my colleagues in the departments of History and Women's Studies at Penn State. Audiences at the University of Delaware, Villanova University, the Schlesinger Library Summer Institute, the Society for Historians of the Early American Republic, the David Library of the American Revolution, and Penn State's Women's Studies Forum challenged me to sharpen my interpretation of Stanton's legacy. Finally, like all students of Elizabeth Cady Stanton and the movement she helped lead, I am indebted to Ann D. Gordon and her associates at the Stanton and Anthony papers at Rutgers University for the gift of their editorial scholarship.

My good fortune in my family and friends is best expressed by noting that there are too many of them to mention; I hope they know how grateful I am for their talents, their teasing, and their love. I want especially to thank Shirley and David Ginzberg and Francine Steiker for their ongoing encouragement; Janet Ginzberg for reading my drafts and listening to my gripes; and Joel Steiker for sharing our home, our vacations, and our daily lives with Elizabeth Cady Stanton, who took up a lot of space.

It is impossible to measure my debt to Jeanne Boydston, who died in 2008. The conversation she and I began on my first day of graduate school more than thirty years ago finds its echo in these pages, as it does in everything I have ever written or ever will.

This book is dedicated to Kate and Eli Steiker-Ginzberg, resident critics.

INDEX

abolition, abolitionism: Anthony as supporter of, 77, 93–94, 115, 120, 141, 168; in Boston, 44–48, 60; Civil War and cause of, 10, 97, 101, 103–10, 111–12, 115; clerical influence in, 31, 38, 53, 67–68; ECS as supporter of, 5, 26–27, 31–41, 44–47, 49, 53, 93–94, 103–104, 119, 120, 141, 190; electoral strategy for, 31, 36, 44, 60–62, 97; in France, 52; Free Soil movement in, 49, 60–61, 62, 66, 69, 87, 88–89, 91, 94, 141; Garrisonian faction in, 19, 36, 38, 44–45, 46, 49, 52, 61, 62, 88–89, 94; in Great Britain, 34–41, 54; HBS and, 29, 30–41, 43–45, 53, 60, 103, 168; Quaker influence in, 55–56, 61; radical ideology of, 19, 26, 31, 37–39, 44–46, 108–109; rift in, 30, 31, 36–38, 44–46, 60, 61–62, 97; at Seneca Falls Convention (1848), 53–54, 57, 59, 60–61, 66, 67–68; woman's rights and, 5, 17, 19, 25, 26–27, 33, 34–41, 44–47, 49, 53–54, 57, 59, 60–62, 66, 67–68, 77, 87–88, 93–94, 97, 103–104, 107–10, 115–31, 141, 154, 180, 190
Abraham (slave), 20
Acadia, 41
Adam, William, 37, 38
Adam Bede (Eliot), 100

Adams, John Quincy, 9, 30
adultery, 136–37, 145
African Americans: citizenship of, 108–10, 115–31; discrimination against, 125–27, 128, 164, 173, 177, 180; as freed people, 115–31, 161–63; intermarriage of, 45, 166–67; military service of, 108, 111; in North, 110–12, 118, 125; prejudice against, 4, 5, 47, 110–12, 120–31, 134, 161–65, 192, 193; in South, 10, 114–20, 125–27, 128, 129–30, 131, 134, 164, 165, 173; support for woman suffrage, 38, 62, 117, 119, 124, 129; voting rights of, 10, 62, 107–10, 115–31, 136, 161–64, 166, 184; white violence against, 125–27, 128; women, 26–27, 64–65, 119, 122, 127, 129; *see also* slavery, slaves
Albany, N.Y., 16, 43, 47, 49, 99, 150–51
Albany County Free Soil Convention, 69
Albany Patriot, 49
Alcott, Bronson, 44
American Anti-Slavery Society, 31, 35, 36–37, 52, 97, 107, 116, 117
American Equal Rights Association, 119, 124
American Revolution, 16, 20, 84
American Woman Suffrage Association, 125, 157, 160, 165–66

INDEX

Woodhull, Victoria, 144–47, 150
Woodhull & Claflin's Weekly, 144
Woolworth stores, 49
Worcester, Mass., 75
Worden, Alvah, 23
Worden, Lazette Miller, 23
working class, 25, 48–49, 65, 68, 83,
    137, 160, 161, 163, 182
Working Women's Association, 137,
    218*n*7
World's Anti-Slavery Convention, Lon-
    don (1840), 33, 34–41, 154

Wright, David, 60
Wright, Fanny, 37, 80
Wright, Martha Coffin, 54, 60, 98, 100,
    139, 143, 146, 151, 180
Wright, Silas, 90
Wyoming, 143, 149

Yale University, 98

Zouave regiments, 104